New Frontiers

in

Formative Assessment

New Frontiers
in
Formative Assessment

Edited by

PENDRED E. NOYCE

DANIEL T. HICKEY

Harvard Education Press

Cambridge, Massachusetts

Library of Congress Control Number 2011928649

Paperback ISBN 978-1-61250-117-8
Library Edition ISBN 978-1-61250-118-5

Published by Harvard Education Press,
an imprint of the Harvard Education Publishing Group

Harvard Education Press
8 Story Street
Cambridge, MA 02138

Cover Design: Sarah Henderson
The typefaces used in this book are ITC Stone Serif and ITC Stone Sans

Contents

Foreword

A decade ago, Paul Black and Dylan Wiliam published a groundbreaking research review establishing the claim that formative assessment can dramatically improve student learning. The promise of this approach—as yet not fully realized in classroom practice—underlies the innovative projects documented in this thoughtful and timely volume.

Despite its fame, few have actually read Black and Wiliam's research review. Most rely instead on an abbreviated article by the same authors or derivative citations and advertisements. Surprisingly, the original review was not a meta-analysis of comparative studies with formative assessment as an intact and well defined "treatment." Rather, it was a narrative review of quite disparate literatures, including studies of goal orientation (from motivation research), student self-assessment, task quality, classroom discourse and questioning, types of feedback, mastery learning, and so forth. Black and Wiliam considered possible theories of formative assessment and offered guidance about which components might be considered essential, but they did not provide a complete theory of how formative assessment was supposed to work nor how the pieces were expected to fit together. As the authors noted, only about twenty studies of the hundreds reviewed could be thought of as testing the effectiveness of formative assessment as a whole, and these were so different from each other—especially in their conceptions of pedagogy—that aggregation would have been meaningless.

In subsequent work, Black and Wiliam and their colleagues took up the challenge of putting research evidence into practice. They worked with teachers who tried out specific formative practices, including improved questioning techniques, comment-only grading, and student self-assessment using traffic lights, to name a few. Other scholars have also developed and evaluated formative assessment projects with both promising and discouraging results. Given the hoopla and euphoric promises of dramatic learning gains, however, the number of well-studied formative assessment projects has been surprisingly limited, and there has been no further synthesis of research findings from the past decade. No doubt limited progress can be attributed to the complexity and difficulty of implementing formative assessment. But energy has also been diverted by definitional debates and by the more prevalent investments in interim and benchmark assessments. It is fair to say, then, that there is not yet a robust literature on formative assessment as a proven teaching and learning intervention.

New Frontiers in Formative Assessment is critical because it treats formative assessment as a complex set of interrelated assessment practices, and it does so with thoughtfully reformed enactments of curricula in each of three subject areas–reading, mathematics, and science. The attention to subject matter is important because the instantiations of formative assessment principles can be more completely worked out in the context of specific curricula. In the selected projects, content focus is also associated with ambitious learning goals aimed at conceptual understanding and—given that reformed curricula might require new teaching practices—attention is also paid to teacher learning. Of course, formative assessment principles could have been applied in traditional classrooms, with a focus on mostly lower-level skills and procedural knowledge. Indeed, in many of the mastery learning studies cited in the Black and Wiliam review, the outcome measures were quite low level; and, consistent with the behavioristic orientation of those studies, the instructional tasks were nearly carbon copies of the final assessments. But, given the worry that runs throughout the book regarding the lack of understanding caused by teaching to narrow external accountability tests, it makes no sense to invest in formative assessment without, at the same time, attending to conceptually richer learning targets.

The formative assessment tools described in a number of chapters are deeply substantive and therefore in sharp contrast to typical interim and benchmark assessments that imitate the formats of accountability tests and invite repetitive practice. Besides changing the cognitive level of assessment content, truly formative tasks change the character of assessment interactions. In recent work studying the use of formal interim assessments, my colleagues and I have drawn the distinction between classroom assessment practices focused on *scores* versus those focused on substantive *insight*. In many cases, students learn about their interim assessment results as a list of standards mastered and a count of the correct items needed to reach proficiency on the remaining standards. This contrasts with the examples in Audrey Poppers's chapter 5 of detailed "writing craft moves," such as the development of an engaging opening or the use of pacing to create suspense, which provide specific direction about how to improve student writing. As several authors here note, it does little good to generate mountains of data for each student if teachers have too little time to wade through it and if yet another step is required to decide on an instructional response. It may be much more worthwhile to develop key tasks or questions to check for student understanding at critical junctures in a lesson or curricular unit. A score, per se, is not needed, but as with good audience response system ("clicker") questions or class discussion of anonymous student work described by Daniel Damelin and Kimberle Koile in chapter 10, consideration of assessment task results can be turned immediately into a high-level, conceptually-focused instructional strategy.

By recruiting curricular reform experts in each of the subject areas, the editors have also ensured that the chapters share more coherently aligned assumptions about pedagogy consistent with contemporary learning theories. Just as learning mathematics or science requires an understanding of underlying principles, effective implementation of formative assessment requires an understanding of the underlying principles from the research on learning and motivation. For example, the feedback literature warns that feedback can actually be harmful if it implies a judgment about the person and is only likely to be helpful if it focuses on the task and provides specific help about how to improve performance on the task. Consider how this key principle informs the distinction made between summary score reporting versus actionable improvement insights. Cognitivist and sociocultural theories also help explain why it is important to elicit student thinking, not only so that teachers can build on what students know, but to develop the skill and habit of explaining one's thinking. As is evident in the chapters focused on formative assessment in science, learning to "think like a scientist" is as important to science learning as mastering scientific "content." Even kindergarteners, in Alison Bailey, Yiching Huang, and MaryLou Escobar's chapter 8, can develop observational and representational skills with carefully designed lessons and explicit attention to these expectations. In Jennifer Tilson, Alison Billman, Seth Corrigan, and Jacqueline Barber's chapter 9, learning to use evidence to justify claims is supported by substantive scoring criteria that show students how to improve: use more than one source of evidence, don't just list evidence but explain how it is connected to claims, etc. Sociocultural theory likewise underlies the centrality of classroom discourse practices in mathematics education reform and can explain why students "finishing each other's sentences," described in the GenScope project by Daniel T. Hickey in chapter 12, was so much more powerful a support for student learning than teacher intruded explanations.

Explicit attention to teacher learning is also important throughout the book especially because formative assessment tools are embedded in larger content-focused reforms. Teachers are not merely adopting one or two formative assessment techniques in the context of their existing practice but rather are engaged in more fundamental instructional change. We know from decades of research on teacher professional development that the kinds of projects described here are the most likely to be successful because they (a) allow teachers extended time to try out new approaches in the context of their own classrooms and (b) provide ongoing support that is *conceptual* (focused on the learning principles underlying the intentions of the reform) rather than merely *technical* (focused on how to access software). The chapters are replete with compelling examples of increased teacher learning about content and pedagogical content knowledge more generally as well as formative assessment per se. In chapter 4, by Kathi Cook, Cathy Seeley, and Linda Chaput, and in Damelin and Koile's chapter 10, the authors surmise that when teachers focused more explicitly on quality feedback to enhance student learning they actually clarified and deepened their own understanding of content. In Poppers' chapter 5, many teachers were not prepared to make use of diagnostic information in students' daily work until they had spent substantial amounts of time learning more about the features of good writing and how these features could be expected to be manifest at the grade level of their own students. In chapter 3, Herbert Ginsburg, Sandra Pappas, Young-Sun Lee, and Cynthia Chiong explain explicitly how learning theory informs their design of formative assessment tools that can enhance both student and teacher learning. Especially, they used the idea of a diagnostic interview as a means for teachers to get beyond exclusive focus on computational proficiency and attend more purposefully to students' invented strategies and mathematical ideas.

The projects described in this book are impressive examples of complex reforms. They illustrate how many pieces must be gotten right to enable fundamental change. Teaching for deep understanding requires setting of ambitious and integrated learning goals as in the blending of science and literacy goals or academic language affordances for English learners. It also requires the development of engaging and authentic tasks with embedded formative assessment tools that allow the benefit of documented patterns in student learning difficulties. Successful systems must be designed for desired participation structures making it customary to explain one's reasoning, discuss alternative solutions, and so forth. And, although there are no guaranteed remedies for every diagnosed learning difficulty, collectively developed and tried-out interventions provide much greater chances for success than leaving every teacher on his or her own to devise follow-up strategies.

In summary, these chapters describe more than specific formative assessment practices. Rather, they provide a detailed look at coherently designed, theory-driven, subject-specific curricular reforms. My partiality to this way of developing formative assessment tools comes in part from the research on teacher learning and subject-specific reforms mentioned above. But it also comes from a very personal lesson learned from a team of teachers as part of an assessment reform project twenty years ago. One group of third-grade teachers was using Marilyn Burns's replacement units, which were quite compatible with the conceptually-oriented problem types we had been using in our assessment project. Because researchers were committed to supporting the development of more insightful assessments within the context of each school's existing curriculum, however, we had not mentioned Marilyn Burns in the other schools. When the third-grade team in another school found out about this, they were quite angry and confronted the researchers at our next meeting. I will never forget the lead teacher holding up a copy of the Burns multiplication unit and saying, in an accusatory tone, "Look, she's worked it all out here." By this she meant that a conceptual pre-assessment, imaginative hands-one instructional activities, and open-ended assessment tasks that could be used formatively in the context of instruction as well as summatively at the end of a unit were already developed and just waiting to be used. Why were we asking teachers to start from scratch in rethinking their instruction and to develop their own assessments? Why not learn while trying out such a well thought-through resource? Indeed, we supported the introduction of Marilyn Burns's mathematics units from that time forward, and noted in subsequent reports that teachers not only learned the underlying principles and implemented the curricular units, but were also able to apply these principles in developing new units in geometry and measurement. As I learned, providing well-conceived curricular tools with theoretical justifications is by no means the same as dictating an instructional script, as I had feared. Rather, theoretically justified tools can be a powerful resource for instructional transformation.

If we acknowledge the complexity of what is being envisioned, as well as the barriers caused by traditional assumptions about learning exacerbated by the pressure to prepare for accountability tests, then projects described in this book are especially appealing because they have each taken up multiple parts of the complex puzzle. In the same spirit, in the future, well-developed curricular and assessment reforms could even take up the problem posed by Hickey in chapter 12 of too great a similarity between formative and summative problem types. An intentional continuum of extensions could be devised whereby learners are always asked to demonstrate their learning in both familiar and new ways. To be sure, conceptual tasks are less susceptible to seemingly proficient performance merely by rote, but I agree with Hickey that students still may rely on some ease of knowing what the problem is *about* based on a familiar problem frame, which means that students may not yet be sufficiently expert to recognize an instance of *x* in an entirely new context. Necessarily then, this should be the next step in assessing and teaching for robust understandings.

The chapters in this book may be regarded as important proofs of concept illustrating the uses of formative assessment in the context of ambitious, substantive reforms. Beyond project descriptions and rationale, the authors have also laid out a research agenda by which projects should be evaluated and underlying theories tested. Formative assessment tools should be examined in terms of their fidelity to cognitively demanding learning goals and the classroom interactions they encourage and support. They should be evaluated as to their feasibility, the utility of information provided, and the teacher learning that occurs under specifically identified conditions of professional development. When results were not uniformly positive, authors here developed the strategy of investigating effects associated with degree of implementation. Multiple authors also attended to measuring learning outcomes and were mindful of the distinction between performances on familiar, project-specific tests versus effects on distal, accountability tests. While formative assessment as defined by Black and Wiliam is still a work in progress, these projects have come a great distance in demonstrating what is possible and what benefits are likely to follow, just as foretold in the research literature.

Lorrie A. Shepard
Dean and Distinguished Professor
School of Education
University of Colorado Boulder

Introduction and Overview

The Elusive Promise of Formative Assessment

PENDRED E. NOYCE

Formative assessment is a powerful learning tool that is too seldom, too haphazardly, and too ineffectively used in the United States. Despite our national fervor to raise standards and see our students boost their performance on every sort of high stakes or international test, we have not found a way to harness the potential of well-planned, ongoing feedback to students about their learning. The purpose of this book is to delve into why this is so and how it can be changed.

For this book, we define formative assessment as the process of monitoring student knowledge and understanding during instruction in order to give useful feedback and make timely changes in instruction to ensure maximal student growth. Paul Black and Dylan Wiliam have characterized assessment *for* learning as any assessment designed or used specifically to boost student learning.[1] Such assessment differs from summative assessment, which is the assessment *of* learning for purposes of accountability or to rank or certify students. Black and Wiliam note, "Such assessment becomes formative assessment when the evidence is actually used to adapt the teaching work to meet learning needs."

In the chapters that follow, readers will find a series of examples of formative assessment programs as they have been developed, tested, and implemented in classrooms across three content areas: mathematics, literacy, and science. All the projects address how educators can move from a traditional approach that focuses on assessment *of* learning to one that builds on assessment *for* learning. Several chapters hint at yet another level of practice, where assessment can be seen as an opportunity for students, teachers, and curriculum developers to learn together as a community: assessment *as* learning.

A number of published studies suggest that formative assessment can lead to significant learning gains, with mean effect sizes ranging from an average of one-quarter to nearly three-quarters of a standard deviation.[2] Studies by Stuart Yeh have concluded that "rapid formative assessment" may be two orders of magnitude more cost effective for raising student achievement than is class size reduction.[3] Yet examples of widespread, systematic use of formative assessment are rare. While the chapters that follow detail some of the barriers to broad use of formative assessment, they also suggest principles and approaches that can help to overcome these barriers.

THE CHALLENGE OF CLASSROOM ASSESSMENT

In its most pure configuration, formative assessment means constantly probing and monitoring student understanding through a combination of formal and informal measures. Teachers ask searching questions, listen over the shoulders of students working together on a problem, help students assess their own work, assign and respond to brief writing prompts, and carefully design quizzes to uncover students' thinking. They may challenge students to discuss difficult concepts or to comment on how to strengthen one another's work. Teachers react to what they learn from this regular scrutiny by adjusting their instruction, leading students to greater understanding.

An ideal teacher makes these adjustments instinctively in the classroom every day, intuitively and seamlessly reacting to student needs. This teacher also analyzes written work for nascent student strengths as well as patterns of misunderstanding or skills that need to be strengthened. The teacher then responds by providing immediate feedback and/or customizing strategies for the next day's lessons that both address the students' conceptual or skills gaps and build on their strengths.

The problem is that this ongoing analysis and customization isn't easy to do. In the press of accountability, teachers often lack the tools, time, and confidence to adjust their lessons (and abandon the pacing plan) on a daily basis. They may lack the depth of content knowledge needed to analyze student misconceptions or see at what branch of reasoning the student went wrong. Their vision of iteratively building on student strengths may lack the support of an administration anxious to find quick fixes for low student achievement. Teachers may become discouraged if they decide that the high standards and deep understanding they value in the classroom are not reflected in end-of-year high-stakes tests.

Moreover, the distinction has become blurred between formative assessment and what has been called "mini-summative assessment" or "interim assessment." In their concern over accountability, many school and district leaders have seized upon assessment tools that can predict whether a student is on track to do well on the high-stakes end-of-year exam. Commercial testing firms have responded by aggressively marketing interim assessments that can be administered quarterly or even more often. Such tests usually mirror the format and content of high-stakes exams, with mostly machine-scored, multiple-choice items, and they can predict quite well how students will do on a similar test. Where they fall down is in providing teachers or students a closer analysis of where the students' difficulties lie and what should be done about it. Thus, they serve more as a tool for monitoring than a tool for improvement.

GOALS OF THIS BOOK

New Frontiers in Formative Assessment is written for practitioners who want to tap into the power of understanding what students are thinking. It is designed for teachers, principals, department heads, curriculum designers, and professional developers. Our purpose is to showcase ongoing work that can push the field of formative assessment forward in key ways. The authors invited to contribute to this volume are themselves all deeply immersed in authentic classroom use of formative assessment. We asked these authors to provide frank examples and illustrations of their work, and to include both successes and challenges. While many of the chapters provide evidence of impact, we did not ask the authors to prove that formative feedback "works." Rather, we asked them to paint a realistic picture of where they are and what they are learning at this point in their work.

One argument arising from the chapters that follow is that formative approaches must be tuned to specific content areas; generic approaches are not enough. The chapters raise issues and offer tools that are specific to mathematics, literacy, and science. They provide guidance in how to select formative tasks in mathematics, how to identify strengths in student writing, and how to encourage young English language learners to share their insights about science. One measure of success will be if this book leads to more focus on the assessment needs of specific content domains. How can we track growth in young students' use of different strategies to solve mathematical problems? How can we unpack what students need to do to comprehend a complex text? Can skills of inquiry be unraveled from knowledge of specific content in science?

A second major focus of the book is the advances in assessment made possible by computing power. Half the chapters that follow address the use of digital technologies in presenting questions, gathering student work, analyzing patterns of response, and adapting materials in real time to individual student needs. The wealth of experience in technology-supported assessment represented by these chapters should prove invaluable to curriculum developers who are contemplating how to embed assessment for learning within digital materials.

By highlighting how the formative potential of assessment is best exploited in specific educational contexts, the editors intend to encourage and provoke educators who want to move their own practice toward ongoing effective monitoring of and response to student learning in their own educational setting. By revealing common barriers to this work, along with a broad range of strategies that projects have devised to overcome the barriers, we hope to inspire educators to take formative assessment to the next level. In discussing areas of controversy, we hope to inspire administrators and professional developers to clearly define their educational goals and values before launching into a major assessment effort. And by presenting several different cutting-edge approaches to using technology for formative assessment, we hope to inspire curriculum developers to consider ever more creative ways to break the boundaries between assessment and learning.

OVERVIEW OF CHAPTERS

We have grouped the following chapters according to the academic domains they address. Chapters 1 through 4 focus on formative assessment in mathematics, while chapters 5 through 7 highlight language arts classrooms. Chapters 8 through 10 present projects addressing student learning in science. Chapters 8 and 9 both consider the integration of literacy assessment into science classrooms, while chapter 10 explores the frontiers of technology-based formative assessment for students who are learning science. We then step back, pause, and in the final two chapters take a longer view. Chapters 11 and 12 present the experience and evolving ideas of two researcher-practitioners who have long used formative assessment to probe student thinking and improve technology-based programs for teaching science. A concluding chapter summarizes common findings, challenges, and controversies, while also suggesting areas for future exploration in formative assessment.

Mathematics Education

Of all of the primary domains, mathematics seems to offer both the greatest challenges and the most direct opportunities for formative assessment. The challenges arise from the ease with which simple-minded multiple-choice questions can reduce the rich conceptual domains of mathematics to bare procedures. The negative consequences of accountability testing on mathematics proficiency were a focus of the 2001 National Academy of Sciences report "Adding it Up: Helping Children Learn Mathematics." A particular concern in that report was the intensive effort that many mathematics teachers invest in attempting to prepare their students for various high-stakes tests. These concerns have intensified in many school systems with the increased use of interim tests. Unfortunately, the types of mathematical questions asked on both interim and high-stakes achievement tests do not lend themselves to classroom instruction that builds the kind of enduring understanding needed for true proficiency. The four chapters concerning mathematics instruction in this volume provide compelling examples of teachers using social and technological tools to ask better mathematical questions, provide feedback to students, and adjust instruction accordingly.

Chapter 1 summarizes one of the more ambitious formative mathematics assessment efforts to date. David Foster and Audrey Poppers describe their efforts supporting middle school teachers in eight districts that collaborated to examine student performance on periodic performance assessments. Foster's intensive work was conducted with a subset of districts participating in the much larger Silicon Valley Mathematics Initiative (SVMI), which ran for nine years. SVMI's efforts were organized around a comprehensive set of highly regarded formative and summative assessments developed by Mathematics Assessment Resource Service (MARS). By starting with these assessments, Foster, working with district math coaches, was able to focus on the additional supports needed to help teachers use such assessments in their classrooms. For example, the chapter introduces an innovative method that streamlined the crucial task-selection process, helping teachers select the ideal formative assessment task for their class while also laying the groundwork for using that task with their students. The chapter also addresses how to help teachers decide what to do once they have examined results and developed a sense of class strengths and weaknesses as well as the unique needs of individual students. Foster's team tackled the thorny problem of differentiating instruction to help students who are falling behind, while still allowing scope for students who have mastered a topic to deepen and expand their understanding. This was accomplished in the classroom via *reengagement lessons*, which ask students to diagnose and discuss different approaches and common error patterns. The districts involved saw impressive gains on both the MARS test and the high-stakes California Standards Test.

Chapter 2, by Wendy Cleaves and Sandra Mayrand, delves more deeply into one key element of formative assessment in mathematics: looking closely at student work. Their chapter describes an innovative extension of the increasingly popular professional learning communities (PLCs) promoted by Rick DuFour and associates. In Cleaves and Mayrand's Mathematics Learning Communities, groups of teachers work with a coach or math facilitator to learn to look at student work systematically and objectively. The focus is on finding evidence of student strengths, of what students already understand and where they need to go next. This work, which Cleaves and Mayrand argue is best carried out in vertical teams that cross grade spans, often uncovers areas where teachers' own understanding is weak. The chapter illustrates how Mathematics Learning Communities can embrace high-quality formative assessment in mathematics. Consistent with the vision behind the PLC approach, team meetings serve as a safe place for teachers to build their own understanding of mathematics and of the role that good mathematical questions can play in the development of mathematical proficiency.

Chapter 3, by Herbert Ginsburg and colleagues, extends the idea of uncovering student understanding of mathematics to the youngest students, those in kindergarten through third grade. Extending work that others had piloted in the field of literacy, Ginsburg's team is pioneering the use of handheld computing devices to help guide teachers through diagnostic assessments and follow-up interviews. This work demonstrates an important extension of the curriculum-based measurement (CBM) approach. While widely used with students with learning disabilities, CBM has encountered resistance more broadly because of its focus on speedy completion of relatively specific arithmetic questions. Ginsburg and colleagues show how CBM can be extended by bringing in two new elements. The first is the inclusion of newer, more conceptual questions focusing on number sense. The second is the introduction of cognitively oriented diagnostic interviews that represent a modification of methods used by developmental psychologists. What is particularly groundbreaking in this work is the pioneering use of computer technology to conduct such interviews alongside a computer-based CBM system. The chapter shows that particularly with young students, seeing students' answers to math problems is not enough; it's also important to examine how their strategies develop over time.

Technology also plays a central role in the formative assessment practices in mathematics described in chapter 4. Kathi Cook, Cathy Seeley, and Linda Chaput describe their efforts working with a product developed by Agile Mind, a company partnering with the Charles A. Dana Center at the University of Texas in Austin. The product consists of a suite of online tools to support teachers of mathematics for grades six through twelve. Among these tools is a set of embedded assessments that serve a variety of functions. Some guide students as they learn, providing hints and feedback. Others gather and organize data on student effort, success, and error patterns, so that teachers can follow the progress of individual students along with diagnosing the strengths and misconceptions arising in the class as a whole. Teachers can customize the assessments to meet the needs of their own students. Meanwhile, student responses provide formative feedback to Agile Mind's developers, allowing them to continually refine the ways the mathematics is presented.

Literacy and Language Arts

Literacy and the language arts are natural domains where assessment practices for learning can be realized. Particularly with writing, many curricular goals lend themselves to open-ended assessment practices. In chapter 5, Audrey Poppers discusses

Every Child a Reader and Writer (ECRW), a multiyear Silicon Valley initiative focused on strengthening student writing in the elementary grades. Poppers presents the tools and processes used, along with examples of student writing showing different strengths and growth over time. ECRW writing workshops provided significant ongoing professional development and support from coaches. The chapter highlights how the open-ended nature of writing, which makes it a natural target for formative assessment, also requires substantial investment by teachers in their own learning and makes major demands on teacher and classroom time. These ongoing requirements present challenges for sustained initiatives. In ECRW, these challenges were compounded by an accountability environment that tested writing only intermittently. Moreover, state tests veered away from the state writing standards and did not appear to value the depth and variety of student work expected by ECRW. Chapter 5 provides a cautionary tale about how the best of tools, professional development, and outside support can be stymied by a poorly aligned policy environment.

Our two chapters on reading highlight the potential synergy between formative assessment and digital technology. In chapter 6, Lisa Lineweaver discusses the introduction in Boston schools of Formative Assessments in Student Thinking in Reading (FAST-R). This program is organized around an instrument that helps teachers diagnose and address weaknesses in students' reading comprehension. FAST-R consists of seventy formative reading assessments developed for grades two through ten. These assessments are used to analyze student capacities and error patterns when finding evidence and making inferences from text passages. Teachers working with literacy coaches use this diagnostic information as part of their cycles of inquiry, making decisions about how to modify their instruction in upcoming units to address the comprehension issues they uncover. What is particularly noteworthy about the FAST-R work is that it fits nicely into the increasingly popular "interim assessment" context, but provides more instructionally useful information and feedback.

Chapter 7 extends the synergy between formative assessment and digital technology to better serve struggling readers, with a particular focus on those who are overcoming learning disabilities. Nicole Cohen and colleagues of the Center for Applied Special Technology (CAST) report on assessment tools built into the Strategic Reader. This program combines an interactive, Web-based reading environment that reflects Universal Design for Learning principles with ideas drawn from curriculum-based measurement. The program supports middle school readers with a variety of tools to help them navigate a set of commonly assigned novels. Students can highlight words for vocabulary help or listen to the computer-read selections. Students can record their own oral reading to help teachers diagnose problems with reading fluency. They also respond to embedded assessment questions in a variety of ways, from speaking their response to typing it into the computer to discussing it online with other students. This variety of response modes encourages student interaction and discourse and allows the teacher to customize instruction and differentiate interventions within the classroom.

Science

Many teachers recognize that the sciences are a promising domain for integrating language instruction. Focusing on the language of explanation is a good way to keep scientific inquiry from being reduced to a collection of specific facts and definitions. But such integration also calls for careful assessment to ensure that neither set of goals gets lost in the combination. In chapter 8, Alison Bailey, Yiching Huang, and MaryLou Escobar report on an effort to bring formative assessment in science to bear on how English language learners transition to using academic language in kindergarten. Here the primary focus is on students' oral production—how they learn to talk about science activities and concepts. A dedicated group of kindergarten teachers from a charter school worked with university colleagues and researchers over three years to improve their practice in three areas: clarifying learning goals, making success criteria explicit and clear to students, and expanding their repertoire of ways to evoke evidence of student learning. Compared to the other chapters in this volume, this chapter presents a relatively immediate type of formative assessment, occurring during teacher-student interactions minute by minute every day. Such an approach can easily be adapted for work with older students and those for whom English is their primary language.

In chapter 9, Jennifer Tilson and colleagues report on Seeds of Science/Roots of Reading, the result of collaboration between leading scholars in science education and reading research. It is one of the nation's foremost programs developed specifically to integrate literacy and science instruction. The chapter presents examples and guidelines that should be immediately useful to others who are using formative assessment to help integrate science and reading. It shows how Seeds of Science/Roots of Reading uses writing prompts to simultaneously assess growing understanding of scientific concepts and growth in specific writing skills such as organization and use of evidence. The authors show how to construct a scoring guide for such integrated assessment tools, and they conclude with evidence that this combined approach leads to improved student learning of science concepts. The authors emphasize that formative assessment needs to come at just the right time in the learning process and that efficient assessment practices are particularly crucial for teachers trying to cover multiple and diverse curricular goals. The authors demonstrate how to increase efficiency by making formative assessment an intrinsic part of instruction, rather than an interruption.

Chapter 10 discusses the use of technology tools and embedded assessments to support growth in conceptual understanding in science. Based on work carried out by the Concord Consortium, one of the nation's leading research centers for technology-supported science education, Dan Damelin and Kimberle Koile present Rhode Island Information Technology Experiences for Students and Teachers (RI-ITEST), and Logging Opportunities in Online Programs for Science (LOOPS). Both projects use cutting-edge technology to capture and respond to student work. Since even student keystrokes can be recorded, the problem is not how to collect enough information, but rather how to manage and present it in such a way that a teacher can quickly respond. Key here is the fact that not just "clicked" answers to multiple-choice questions but student-created artifacts such as graphs, labeled diagrams, or commentary can be shared in real time with a teacher or with other students in a way that facilitates discussion.

Perspectives and Reflections

Following the presentation of these eleven specific projects, the book's final two chapters seek to provide a first-person perspective on where formative assessment in the

United States has come from and where new work is pressing against the frontiers. Perhaps not surprisingly, both chapters focus on the promise and problems inherent in ever-evolving technology. In chapter 11, Paul Horwitz takes a long view of the use of computers in science instruction. He describes advances over the past thirty years in what technology allows, and how those advances have affected his own thinking about what computer-based models can teach and how to tell what students are learning. Helping lay the groundwork for the coming explosion of educational computer games, he explains how computer-based models allow assessments that feel like games. The challenge inherent in taking this approach is ensuring that success in the game translates to evidence of understanding in other settings—the perpetual problem of learning transfer. Horwitz also muses on the future of technology-based assessment, asking how group learning can best be assessed, what role teachers should play in a classroom where students spend much of their time on computers, and how the psychometric community can respond to the challenge of performance assessments that employ more open-ended item formats.

Finally, in chapter 12, Daniel T. Hickey provides a "gentle critique" of prevailing approaches to formative assessment. He discusses how evolving views of the nature of teaching and learning affect how we think about establishing "coherence" between formative and summative assessment and shares some concerns about possible negative effects of growing national interest in formative assessment. He considers how emerging situative theories of assessment and participatory approaches to instruction offer a rather different way of thinking about the range of formative and summative assessment. Based on continued experience with the GenScope project and other technology-based curriculum projects that built assessment into their design, he argues for the value of more informal formative assessment practices. These practices begin with student-oriented *feedback conversations* that build on shared representations arising from technology-supported inquiry. Hickey argues that improved conceptual understanding can and should come as a by-product of that shared discourse. He suggests that the conceptually oriented individual problems typically used in formative assessments should be used for evaluating feedback conversations and refining curriculum, rather than for providing direct formative feedback or for adjusting instruction. He also attempts to resolve the enduring tension between summative measures of group achievement and formative assessments of individual understanding by treating both as particular forms of educational discourse. Hickey concludes by suggesting that new approaches to instruction and assessment need to pay particular attention to the context in which learning is taking place, if that learning is to be useful in fast-changing twenty-first century knowledge networks.

CONCLUSION

For the reader who wonders what to make of this collection of chapters, drawn from across the content areas and covering classrooms from kindergarten through high school, our concluding chapter points to common findings, challenges, and controversies. In the conclusion, we draw the findings together both across content areas and in relation to specific content domains.

Common Findings

Any program of formative assessment, whether oral, written, or based on technology, must start with a series of decisions about not what is easy to ask but what is most important for students to learn. A second important finding is that working with formative assessment can be a valuable professional development opportunity for teachers, in which they not only learn new pedagogical techniques but also come to understand fundamental content in a more profound way.

The chapters demonstrate that a set of common tools, ranging from low-tech organizers to high-tech systems for gathering and displaying information, can reduce the burden of interpretation for individual teachers. But digital technologies do more than organize data: they can fundamentally change the relationship of assessment to curriculum, embedding assessment so thoroughly that students sense no discontinuity and assessment becomes just another stage of learning.

Much formative assessment work has focused on getting the diagnostics right, but even with the best of information, teachers are faced with the question of what their next instructional moves should be. We note that formative assessment often leads to teacher demand for additional practice-oriented professional development, and that feedback and next steps require careful attention to teacher-student and student-student discourse.

Finally, we note that successful implementation of formative assessment requires strong leadership and sustained administrative support, which means providing the tools (such as working networked computers), the time to collaborate, and the professional development that teachers need if they are to gather diagnostic information and act on it in useful ways. But beyond leadership, the durability of systems for formative assessment appears to depend on how well the external accountability system aligns with and supports classroom goals. The fact that this compatibility of goals is often a changing picture, and one outside the control of teachers and program developers, presents a challenge and leads to difficulty in finding "proof" that formative assessment "works." We offer different approaches developers may take to address this dilemma.

Controversies and Frontiers

Like any field, the field of formative assessment has its controversies. One of these is just what kinds of assessment deserve to be called "formative." Practices associated with interim assessment and curriculum-based measurement raise concern for many educators. Similarly, the question of whether formative assessment should move away from focusing on conceptual growth among individual students toward a more situated, shared system of mutual feedback is clearly controversial. We offer a way of thinking about how these different approaches can find their place within a comprehensive assessment system.

Finally, we make some predictions about the forces that will affect formative assessment in coming years. Digital technologies will continue to burgeon and diversify, and even as the nation moves toward a common core curriculum and shared high-stakes tests, it is likely that the modes and settings of education, including home schools, charter schools, and online courses, will continue to diversify as well. Those creating assessment tools need to keep in mind that the role and identity of the teacher are likely to change. Researchers and psychometricians, too, will need to move quickly to develop new theory and ways of measuring student interaction with complex material.

WHY FORMATIVE ASSESSMENT MATTERS

We hope that together these chapters will stimulate readers to think about what formative assessment has to offer the science, mathematics, or literacy classroom. Clarifying goals, providing systematic feedback to students and teachers, and carefully planning the next instructional steps can be a powerful way of motivating and organizing efforts to improve learning in a core content area. Nevertheless, one of our central concerns in organizing this volume has been to caution those who might look to formative assessment as a quick fix for raising scores on standardized measures of achievement. With thoughtful implementation, student learning will become stronger and richer, but initial growth in test scores is unlikely to be explosive. Rather, formative assessment is a tool for curriculum developers, teachers, *and students* to use in furthering their own understanding of knowing and learning. Formative assessment probes to the heart of what education is about: it allows educators to explore how students' understanding and knowledge change in response to what teachers do. This exploration can be tremendously motivating for everyone involved. Close investigation of how students learn can motivate educators to renew their participation in the educational enterprise in order that students may learn more deeply and with more joy.

PART I

Mathematics Education

CHAPTER 1

How Can I Get Them to Understand?

Formative Assessment and Reengaging Students in Core Mathematics

DAVID FOSTER AND AUDREY E. POPPERS

Consider Mr. Avery, a seventh-grade math teacher in Hilldale, California. The state and district are moving toward a mandate that all eighth-grade students enroll in Algebra I. As a result, seventh-grade teachers have been issued pacing guides to ensure that they cover the prerequisite material. It's now February, and a benchmark assessment has been administered across all of seventh grade. When Avery receives his students' score sheets, he is distressed but not surprised to see that many of them are performing at a level that predicts they won't be proficient on the end-of-year California Standards Test (CST). Unless something changes, these students will be unprepared for eighth-grade algebra.

But exactly which skills and concepts Avery's students are missing is unclear from the broad reporting categories of the benchmark assessment. Moreover, the structure of the school day allows him no extra time with these struggling students, and the district pacing guide insists that Avery move quickly to the next section of the district-mandated text. Avery sighs. He can offer the struggling students afterschool help sessions and extra homework, but he worries they'll be too discouraged to take him up on the offer. Worse, he's not sure where to focus or what to do differently in review sessions to make his students understand the material better a second time through. He faces another batch of students passing on without mastery; next year he'll try to do better.

CURRENT STATE OF MATHEMATICS ASSESSMENT IN THE UNITED STATES

A growing number of researchers and educational leaders are making a case for the promise of formative assessment to improve student learning. Paul Black and Dylan Wiliam's review of the research cited compelling data to indicate that formative assessment focused on student thinking can inform future instruction and learning.[1] However, there is little evidence that assessment-driven analysis of student understanding has been used to drive instruction in the typical mathematics classroom in the United States.[2] Textbooks, pacing guides, state tests, and courses of study govern and limit the topics that are taught, the time spent on each topic, and the depth of what is taught.

These practices continue despite the results of international, national, state, and college entrance tests indicating that American high school students have not learned adequate mathematics to support their own futures and career opportunities, nor to support the future success of America in a globally competitive world.

The information that is most valuable for teaching must focus on student thinking. Marnie Thompson has stated, "The central idea of formative assessment, or assessment for learning, is that evidence of student learning is used to adjust instruction to better meet student learning needs."[3] She describes formative assessment practice as students and teachers using evidence of learning to adapt to meet immediate learning needs, minute to minute and day by day. Most teachers don't actively use these practices. In fairness, very few teachers are trained to use formative assessment, and most have no apprenticeship in implementing its use in classrooms.

Educators and school districts often claim to use formative assessment but fail to focus on student thinking. Testing in schools is prevalent, yet traditional testing is usually conducted to produce grades or to place or sort students—all summative approaches. Seldom do the findings from these summative assessments directly drive learning by informing teachers' instruction.

During the past decade of high-stakes accountability, states have developed standardized tests, and schools have been held accountable for how their students perform. The schools' stakeholders focus on test results and the improvement of student scores. As a result, schools often introduce benchmark tests to predict how students might perform on a summative high-stakes exam. A significant industry has grown up around these instruments. While some educators characterize benchmark tests as formative assessments, they don't match the true definition and purpose of formative assessment. Instead, benchmarks are mini-summative tests that may accurately predict future success on another test but do not provide specific information to guide instruction. Dylan Wiliam labels them "early warning summative assessments."[4] The reports produced by benchmark tests usually provide a scale value on a continuum of scores and may list topics where students have been successful and unsuccessful. But interim tests are so removed in format and time from the actual curriculum, this information is insufficient to help teachers truly grasp what students know, what errors or misconceptions are hampering their understanding, or what approaches in reasoning were successful and where students met challenges or struggled. This information is essential to helping advance the struggling student and for successful refinement of future lessons.

Educational practice has a long history of substituting superficial practices for more rigorous approaches, thus rendering them ineffective. The subsequent lack of success is then regarded as proof that the recommended practice is ineffective. Continued use of these mini-summative benchmark assessments and the mislabeling of them as formative assessments threaten to undermine the effective use of formative assessments and their potential for promoting improved instruction and student achievement.

There are multiple reasons for the superficial attempts to implement formative assessment in the United States. These include outdated or simplistic beliefs about the nature of teaching and learning, the current structure of schooling, the lack of in-depth professional preparation for teaching, and shallow understanding of the particular domain. In addition, in the United States, there are few examples of widely used models of formative assessment from which teachers can learn. The Silicon Valley Mathematics Initiative (SMVI) has attempted to develop one such workable model.

THE SILICON VALLEY MATHEMATICS INITIATIVE

In response to low mathematics performance among California students, the Noyce Foundation created the SVMI in 1996. SVMI was a partnership of the Santa Clara Valley Mathematics Project (part of the California Subject Matter Projects) at San Jose State University with more than thirty-five member school districts. Its primary components are formative and summative assessment systems, pedagogical content coaching, and ongoing professional development and leadership training. SVMI contracts with the Mathematics Assessment Resource Service (MARS), a National Science Foundation–funded international project that involves UC Berkeley and the Shell Centre for Mathematical Education in Nottingham, England, to develop performance exams and scoring materials. For summative performance assessments, teachers, coaches, and SVMI leaders collaboratively scored the MARS exam, as has been discussed in past articles.[5]

Participation in SVMI professional development, formative assessment, and coaching was voluntary, and schools could pick and choose from among the various services SVMI offered. Coaches worked with a limited number of teachers in grades K–10 every year; more teachers attended professional development; still more used formative assessment; and some schools used MARS summative performance exams schoolwide. Only in 2006, as described later in this chapter, did we begin more intensive work with nine middle schools to test the impact of full, schoolwide implementation of formative assessment.

SVMI Theory of Action

Over time, our observations have confirmed what many researchers have concluded: most teachers lack the in-depth understanding of mathematical concepts and strategies needed for effective instruction. Without such depth of understanding, it is impossible for teachers to design instructional experiences that drive significant student achievement. The SVMI theory of action is based on the premise that teachers can improve their instructional effectiveness by using a cycle of formative assessment practice. As they examine the student thinking revealed in assessment tasks and consider each student's current knowledge and misconceptions, teachers also clarify and strengthen their own understanding of mathematical concepts.

As a result, we designed SVMI to support two parallel lines of thinking, with a complementary focus on teacher learning and student learning. The SVMI process aims to engage teachers in an integrated effort to deepen their own understanding of the mathematics behind a given concept as they simultaneously seek to understand their students' thinking about that concept. Building on both the accurate knowledge and the misconceptions students demonstrate in a task, teachers can design new instructional approaches that target students' current needs.

While we believe that the most effective use of formative assessment practices occurs on a daily basis, this means supporting the teacher's minute-by-minute decision making. We have found that very few teachers are adequately prepared to successfully implement that level of practice. Therefore, the SVMI sought to develop tools and procedures to provide scaffolding for teachers' learning.

This is not a quick intervention. At first, teachers need informed and skillful guidance to boost their motivation and success with the assessment cycle. Once they begin to realize that both they and their students are looking more deeply into mathematics concepts, they find the process to be highly engaging and generative. We believe that investments in rigorous teacher learning, structured to support application in the context of one's own classroom, can promote significant student learning.

The SVMI Formative Assessment Cycle and Tools

The SVMI cycle mirrors common conceptions of formative assessment; SVMI's contribution lies in the development of tools and procedures to support teacher learning and implementation. This work is organized around a continuous cycle with four stages: (1) selecting and administering a worthwhile assessment task, (2) examining and analyzing student work, (3) using the findings to inform and enhance teacher knowledge, and (4) designing and teaching lessons to address the learning needs of students. One of the things we learned early on was that teachers needed significantly more support with every part of the assessment cycle than we had assumed. Teachers' responses and struggles provided formative information for our SVMI team, leading us to develop tools and procedures to build teachers' understanding as they worked to develop both their formative assessment skills and their deeper understanding of mathematical ideas. Following are the procedures and tools associated with each of the cycles.

Select and administer tasks. At the outset, SVMI focused on finding worthwhile assessment tasks. Reflecting the extensive effort that went into developing them, we found the MARS tasks to be strong in assessing math concepts, relatively easy to use, and powerful for providing valuable feedback about student thinking and understanding. The databank of MARS assessment tasks includes an extensive range of concepts and levels, covering the most important mathematical ideas from second through tenth grades. This rich collection of tasks proved to be a crucial resource. Good formative assessment tasks are difficult to find and very difficult for the average teacher to create.

A worthwhile assessment task provides instructionally useful information for the teacher. The task must address the core mathematics and also capture the potential range of student performances. A task provides little formative value if students are totally unsuccessful with the mathematics—equivalent to receiving a zero score. This may well mean that the student simply does not understand that concept that is being assessed. A well-designed and well-selected task provides access so nearly all students can demonstrate some level of success.

The MARS tasks are designed to assess a wide range of knowledge. The tasks gradually increase in complexity and cognitive challenge as the core mathematics is assessed. A well-designed task delves deeply into the core mathematics, probing for understanding and requiring explanations in order to provide evidence of students' thinking and knowledge. The final stage of the task requires an elaborated level of understanding of the core math; at this level, the task may challenge students to demonstrate strong conceptual understanding, generalize from a situation, justify a finding, or make a connection. Success at the elaborated level is the best indicator of future success on related mathematical ideas.

Initially, many teachers need support to select an appropriate task. The MARS Task Anticipation Sheet was developed to assist teachers with this process. It asks teachers to record their thoughts about a given task in three sections. First, they designate areas where students are likely to be successful and what this indicates about what students know and can do. It is essential for the teacher to anticipate how students could be successful and to consider multiple ways students might approach the problem. Second, teachers anticipate areas where students are likely to struggle and what this indicates about skills or concepts they still need to learn. Finally, teachers record their proposed plan for teaching. Based on this anticipatory work, the teacher selects a worthwhile task that matches the learning trajectory of her students. Answering the questions frames the mathematical ideas and processes to be learned and assessed, and focuses teacher attention on evidence of student thinking that will appear in their work. In other words, the procedure and tools that SVMI developed to help teachers *select* a worthwhile task also helps prepare teachers to know when and how to offer the task to students to further instruction.

Teachers may use the Task Anticipation Sheet individually or in collaboration with others. A promising method for considering a potential task begins with the teacher actually doing the task as a learner would. In this manner, the teacher is able not only to examine the core mathematical ideas embedded in the task, but also to develop an appreciation of the mathematical thinking the students must engage in and the complexity of the steps and strategies students will encounter. When this is done collaboratively, it gives teachers practice and experience in discussing underlying concepts with their students, which is helpful.

Examine and analyze student work. Students' completion of a well-selected and well-designed task provides a goldmine of information that can drive significant teacher and student learning. However, mining the student work is not simple. Examining student work to determine trends, identify misconceptions, categorize successful strategies, and extract important findings is a learned art. Those who have become accomplished at this important investigative work are often self-taught, driven by a passion for understanding how their students think. Our goal was to help every teacher develop these proficiencies.

Because of our belief that analyzing student work is core to becoming an effective teacher, the SVMI team created tools and protocols to help teachers with this stage of the process. The analysis process usually begins with scoring. This process can initiate a transformational shift away from teachers' traditional scoring practice—that of merely correcting mistakes or assigning a grade to a student's work. In our view, scoring can help teachers learn the mathematical content, recognize different approaches to successful solutions, and develop a critical eye for examining student work. Collective scoring can help teachers learn these things *and* learn to discuss them with others.

The MARS tasks come with rubrics and fifteen student responses that illustrate the range of student performances on the task. Consider the fifth-grade task "Candies," shown in figure 1.1, which assesses students' knowledge of fractions, ratios, and proportional reasoning. The first part of the task provides access for students. The prompt

FIGURE 1.1   Candies task

This problem gives you the chance to:
- *work with fractions and ratios*

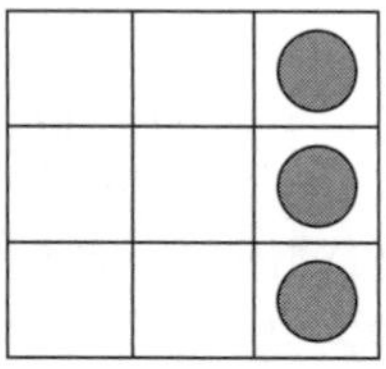

1. This is Amy's box of candies.
   She has already eaten six of them.

   What fraction of the candies have been eaten?

   _____

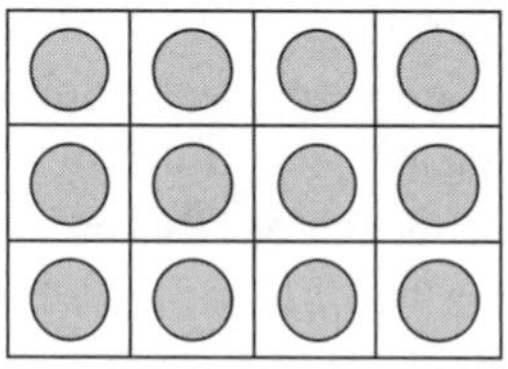

2. From this box Valerie shares out 12 candies.
   She gives Cindy one candy for every 3 candies
   she eats herself.

   How many candies does Cindy eat? _____
   Show how you figured this out.

3. In a packet of mixed candies, there are 2 fruit centers to every 3 caramel centers.
   There are 30 candies in the packet.

   How many caramel centers are there? _____
   Show how you figured this out.

4. Anthony makes candies.
   First he mixes 1 cup of cream with 2 cups of chocolate.
   In all he needs 9 cups of these two ingredients.

   How many cups of chocolate does he use in this candy recipe? _____
   Explain how you figured this out.

   _____

   _____

includes a visual model and asks the students to name the basic fraction of the candies eaten. In parts two and three, the core mathematics is assessed. Students must demonstrate knowledge of ratios and proportional reasoning. The fourth part is the elaborated level for fifth-grade students. The students must solve a multistep problem involving a proportional relationship and a sum of ingredients. Figure 1.2 shows the scoring rubric for the Candies task.

The scoring process guides teachers to match evidence in their students' papers to points on the rubric, calibrating their judgments with those of other teachers in order to score reliably. In the scoring process, teachers see a wide variety of successful mathematical approaches, as well as common misconceptions and errors found in unsuccessful

FIGURE 1.2   Scoring rubric for candies task

The core elements of performance required by the task are:
• *work with fractions and ratios*

Task 1: Candies	Rubric	
Based on these, credit for specific aspects of performance should be assigned as follows:	Points	Section points
1. Gives correct answer: **2/3** or **6/9**	1	1
2. Gives correct answer: **3**	1	
Shows work such as: 1 + 3 = 4 12 / 4 =		2
Accept diagrams.	1	
3. Gives correct answer: **18**	2	
Shows work such as: 2 + 3 = 5 30 / 5 = 6 6 x 3 =		
Accept diagrams.	1	3
4. Gives correct answer: **6**	1	
Gives a correct explanation such as: Anthony mixes a ration of one cup of cream to two cups of chocolate. The ratio stays the same for different amounts. So I wrote the numbers in a chart like this 1 to 2 = a total of 3 2 to 4 = a total of 6 3 to 6 = a total of 9		
Accept diagrams.	1	2
Total points		8

efforts. Uncommon but valid approaches can make scoring difficult; however, considering these solutions deepens the teacher's understanding of the mathematics and the range of student thinking.

The analysis process is typically led by a math coach or mentor until teachers have gained sufficient skills at analyzing and learning from student work. The MARS Task Analysis Sheet, parallel in format to the Anticipation Sheet, provides a frame for tracking evidence of understanding or difficulties in student work. Teachers record where students were successful or struggled with the task, and outline a plan for teaching based on their analysis of strengths and gaps in student understanding. Systematically recording important evidence and findings from student work in this way is the first step in enhancing the teacher's ability to address the learning needs of the students.

Inform and enhance teacher knowledge. During the first years of SVMI, we carefully examined a few tasks given across the initiative in order to determine patterns of student response. We documented common errors in students' answers and their problem-solving processes; common methods that produced successful solutions; and unique, interesting and/or unusual solutions. Realizing that teachers could benefit from the insight we gained, we collated our findings in an instrument called Tools for Teachers, often referred to as simply "the toolkit."

Tools for Teachers contains data describing common features of student performance along with examples of student solutions—both those that are well conceived and well communicated and those that contain examples of common errors or invalid reasoning. The toolkit also features unique or unusual approaches that show interesting mathematical thinking. We developed a commentary for each piece of student work, pointing out important features of the work and why we selected it.

In the initial stage of development, the toolkit was merely a report of findings from a significant sample of students. As we became more sophisticated, we adapted it to use interactively with actual student work, allowing teachers to compare their current students' work against the performance of the large normative set. By charting their own student work to see trends and patterns of performance, teachers can identify their students' strengths and varied approaches. They can also compare their students' errors and struggles in light of commonly identified misconceptions and challenges that appear in the larger sample.

For each task analyzed in the toolkit, we first provide a graph and analysis of MARS task data showing the frequency distribution of scores from the thousands of students who have attempted the task. Next we provide student work samples, including examples of well-conceived and well-communicated solutions (figure 1.3), examples of common errors or invalid reasoning that resulted in unsuccessful attempts at solving the problems (figure 1.4), and unique or unusual approaches that show interesting mathematical thinking. These examples help teachers learn different methods that successful students use in problem solving. Often these solution paths are based on strong conceptual foundations and show sound logic and reasoning. Encouraging multiple solution strategies is important in class, and the toolkit can be a rich resource for ideas and approaches.

An important feature in Tools for Teachers is a chart for each task, elaborating particular point scores with the common understandings and misunderstandings of students who attained the score. These charts generally consist of a matrix that makes explicit the areas of student need.

Over the years, the toolkit became more sophisticated and rich with information. The section on implications for instruction grew, providing numerous instructional suggestions and curricular resources. This toolkit provides teachers with important information to enhance their mathematical and pedagogical content knowledge. However, teachers still needed specific help in acting on this information.

Inform instruction. The fourth phase of the cycle—supporting teachers to create follow-up learning experiences—took a while to develop. Originally, we were content to help teachers access information, assuming that they would know what to do next as a result. In some instances, teachers did learn about student performance and then adjusted instruction in subsequent years to prevent common errors, confusion, or misconceptions. However, we were disappointed at teachers' efforts to use the information to improve the learning of their current students. When teachers were uncomfortable with the amount their class had learned, some retaught a lesson, but the reteaching was usually a review of the original lesson or one very similar to the origi-

FIGURE 1.3   Student work on candies task

Student A, who receives a full score of 8, uses three models to think about ratios. In part 2, the student uses a dealing-out strategy; 1,2,3 for Valerie, then 1 for Cindy, etc. In part 3, the student uses a table that shows equivalent ratios. In part 4, the student uses a scale factor of three to solve the problem.

1. This is Amy's box of candies.
   She has already eaten six of them.

   What fraction of the candies have been eaten?

   2/3 of the candies ✓

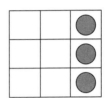

2. From this box Valerie shares out 12 candies.
   She gives Cindy one candy for every 3 candies she eats herself.

   How many candies does Cindy eat? _3 candies_ ✓
   Show how you figured this out.

   1, 2, 3 candies = Valerie has eaten before Cindy 1.
   1, 2, 3, 1,   1, 2, 3, 2   1, 2, 3, 3

3. In a packet of mixed candies, there are 2 fruit centers to every 3 caramel centers.
   There are 30 candies in the packet.

   How many caramel centers are there? _18 caramel centers_ ✓
   Show how you figured this out.

fruit	2	4	6	8	10	12
caramel 1	3	6	9	12	15	18

   12 + 18 = 30

4. Anthony makes candies.
   First he mixes 1 cup of cream with 2 cups of chocolate.
   In all he needs 9 cups of these two ingredients.

   How many cups of chocolate does he use in this candy recipe? _6 cups_ ✓
   Explain how you figured this out.

   3 × 2 is 6.   3 × 1 is 3.   3 + 6 equals 9.

---

nal. Instead of using the findings to define what specific experiences would promote further student learning, teachers regarded the findings as prompts to go back and do the lesson again with minor changes in emphasis.

Reengagement Lessons

We realized that even when teachers were reteaching concepts, they often did not appreciate the need to engage their students in thinking about the concepts in a new

FIGURE 1.4   Student work on the scale factor

Students had difficulty understanding what to do with the scale factor. Student F loses points on part 3. The student is able to think about the part/part/whole relationship in 2 and 3 (3+1 makes a group of 4, 3+2 makes a group of 5). The student solves part 2 by counting the number of groups of 4, which is the same as the number of candies. The student then counts how many groups of 5 there are in 30. Why does this strategy no longer work? What is different mathematically in part 3?

2. From this box Valerie shares out 12 candies.
   She gives Cindy one candy for every 3 candies
   she eats herself.

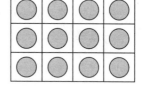

   How many candies does Cindy eat? __3 candies__ ✓
   Show how you figured this out.

$$3 + 1 = 4 \quad / \quad \overset{1}{4} + \overset{2}{4} = 8 + \overset{3}{4} = 12$$

3. In a packet of mixed candies, there are 2 fruit centers to every 3 caramel centers.
   There are 30 candies in the packet.

   How many caramel centers are there? __6 caramel centers__ ✗
   Show how you figured this out.

$$3 + 2 = 5 \quad / \quad \overset{1}{5} + \overset{2}{5} = 10 + \overset{3}{5} + 15 + \overset{4}{5} = 20 + \overset{5}{5} = 25 + \overset{6}{5} = 30$$

4. Anthony makes candies.
   First he mixes 1 cup of cream with 2 cups of chocolate.
   In all he needs 9 cups of these two ingredients.

   How many cups of chocolate does he use in this candy recipe? __6 cups__ ✓
   Explain how you figured this out.

   Since 1 + 3 = 3 I times it by 3 because I know that it equals 9. But I knew
   I have to times three by 2 witch equals six.

way—the need to reengage them differently in the mathematical ideas. In order to distinguish this type of lesson design from more traditional reteaching or review, we began to talk with teachers about the idea of reengagement and to develop tools to support the practice of designing lessons that were directly tied to the results of formative assessments.

Reengagement lessons are constructed to involve students in the core mathematical ideas of the assessment task in order to deepen their understanding and build a better conceptual foundation to learn further mathematics. The follow-up or reengagement lessons featured in Tools for Teachers suggest ideas for designing lessons using the formative findings. It is common for test results in a class to range from students indicating little success to those students who successfully complete the task. A well-designed reengagement lesson addresses students' learning needs across this continuum.

First, the lesson provides access and develops a conceptual foundation for understanding the core mathematics so that all students know how to approach and attack future problems. While this is the goal in most review and reteaching lessons, it is usually unsuccessful. If students cannot connect the mathematics to what they already know and develop an understanding of the core concept that underlies the problem, they will be doomed to forget and fail to solve future related problems. Surfacing the concept in a manner that helps students make connections and see relationships is a necessity for learning. Even for students who have successfully completed a task, further challenges that require thinking critically and diving deeper into the mathematics can solidify their understanding. This is accomplished as students reengage in the conceptually deeper aspects of the task.

Although there are no formal templates for constructing reengagement lessons, certain principles might be considered. The lesson should address the learning needs of the entire class by:

- Providing access to the task.
- Solidifying foundational math concepts.
- Addressing the core mathematics.
- Surfacing errors and misconceptions in the students' work.
- Using student work examples and thinking for others to critique.
- Promoting higher thinking at the elaborated level of the task.

One interesting method for exploring these challenges is to use actual student work from the class or the toolkit. The work is transcribed to assure anonymity. Students are asked to examine the work, determine if it is mathematically sound, and either justify the findings or show where the work lacked mathematical accuracy or logic. The challenge of critiquing and explaining other students' thinking and misconceptions requires and develops high cognitive skills.

Asking the class to explore the student thinking in unique or mathematically interesting approaches or in intuitive and logical approaches that contain mathematical flaws is a productive way to deepen understanding. Comparing alternative approaches is also valuable. The teacher may select a few different approaches and have the class examine and compare the methods to make connections between ideas and representations.

A sample reengagement lesson. This example of a reengagement lesson was developed as a result of fifth-grade responses to the MARS Candies task introduced earlier. The core mathematics of the task involves understanding and using proportional reasoning, including the use of both part-to-part and part-to-whole comparisons. At the elaborated level of the task, students must work through multistep proportional reasoning problems.

The first question from the assessment task shows a candy box with three candies and six missing pieces. The question states, "This is Amy's box of candies. She has already eaten six of them. What fraction of the candies has been eaten?" The responses of this fifth-grade class revealed that a few students struggled with the access level of the assessment task—developing the ratio between the candies eaten and the total candies in the box. Some students counted the missing candies and compared that with the total number of candies to determine six-ninths. Other students used traditional procedures to simplify the fraction to two-thirds. About 10 percent of the students were unsuccessful in arriving at a correct ratio.

At the beginning of the reengagement lesson, it was important to revisit the access level for the 10 percent who were confused and to refresh the memories of those students who were successful. Understanding this level is important for providing access to the more complicated understanding at the core and elaborated levels. The class was presented with the same illustration and the first question from the assessment, but this time the answers six-ninths and two-thirds were also shown. The teacher asked the class to use the drawing to illustrate how one could know the answer was six-ninths. Students first paired up to discuss and share their answers; the teacher then gathered the whole class together to discuss the question. Individuals shared that they counted the missing pieces to determine the six and then counted all the squares in the box to determine the total number of candies, which was nine; therefore, the fraction of eaten candies was six-ninths.

Next the teacher asked the class where two-thirds was represented in the picture. After a think-pair-share process, a student described how she saw three separate columns. Two of the three columns had all pieces missing; thus, the fraction of eaten pieces to total pieces was two-thirds. In this manner, the simplification process was reinforced as a conceptually accurate solution to the original task, a connection that is often missing in math classrooms.

The second question in the Candies task addresses the core mathematics—understanding ratios and solving a proportional reasoning problem. The task provides a new illustration of a rectangular candy box, arranged in three rows by four columns. The prompt indicates that, "Valerie shares out 12 candies. She gives Cindy one candy for every 3 candies she eats herself. How many candies does Cindy eat? Show how you figured this out."

In order for the class to consider different approaches to the second question, the teacher used two different student work samples. The teacher asked the class to look at the method the first student used to solve the problem, as shown in figure 1.5. She

FIGURE 1.5   First student work for problem 2, reengagement lesson

asked the students whether it was correct, and if so, how the student was illustrating a correct solution. After pair-share discussions, one student suggested the following reasoning: The person must have worked down the column, giving three to Valerie and one to Cindy; next, continuing down the second column the person gave three more to Valerie and one more to Cindy. The person continued this process until all the candies were distributed. By counting, one could see that a total of nine candies went to Valerie and three to Cindy.

The teacher then showed the second sample (figure 1.6), and students were asked again to consider how the students approached the problem. After the students had a chance to discuss the work in small groups, the students shared ideas. A common idea the class shared was that the student used rows to first distribute three to Valerie and one to Cindy. In this manner, students analyzed two different approaches to tackling the problem. Comparing and contrasting different approaches to a mathematical task raises the students' analysis to a higher level of cognition, links mathematical representations, and encourages varied attacks on problems.

This example concerns operations on fractions, which have traditionally been taught in fifth grade. It illustrates that the concept of a fraction as a ratio is often misunderstood. Because the students are abstracting, their understanding of part-to-whole, part-to-part, and part-to-part-to-whole can be challenging at this level. The real impact of the lesson comes with the third question of the task, which assesses the core mathematics of proportional reasoning at a deeper level by building on the context provided by the first two questions. Because proportional reasoning is a major topic in most sixth-grade math curricula, every struggling fifth grader should have these sorts of opportunities to reengage with this developmentally crucial concept.

The final problem in the Candies task takes the core concept to an elaborated level and once again assesses students' conceptual understanding of proportional reasoning. The problem states, "Anthony makes candies. First, he mixes 1 cup of cream with 2 cups of chocolate. In all, he needs 9 cups of these two ingredients. How many cups of chocolate does he use in this candy recipe?" Instead of having students just rework the problem, the teacher used actual student work in the reengagement lesson to promote deeper understanding. She showed two different solutions, one using representations of measuring cups and one involving representations of segmented rectangles. In each

FIGURE 1.6   Second student work for problem 2, reengagement lesson

V	V	V	C
V	V	V	C
V	V	V	C

case, she asked the class to consider how the student approached and solved the problem. The class needed to determine whether the solution was correct and to explain either the correct reasoning or the faulty logic.

The class attempted to make sense of the student's reasoning, shown in figure 1.7. Originally, before the whole-class discussion, the line did not appear on the table in the sample. Members of the class added the line to help explain where the student went wrong. Some classmates argued that the student was confused over the nine cups in the problem. Instead of thinking it meant a total of nine cups, the student believed that it was nine cups of chocolate. The class reasoned that since the pattern of chocolate cups grew in an even-numbered pattern of two cups, four cups, six cups, eight cups, ten cups, and so on, nine cups would never appear in the table. Therefore, they argued that the student must have stopped short of nine, stopping at eight cups. They pointed to the table and the highlighted eight cups as their evidence.

Next the teacher asked the class to consider a second solution to Anthony's problem (figure 1.8). After puzzling over the thinking behind the student's approach, the class suggested that the student must have been confused by what was meant by the total number of cups being nine. Instead of understanding that there were just nine cups in the batch, the student must have thought that the number of cups of each ingredient was a factor of nine. As the students in the class made sense of the error, the teacher recorded where the actual nine occurred by circling the three sets of three cups that total nine.

This level of reasoning about another student's work represents a high level of mathematical understanding. It is called for in the Common Core State Standards for Mathematics, Standards of Mathematical Practices—Practice 3. Construct viable arguments and critique the reasoning of others. As students learn to reason and justify, it is equally important for them to know why some arguments are mathematically invalid. A reengagement lesson deepens the mathematical understanding rather than merely revisiting the original content. It is important that those students who were unsuccessful develop an understanding of the core mathematics in the task, and that all students go deeper and develop conceptually sound foundations. This work prepares students for more advanced thinking in the future.

FIGURE 1.7   First student work for problem 4, reengagement

1c	2ch
2c	4ch
3c	6ch
4c	8ch

8 cups

FIGURE 1.8   Second student work for problem 4, reengagement

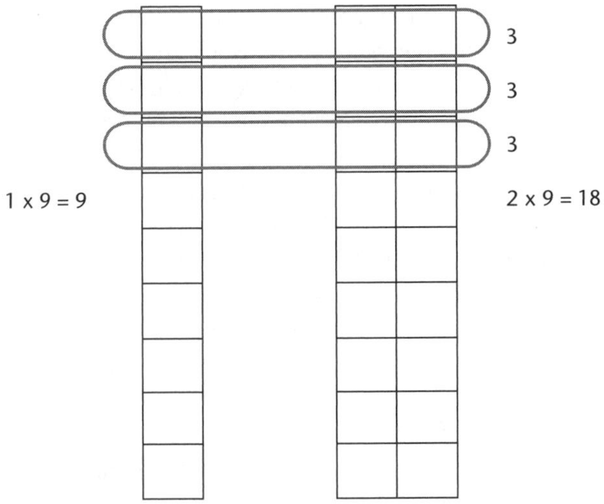

$1 \times 9 = 9$ 3
3
3
       $2 \times 9 = 18$

1 creams   2 chocolate

IMPLEMENTATION AND APPARENT IMPACT

In the fall of 2006, the Noyce Foundation selected nine SVMI member districts to work together more intensively as part of the First in Mathematics Collaborative (FiMC). Districts were selected for their strong leadership and their willingness to engage fully with a program of professional development based on formative assessment. FiMC pursued goals and strategies similar to SVMI's, but incorporated a more intensive focus on supporting a structured implementation of formative assessment practices. The Noyce Foundation conducted an internal study of FiMC. Eight of the nine FiMC districts participated in the three-year effort. One district withdrew in 2008, citing competing professional development demands. During the 2007–2008 and 2008–2009 school years, all of the middle school teachers from the eight FiMC districts participated in relatively intensive professional development in the strategies described earlier. All of the teachers engaged in a minimum of fourteen formative assessment cycles. Working together within their math departments, teachers (1) selected and administered a series of common MARS performance assessment tasks, (2) met to score and analyze the student papers, and (3) identified successful practices, common errors, and misconceptions. They used Tools for Teachers documents to research student performance and compare their students' work to the general findings. This process helped teachers gain greater knowledge about both math content and pedagogy and to craft and teach new lessons that reengaged their students in the key math concepts.

Before examining learning outcomes, we set out to document how faithfully the FiMC teachers had implemented the formative assessment practices. In 2009, using teacher surveys and double-checking results with math coaches, we learned that almost

90 percent of middle school math teachers in the eight FiMC districts reported engaging in formative assessment practices using the MARS bank of released tasks. About two-thirds of FiMC teachers reported completing the formative assessment cycle, including designing and teaching reengagement lessons. In addition, most of the teachers who engaged in this intensive professional development reported that they planned to continue to use the MARS formative assessments. In addition, every one of the participating middle schools reported that they had continued to administer and analyze student work using MARS performance assessment tasks as a regular part of their mathematics curriculum during the 2009–2010 school year. These commitments were made despite the fact that formal funding and professional development sponsored by the Noyce Foundation had ended the year before. Given the face validity of high-quality formative assessment practices, this persistence alone suggests that the participating school systems saw substantial value in the approach that was pioneered in this project.

Impact on Understanding and Achievement

To consider the impact of these practices, we compared the mathematics performance of eight FiMC districts with that of nineteen non-FiMC member districts in the SVMI. Baseline data collected in 2006 showed that the demographic composition of the two groups was quite similar: the overall percentage of students who qualified for free and reduced lunch, who were English language learners, who were nonwhite, and whose parents did not attend college were all within three points for the two groups. Initial student achievement of the two groups was also quite similar, though slightly lower in the FiMC districts. In 2006, the 2,747 eighth graders in the FiMC included 32 percent passing the CST and 27 percent meeting standards on the MARS summative assessment; 51 percent of them were enrolled in Algebra I. That same year, the 6,778 eighth graders in the non-FiMC districts included 35 percent passing the CST and 31 percent meeting standards on the MARS summative assessment; 52 percent were enrolled in Algebra I.

Given the similarity of the two groups, it seemed reasonable that the nineteen non-FiMC districts could be used as a comparison group to the FiMC treatment group. Nonetheless, this research design presents an obvious selection bias. In selecting and then retaining districts that were more able to participate in a relatively comprehensive professional development effort, the FiMC likely ended up selecting the districts with relatively coherent mathematics curriculum and accountability practices, while excluding the districts that were less coherent. This alone would be expected to give the FiMC students some advantage in mathematics proficiency in the subsequent years. Thus, the results we report next should be seen more as an existence proof than as the results of a rigorous controlled trial.

The 2006–2007 school year was spent recruiting, selecting, and inducting districts into FiMC. This was followed by two years of intensive professional development, utilizing the formative assessment cycle as the major strategy. We evaluated the impact of the program by examining performance on the MARS summative performance assessment and the multiple-choice CST. Both assessments were carefully constructed, and each had carefully set levels needed to qualify for grade-level proficiency. We hypothesized that by the third year of the program (2009), the percentage of students scoring at the proficient level or above in the thirty-two schools in the eight FiMC districts would be dramatically higher on the MARS summative test (which was similar in content and format to the formative assessments) and significantly higher on the CST (which was aligned to the entire set of grade-level standards and used a very different item format), compared to the students in the nineteen non-FiMC districts.

Our expectations were borne out across all three grade levels. On the MARS summative assessment, 69 percent of the FiMC sixth graders were proficient versus 45 percent of the non-FiMC students. In seventh grade, the difference was 45 percent versus 28 percent, while the difference for eighth graders was 38 percent versus 20 percent. In summary, the advantage across the three grades for the FiMC students was 24, 17, and 18 percentage points. Compared to other large-scale professional development efforts, these are very large differences and appear to be substantially more than could be explained by the manner in which the FiMC schools were selected. In our opinion, the magnitude of the difference is compelling evidence that FiMC students became stronger in working at high cognitive levels, using nonroutine approaches, applying conceptual understanding, and explaining and justifying their conclusions. Given the nature of the professional development, we assume that teachers also advanced their understanding in this regard.

Of course, the MARS summative assessments targeted the same levels and types of reasoning that teachers in the FiMC had been focusing on. Relative to the less sophisticated reasoning that is typically captured using multiple-choice formats, we believe that this kind of mathematical reasoning is far more important. Nonetheless, the curriculum-oriented MARS assessments necessarily introduce an undetectable level of bias, relative to an externally developed standards-oriented measure. Consider, for example, that a skeptic might argue that FiMC and the MARS summative assessments might have both targeted a relatively narrow range of concepts. If so, then an independent measure that captures nontargeted concepts and forms of reasoning might reach the opposite conclusion. To this end, we accessed scores on the mathematics subtests of the CST for all students in the SVMI districts.

On the multiple-choice CST, 65 percent of the FiMC sixth graders met the grade-level standard (proficient or advanced), compared to 50 percent of the students in the other districts in the SVMI. For seventh graders, 59 percent of the FiMC students reach the proficiency standard, compared to 48 percent for the non-FiMC students. For eighth graders, 48 percent of the FiMC students reached the proficiency standard, compared to 35 percent. Thus, the achievement advantage that was presumably the result of the FIMC was 15 percent, 11 percent, and 13 percent across the three grades. Given that such external standardized measures have proven to be quite resistant to large-scale professional development interventions, the magnitude of these differences is quite compelling. The fact that the pattern of the CST gains across grades presented a nearly perfect echo of the gains on the MARS summative assessment across grades adds further support that these advantages were the result of the FiMC professional development.

California state policy sets Algebra I as the grade-level course for all eighth graders. Since a No Child Left Behind audit in 2006, students who take a general eighth-grade course and achieve proficiency on the state's general eighth-grade exam are considered to be achieving at below grade level. To meet this new requirement, many districts throughout the state significantly increased the number of students enrolled in Algebra I in eighth grade. Across the state, this policy had a negative impact for many students. Many failed the course. In fact, more eighth-grade students failed Algebra I in 2008 (560,000) than took the course in 2003 (506,000).

That was not the case for the FiMC eighth-grade students. The results for FiMC eighth graders were particularly compelling, because a higher bar had been set for meeting standards at that grade. Only eighth graders who were proficient or advanced on the CST or who achieved levels three or four on the MARS Algebra I or Geometry exam were counted as meeting the standard of *proficient*.

Impact on Enrollments

We also examined changes in enrollment patterns to search for evidence of the formative assessment practices' impact. We expected that the cumulative effect of the FiMC would result in an increased percentage of eighth graders enrolling in Algebra I or Geometry. This is precisely what we found. From 2006 to 2009, the percentage of students enrolled in Algebra I and/or Geometry in FiMC districts grew from 51 percent to 76 percent. The non-FiMC districts' Algebra I and Geometry enrollment also increased, but at a much slower rate, growing from 52 percent to 60 percent over the same time.

Given that increasing the proportion of eighth graders enrolled in algebra or geometry was a central goal for statewide reform efforts, the increase of 25 percentage points in the FiMC districts is quite impressive compared to the increase of just 8 percentage points in the other districts. This increase in taking advanced courses is particularly impressive, given that the percentage of the students meeting the standard on both the CST and MARS tests also increased. Increases in enrollment began in 2006–2007, at the start of the project and prior to intensive work in formative assessment. The initial enrollment increase was accompanied by a dip in the percentage of students meeting the standard in CST tests in the more advanced courses. However, in the two subsequent years, student achievement increased significantly. By spring of 2009, the combined impact of enrollment increases and improved performance meant that the percentage of all eighth graders in FiMC districts who scored at the proficient or advanced level on the CST Algebra I or Geometry test had grown from 32 percent to 48 percent. This was a tremendously gratifying outcome for FiMC.

CONCLUSION

During SVMI's research and development work, we realized that our initial four-stage conception of a useful system of formative assessment was too simplistic to adequately guide and support a rigorous and effective process. Figure 1.9 provides an elaborated view of the cycle, including those activities that proved to be crucial to the efficacy of each step, and for which teachers needed models and guided practice. Key activities that are subsets of each of the major steps in the cycle are shown in the boxes. SVMI tools provide a scaffold for learning as teachers move through each of the steps or phases of the cycle.

FIGURE 1.9   SVMI formative assessment cycle

Key activities which are subsets of each of the major steps in the cycle are pictured in the boxes. SVMI tools provide a scaffold for learning as teachers move through each of the steps or phases of the cycle.

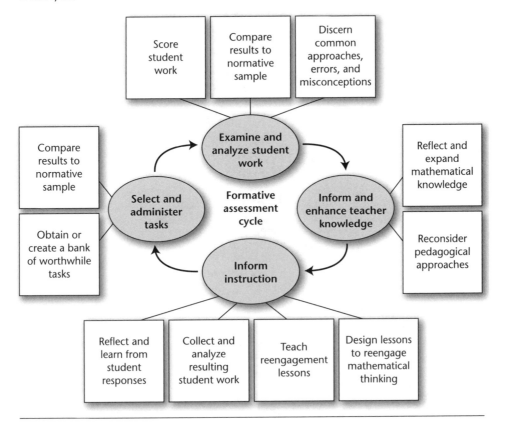

The tools developed in SVMI were employed in the FiMC work to support teacher learning and systematic implementation of formative assessment practices. The tools described in this chapter provide a useful model for teachers as they move toward independent and daily use of formative assessment practices.

Although the Noyce Foundation sponsorship of the FiMC and SVMI initiatives ended in June 2009, the work lives on as the Silicon Valley Mathematics Initiative. (More information is available at www.svmimac.org. A rich archive of tasks and video of reengagement lessons can be viewed at http://www.insidemath.org.)

CHAPTER 2

What Were They Thinking?

A Closer Look at Student Work in Mathematics Learning Communities

WENDY CLEAVES AND SANDRA MAYRAND

"Sometimes the only thing I know about [a] new student is what is written on his or her worksheet or homework paper. This is my data—this is what I need to be able to analyze."

—MLC member, Lowell, Massachusetts

School districts today strive to be data-driven, yet no greater source of data exists than written student work, which unfortunately is not used often enough to its fullest potential. Often, K–8 teachers work in isolation with little to no time to reflect on their practice and consider how students understand mathematics concepts. Teachers, for the most part, assess students' mathematical understanding by the number of correct answers on math problems in an assignment, quiz, test, and so on. But what happens when a child gets the correct answer with the incorrect reasoning or, conversely, the wrong answer with the correct reasoning? If a teacher is only grading for the right or wrong answer, she or he may be missing important mathematical thinking that could inform daily instruction and help students evolve into strong math students.

WHY USE STUDENT WORK?

How does a teacher make the leap from seeing what is written down on the student's paper to knowing what information the student knows, understands, and is able to do? How can a teacher gather that information? How can he or she identify evidence of understanding within a student's written work? How can a teacher develop this skill in order to improve his or her own understanding of mathematics teaching and learning?

A group of teachers and professional developers working in central Massachusetts decided in 2002 to investigate this challenge more fully. We knew from experience that teachers need a solid background in the mathematics they teach. Yet taking math content courses does not always provide teachers with the skills they need to connect that knowledge to how students understand mathematics and to their classroom practice. We also knew that a collaborative school culture fosters continued learning by teachers. By linking mathematics content and the practice of formative assessment in a professional learning community (PLC), we were able to focus specifically and productively on the needs of the classroom teacher.

PROVIDING A STRUCTURE FOR A PLC IN MATH

According to Richard DuFour and Robert Eaker, a school that develops a culture of a PLC should have a shared vision, values, and goals; use collaborative teams; implement collective inquiry in order to participate in action orientation and experimentation; seek continuous improvement; and maintain a results orientation.[1] In addition, teachers involved in a PLC work on the following key areas:

1. *Standards*—What are students expected to know and do?
2. *Evidence*—How do we know when students have learned?
3. *Differentiation*—What do we do when students have not learned?
4. *Enrichment*—What do we do when students already know the content?

Using these PLC guidelines to inform the work and drawing on our own experience in providing professional development, we decided that guidelines and structures needed to be in place for a purposeful discussion. In designing the Mathematics Learning Community (MLC) project and researching existing materials, we learned that generic learning-community protocols do not have the specificity to delve deeply and purposefully into how students understand mathematics. Without a framework for the discussions, the conversations might not be deep, probing, and focused enough to transform how a teacher or school thinks about students' mathematical understanding. However, within this framework, we could maintain flexibility based on the constraints and needs of a district or school using these materials. For example, some schools hold the MLC sessions during contractual time and all teachers attend. In other schools, participation is voluntary. Both have been successful. We created the MLC to exemplify what a PLC should look like in math in order to avoid the top-down implementation of PLCs that end up being nothing more than traditional staff meetings.

MATHEMATICS LEARNING COMMUNITY

The art of teaching combines the teacher's content knowledge with pedagogical skills that come to bear in a classroom. Coordinated, classroom- and content-focused professional development should link challenging learning standards and curriculum to specific problems hindering student progress and thereby provide the support teachers need for effective teaching. In this environment, the MLC project was born with the goal of developing materials for teachers to use in a school-based MLC that focuses on analyzing student work. Analysis of authentic student work is the main vehicle for discussion and communication within the MLC due to its importance in the daily life of a classroom teacher. An MLC seeks to provide content-focused, school-based professional development for mathematics teachers.

People enter the teaching profession with a basic interest in how children think and learn, yet the business of a school day often overshadows that interest. Looking at student work (LASW) collaboratively as a formative assessment in a learning community provides a teacher the time, safe environment, collegiality, and expertise of other teachers to improve and enhance the practice. Along the way, we also learned that an MLC can do much more when it gains such a focus.

MLCs are content-based learning communities ideally made up of seven to fifteen members and cofacilitated by teacher leaders and/or math coaches. MLCs are meant to provide math teachers an opportunity to collaborate with peers, both at the same grade level and at other grade levels, to connect important mathematics content and pedagogy to their own work in classrooms. During MLC meeting time, which is designed in two-hour sessions, teachers engage in math metacognition, problem solving, looking at student work, and making connections to classroom practice, with the bulk of the time and discussion spent on following the protocol for LASW.

A typical MLC session follows an agenda that contains five sections. The first section (Mathematical Background—twenty minutes) focuses the teachers on the mathematical background needed to successfully complete the tasks within the session. This gets everyone on the same page and reviews what the session is about mathematically. During the second section (Math Metacognition—twenty-five minutes), teachers solve problems, often mentally, and then share thought processes and solutions. Facilitators chart the thinking of the group and refer to this information throughout the remainder of the session. In the third section (LASW—fifty minutes), group members analyze student work using the specific MLC protocol for LASW to identify evidence of student understanding. In the next section (Our Learning—twenty minutes), teachers connect their learning to classroom practice using methods such as writing a problem that would relate the content of the session to the grade level at which they teach. The final section (Feedback and Wrap-up—five minutes) is used to elicit feedback about the session itself and encourage teachers to reflect on their individual learning in a quick write-up. MLC sessions are set up in this way to provide a structure for collaboration that focuses on student learning. Because so many school districts and teachers are strapped for extra time, it is important to spend that time wisely. With a structure and protocol in place, teachers can use even an hour of professional development time effectively and avoid wasting time on unproductive discussion.

LOOKING AT STUDENT WORK

By paying attention to what a student understands and how he or she understands a math concept (strengths model), a teacher is better able to know where the student is mathematically and support the next steps in the student's learning. Looking at what the student does not know (weaknesses model) provides less information to the teacher. Figure 2.1 gives a student work sample from MLC session 3. The student work was analyzed from two different viewpoints, explained in table 2.1.

It is evident from analyzing the samples that this student does indeed understand some important mathematics, as stated in the strengths model example. Since the task itself required the student to write a word problem for the given number sentence, it is important to focus on the story provided. The student did correctly find the missing addend, used the inverse operation of subtraction to solve the addition problem, and attempted to write a story problem with at least one of the quantities represented. The

FIGURE 2.1   Student work sample, MLC session

Write a story problem for this number sentence: 18 + <u>54</u> = 72

$$\begin{array}{r} 7\overset{\scriptscriptstyle 1}{2} \\ -\ 18 \\ \hline 54 \end{array}$$

Ther were 18 boats
and 3 What away.
how many does
boat are left?

Source: Student Work Sample, MLC session 3, © Commonwealth of Massachusetts, DOE

---

teacher analyzing the student work from the strengths model goes on to suggest possible next steps in instruction ("draw pictures to help write a story"). This teacher does make an assumption that the student has a low level of literacy or writing skills based on the grammar used to write the sentence in the work; this may or may not be true and would need further assessment.

To work effectively with this new style of professional development, teachers need training in how to objectively examine student work for evidence of understanding, partial understanding, and misunderstanding. Although this way of looking at student work is a common strategy, it is not done well without guidance and practice. The skill of objectivity is developed throughout the MLC by analyzing anonymous yet authentic student work samples. Such samples allow teachers the opportunity to analyze the work without feeling ownership about their teaching (i.e., fear that the student work will reflect poorly on their instruction) and to avoid seeing things within the work that do not actually exist (i.e., making assumptions about what the student understands based on what was taught to that student during class). Only after meeting for a mini-

TABLE 2.1   Student work analysis, strengths model versus weaknesses model

Strengths model	Weaknesses model
Correctly identified the missing addend.	Does not connect the numerical representation to a real-life event.
Used inverse operations to correctly find missing addend.	Made a number story that was unrelated except for one of the numbers.
Student struggled with the story aspect of the question. Very low literacy level.	
He used 18 in the problem but chose 3 instead of 54 and 72—the idea of a story problem is there.	
But lacking literacy skills to see it through.	
If this student fully understood combinations, despite low literacy skills, he would have the translation piece.	

Source: Student Work Analysis—Strengths Model vs. Weaknesses Model, Work from MLC Facilitator Training Participants, 2009.

mum of six sessions do we recommend that teachers begin to bring in student work from their own classrooms, and even this is done in a controlled way so as to maintain focus on the evidence within the work itself.

The MLC protocol for LASW in figure 2.2 was developed to provide the necessary structure for focused conversations.

Each step of the protocol not only develops an important component of the skill of LASW but also contributes to the mathematical discussion as a whole. The steps of the MLC protocol will be explained later, using the following LASW problem from MLC session 4:

> *Jackie and Sara collected shells at the beach. Jackie collected 48 shells in all. She collected 13 more shells than Sara. How many shells did Sara collect? Use pictures, words or numbers to show how you got your answer.*

MLC protocol step one: Read the problem and discuss what it is assessing. Figure 2.3 shows a usual outcome of this step. Typically, this step helps to establish important math concepts and skills embedded in the problem. By proactively discussing the goal of the problem, potential misunderstanding of the problem statement is avoided; the

---

FIGURE 2.2   MLC protocol for looking at student work

1. Read the problem and discuss what it is assessing.

2. Solve the problem individually.

3. Share your thinking with a partner.

4. Discuss the mathematics of the problem as a whole group.

5. Look at how students solved the same problem.

6. Identify evidence of understanding by using guiding questions.

7. Discuss evidence of student understanding as a whole group.

Source: MLC Protocol for LASW, © Commonwealth of Massachusetts, DOE

FIGURE 2.3   Jackie and Sara

Example of a poster charting out the concepts and skills involved in the shells problem

Operation Adding/subtracting

Terminology   "in all"
                     "more than"
                     "how many"

Comparison model
                     For subtraction/relates to addition

Parts and whole model

Missing piece/What is the question asking?

Methods/representing their solution

---

facilitator gets a sense of the teachers' understanding of the mathematics and uses the meeting time effectively. Additionally, this step helps to model the process of teachers identifying specific learning objectives of a given problem or task. For this particular problem, MLC members decided that it assesses the operations of addition and subtraction; the terminology of "in all," "more than," and "how many"; the comparison model; and parts and whole model.

MLC protocol step two: Solve the problem individually. Teachers identify what is needed to solve a problem and assess student understanding of the concepts and skills involved in a problem by doing it first themselves. For this particular problem, teachers' solutions included various pictorial representations, including bar and line models, as well as algebraic equations and numerical expressions.

MLC protocol step three: Share your thinking with a partner. This step allows teachers to try out their reasoning and problem-solving strategy with a neighbor before sharing with the group as a whole.

MLC protocol step four: As a whole group, discuss the mathematics of the problem. MLC facilitators select particular strategies or solutions to share with the whole group. A document camera facilitates this sharing. Solutions or strategies shared usually range from concrete to abstract and/or vary in representation (i.e., numerical, graphical, symbolic). If there is incorrect thinking within the group, the facilitator can address it at this point.

Figure 2.4 shows the possible order in which MLC facilitators would select solutions to be shared for this particular problem, along with the mathematical reasoning behind each choice.

MLC protocol step five: Look at how students solved the same problem. Usually four samples of student work are provided for MLC facilitators to then distribute to MLC members. Depending on available time and format, teachers may analyze anywhere from one to all four samples during an MLC session.

For example, the students' work provided for this session showed approaches from four students that almost all differed from the sample teacher solutions. Three students drew diagrams to illustrate the problem, using a symbol to represent one shell (i.e., 0 or Δ). Two students used subtraction models to solve the problem—one used the take-away model with an equation ($48 - 13 = 35$), while the other showed subtraction as comparison (48 empty circles drawn, then 13 of those circles crossed out, resulting in 35 empty circles). Unfortunately, the latter student miscounted the total number of circles and represented the solution as $48 - 13 = 37$.

MLC protocol step six: Identify evidence of understanding by using guiding questions. Through the use of both specific and general guiding questions, teachers are able to pinpoint evidence of understanding, partial understanding, and misunderstanding within the student work. Teachers are also able to identify areas of difficulty, concern, or possible follow-up with the student. This approach supports the strengths model of LASW by asking specifically for what students know and understand. The guiding questions grid helps teachers to systematically identify what each individual student knows and un-

FIGURE 2.4   MLS protocol for looking at student work

Sharing teacher solutions to the shells problem

Solution	Reasoning for sharing with the whole group
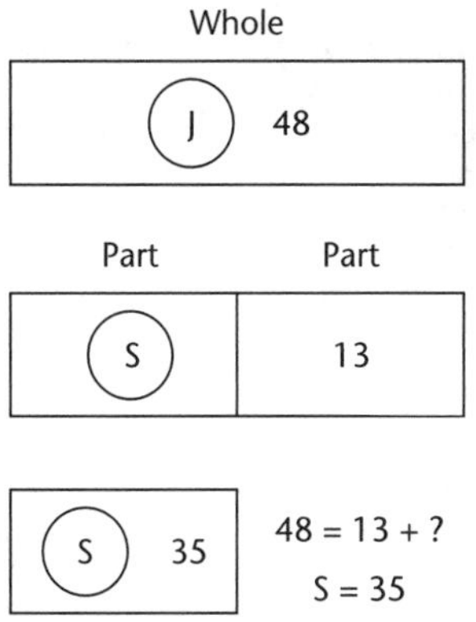 Whole J 48 Part Part S 13 S 35 48 = 13 + ? S = 35	MLC facilitators wanted to begin by sharing a picture or a model that would be accessible to as many MLC members as possible. Here, this is a picture representation of a part-part-whole model, where the whole represents Jackie's shells, and the parts are Sara's shells (one part is the 13 and the other is the missing addend).
J = 48 13 + S = J 13 + S = 48 48 – 13 = S 35 = S	Next, the MLC facilitators shared this solution that is a symbolic representation, using algebraic equations. This solution method was used by the majority of teachers but not by all, so facilitators felt it was important enough to bring forward to share with the group as a whole.

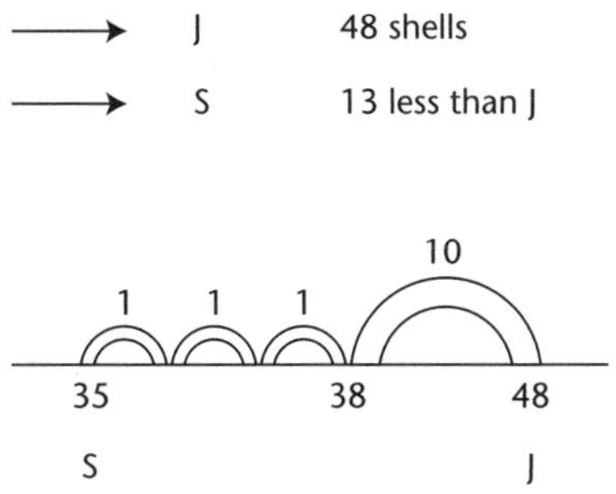 ⟶   J   48 shells
⟶   S   13 less than J
 	
          10
   1   1   1
  35   38   48
  S   J
	Here, the problem is solved using subtraction on an open number line. MLC facilitators chose to share this solution last to expand the thinking of the group as only one person chose to solve the problem in this way. In addition, they wanted to have the group preview the open number line model that will be discussed during MLC Session 5.

Source: Carol L., MLC facilitator in Springfield, Massachusetts.

derstands based solely on the written work provided. Guiding questions focus attention to particular parts of the work and also to the discussion among MLC members.

Facilitators use the grid in table 2.2 to guide the discussion about important mathematics in the student work samples. The grid captures the teachers' responses to the guiding questions as they analyze the shells problem shown earlier. In later sessions, the teachers are invited to formulate their own questions for the grid.

TABLE 2.3   Analysis of student work

Example of a completed guiding questions grid

Student	What strategy does the student use to solve the problem?	What evidence exists that the student understands the connection between the operations of addition and subtraction?	If the student drew a picture, does the student use it to solve the problem or represent the solution?	Do all representations match (pictures, numbers, words)? If not, what does this tell you about the student's understanding?
A	Subtracts 13 from 48 to get 35	Represents as sub-traction problem in written explanation of procedure uses "took 13 from 48" (subtraction)	None	Yes—number sentence shows sub-traction and words describe procedure
B	Draws out rows of 10 triangles and then rows of 7 tri-angles (should be 8) for 48 shells, subtracts 13 from 48	Checks work with re-lated addition sen-tence, 48 – 13 = 35 so 35 + 13 = 48	Picture represents 47 shells—if it were used would it have led to the correct solution?	Picture doesn't match numbers in problem, words re-state what problem is looking for
C	Draws out 48 cir-cles to represent 48 shells then counts back 13 to arrive at 31 (should be 35)	13 as part of the whole 48	Picture used to lead to solution. 13 counted but 35 not counted correctly	Picture represents 48, 35, and 13 shells, number sen-tence should be 48 – 13 = 35
D	Draws out a group of shells for each of 2 girls, Jackie—30, Sara—words describe picture	No number sentence or description of how/why 30 (maybe a lan-guage issue—13 vs. 30)	Correct for Jackie, incorrect for Sara	Pictures and words describe Jackie with 48 and Sara with 30

Source: Carol L., MLC facilitator in Springfield, Massachusetts.

MLC protocol step seven: Discuss evidence of understanding as a whole group. The group as a whole discusses student work using specific examples (evidence) in the student work that tell the group how the student understands an idea in mathematics (claim). Teachers use the guiding-questions grid to help support claims made. This final dis-cussion highlights important mathematical information for the teachers. MLC facilita-tors help guide this conversation using carefully selected questions or probes. Issues an MLC facilitator might raise include some of the following:

1. Let's focus our discussion on the second question listed—and discuss what evi-dence exists that each of these four students has an understanding of the inverse relationship between addition and subtraction.

2. What question would you use to follow up with this student? Or where might you go next with this student based on what you see here?

3. How can you connect what you see in Student A's strategy to Student C's? How can you connect what you see in Student A's strategy to one of the strategies shared by the group?

Often during the whole-group discussion, teachers will express frustration at being unable to know exactly what the student was thinking when he or she solved the problem; and since the work is anonymous, there is no possibility of follow-up with that student. However, what has come from this line of conversation is the notion that teachers *can* and should question their own students when written work is unclear or needs further clarification. In this way, and in others, teachers see that the work and discussions of the MLC can model effective classroom practice.

In addition, teacher misconceptions and misunderstandings can be addressed through the lens of the student work. If a teacher does not understand a particular concept or procedure, the group can uncover that misunderstanding within the student work, taking the onus of not knowing off the shoulders of the teacher.

WHO LEADS THE MLC?

Although it is possible to use the very detailed MLC curriculum materials without any professional development, we have found that the most effective MLCs are led by trained MLC facilitators. Coaches and/or lead math teachers who possess both a strong content background and respect from their peers often make excellent facilitators. MLC facilitator training, completed over five days, mimics the experience of a high-functioning MLC by using the LASW protocol with the purposefully selected student work in all the sessions. The facilitators also learn the intention and purpose of all the student work samples, as well as the reasoning behind the LASW procedure. Facilitators are able to experience the protocol and materials in the sessions as MLC members, and then are given an opportunity to practice their facilitation skills with the MLC materials, learn how to solve typical facilitation dilemmas, and observe group dynamics with a facilitator's eye.

Since an in-district teacher or coach facilitates the learning community, it can be done with little expense to the district, aside from teachers' time. In this way, implementing MLCs can serve as a cost-effective way to transform professional development, staff meetings, or common planning time into a valuable experience for teachers of mathematics to learn and grow in their own content knowledge and to become better at teaching and supporting students' learning. One teacher reflected that, as a result of MLCs, her common planning time "is now not just a time for chit-chat." MLC leaders provide agendas with allotted time to particular topics in order to keep the group on task and make limited meeting time as productive as possible.

MLC IMPACT: BUILDING COLLEGIALITY AND VERTICAL ARTICULATION

When professional development is designed around improving student learning, it is a win-win situation if it also improves teacher collaboration and school culture. The MLC addresses the concern that too many teachers work in isolation, when in fact collegial teacher conversations are vital for diagnosing root causes of student thinking and developing strategies to move students forward with correct math understanding. The structure of the MLC provides time for discussions on how children developmentally increase their mathematical understanding.

When MLCs comprise teachers representing different grade levels, vertical articulation of mathematical concepts and skills is possible. This articulation then promotes new levels of understanding for all involved. For example, one MLC member commented on how helpful it was that the MLC was a vertical team made up of teachers representing grades three through seven because she was able to see work from the adjacent grade levels to her own, since she is always working with students who are performing off grade level. In this way, regular education teachers, special education teachers, and teachers of English language learners are able to see what grade-level work looks like and how the work of their own students compares. Teachers can then use the MLC as a forum to communicate expectations of mastered concepts and skills from one grade level to the next. Opportunities also arise for colleagues to address concerns that mathematical concepts or skills may be "too hard" for students to master.

Another added benefit to a vertical MLC is to bridge the divide between elementary and middle schools. An MLC can serve as a place for teachers to find common ground on mathematical vocabulary used within a district (i.e., determining the level of formality for a given term and/or the use of curriculum program–specific vocabulary). Without such communication, middle school teachers may not be aware of vocabulary used at the elementary level, or vice versa. In fact, one teacher commented on how her MLC was raising awareness of the need for "accountable talk" and an appropriate and accurate mathematical vocabulary—both from the teacher's and the student's perspectives. In addition, a sense of cohesion and camaraderie is built among teachers working in different buildings.

Another example of how a district can benefit from an MLC that spans elementary and middle grades is through the connections that can be made between whole numbers and rational numbers and between number sense and algebra. In this way, students can be more successful as their teachers make necessary connections to prior knowledge.

One MLC was able to explicitly draw connections between the work done with whole numbers, computation, and number sentences in elementary school and how that same content translates into algebraic reasoning and working with equations in middle school. Teachers were asked to solve the problem shown in figure 2.5.

In the problems in figure 2.5, you can see that the quantities represented are the same (72 and 18, with a solution of 54), yet the units, context, and structure of the problem vary. In the elementary version, the whole is 72 flowers in a garden, with the parts being 18 roses and the missing number of daisies. The group then shares a possible solution method that an elementary student might take to solve the problem—counting on from 18 by 10s until 68 and then adding 4 more to reach 72. In the middle school version, ages of family members is the context, with Jim's grandfather's age acting as the whole and Jim's and his dad's ages representing the parts. Jim's age is given, while his father's is the missing addend (similar to daisies in the elementary version). This group also shares a possible solution method, one that would be typical of a mid-

FIGURE 2.5   Elementary and middle school samples

Elementary and middle school–level problems written during a MLC in Springfield, Massachusetts

LASW Problem
Write a story problem for this number sentence: 18 + _____ = 72

Elementary Solution	Middle School Solution

There are 72 flowers in Joyce's garden. 18 are roses.
 	
How many are daisies?
 	
18 28 38 48 58 68 + 4
    10 20 30 40 50   (50 + 4 = 54)
 	
1
54
+ 18
———
72
	Jim's grandfather is 72 years old. The sum of Jim's age and his father's age is equal to grandpa's age. Jim is 18 years old.
	
	How old is Jim's father?
	
	$J + F = G$ $\overset{6\;1}{\cancel{7}2}$
	$18 + F = 72$ $- 18$
	$F = 54$ ———
	    54

Source: MLC Materials Session 3, MA DESE.

dle school student—setting up and solving equations ($J + F = G$, $18 + F = 72$, $F = 54$). Teachers examining problems such as these during the MLC would then be able to draw such parallels between different problems and contexts.

Much of the student work provided during the MLC sessions is for grades two through six, so elementary teachers have a lot to gain from seeing work at the grade level they teach. However, in some ways, middle school teachers have even more to gain from this experience as they can learn to capitalize on methods and strategies used and developed in elementary school in order to apply them to more difficult or abstract ideas in middle school. Students can be more successful as their teachers are able to make those necessary connections to prior knowledge.

MLCs that bridge elementary and middle schools provide opportunities for content development and support as teachers collaborate. An example of such a conversation between elementary and middle school teachers occurred during one session of an MLC held in New Bedford, Massachusetts. The teachers in this example are working on the LASW problem from MLC session 5:

–16 is 9 less than a number. Find the number.
Show your thinking using a picture or a number line.

In the following dialogue, an elementary teacher is having trouble wrapping her head around why the solution is –7 and not –25. Several of her elementary colleagues try to explain their own way of thinking, but nothing seems to click. Instead, the confused teacher jumps up to move toward the two middle school teachers in the group to see if they can help her understand where her thinking has gone astray. In addition, one of the MLC facilitators helps her to finally understand the mistake she made.

> *Elementary teacher (E):* What did I do wrong, please?
>
> *First middle school teacher (M1):* Subtracted 9 when you should have added.
>
> *E:* Why? It says less than. I don't get it.
>
> *M1:* Okay, –16 is less than a number.
>
> *E:* Mm-hmm.
>
> *M1:* So in order to get what that number is you have to add that 9 back.
>
> *E:* Why?
>
> *Second middle school teacher (M2):* Can I try? . . . 9 is less than a number. So you could say a number, less 9. So a number minus 9.
>
> *M1:* If you have 10 dollars and now you have 9 less. 9 less than 10. How much do you have? You have a dollar. So you have –16, you're missing 16 dollars, but you have 9 less than me, how much do I have? How much am I missing? If you have 9 less than what I am holding? Do I have more than you? Or less than you?
>
> *E: [Puts head in hands and shakes her head.]*
>
> *Facilitator (F):* The way you have this written, right, you're saying
>
> *E:* –16 – 9
>
> *F:* Is the 9 being compared to the 16?
>
> *E:* I have no idea.
>
> *F:* They're saying, what is less than what? Is it the 16? Are they saying it's less than?
>
> *E:* I don't know. I'm keeping . . . I like my number line.
>
> *F:* Read this again . . . what does it say?
>
> *M2:* What about this . . . "Is" is a word for what?
>
> *F:* Equals.
>
> *M2:* So –16 is by itself on one side of the equal sign.
>
> *F:* Do you get that?
>
> *E:* Yes!
>
> *[E writes on her paper: –16 = n – 9.]*
>
> *F:* See, they're taking the 9 away from the number. Not from the 16.
>
> *E:* All right. That makes sense.
>
> *[clapping]*
>
> *F:* So what you were doing was taking the 9 away from the 16.
>
> *E:* Yes.
>
> *F:* It's not. The 9 is from the number, some number that we don't know . . . This is why we are pushing you beyond your comfort zone.
>
> *E:* Thank you.

What becomes evident from watching the videotape of this MLC session is that the elementary teacher had an "aha" moment once the connection to the equal sign was made. Up until that point, the teacher had trouble making sense of the problem. Once she saw how the "is" in the problem statement could be represented with the equal sign, then she could recognize that there were two distinct, yet equal, quantities (–16) and (9 less than a number or "n – 9") and that her initial way of thinking about the problem was incorrect.

This dialogue between elementary and middle school teachers within the same MLC occurred as a result of both the hard work on the part of the cofacilitators and the collaborative norms set by the group for their work together. This particular MLC had met on four previous occasions, and facilitators reflected that such a discussion had not happened in the first few sessions—it took some time for everyone to feel comfortable enough with one another to discuss their own questions and math understanding. In this case, as well as in many others, the MLC has become a forum for discussing important ideas about mathematical content and pedagogy.

IMPACT IN THE CLASSROOM AND SCHOOL

In addition to understanding how their students think about mathematics and to adapting their practice to support increased learning, teachers are bringing the model of an MLC into the classroom and schools. In follow-up conversations with learning community teachers, they report that now they are asking students to explain their thinking and are encouraging student-to-student dialogue about different ways to represent and solve math problems. Teachers are seeing the importance of understanding students' prior knowledge and looking for error patterns in the work, which is helping them to differentiate lessons.

The math dialogue among teachers has likewise increased both within the MLC and in the school hallways and teacher lunchrooms. An MLC with teachers of special education students, English language learners, and regular education students is a powerful community in which everyone can share his or her specific expertise about student learning with each other. For example, teachers of English language learners have experience with how students from different language backgrounds can misunderstand the meaning of certain words in word problems. Special education teachers can share a variety of strategies to help students learn. Regular education teachers often have specific training in math concepts. This diverse expertise in a learning community can help a teacher decide what next steps to take in helping a student move forward. The culture of how teachers collaborate, learn, and improve their practice has changed significantly.

In many schools, the document camera is now an integral part of the math class to facilitate these rich math discussions, much as it is in the MLC. Classrooms have become more student-centered and interactive. Students are taking more risks in problem solving, delving deeper to find answers, asking better questions, and completing open-response work that shows more varied representations and justification of answers.

District leaders, through the MLC conversations, can ascertain what specific professional development will be most helpful for their teachers to continue their growth as practitioners. The level of learning community discussion and professional development continues to spiral upward in supporting enhanced teacher practice and increased student achievement. As a result of these changes in school culture and classroom practice, schools and districts have incorporated the MLC into school improvement plans and as a professional development model.

SUCCESSES AND CHALLENGES

During the pilot year of MLC implementation in Massachusetts, MLC facilitators reported on the successes and challenges with respect to teachers' engagement in dialogue, reflection, and inquiry of mathematics teaching and learning. The opportunity for teachers to share math strategies and mathematical thinking and bring ideas back to the classroom was seen as a benefit of the MLCs. As a result of the MLCs, the upper-level teachers have a better understanding of the early foundations in math. No matter what grade level, teachers have a better understanding of the standards and a strong realization of the connections across all grades.

The biggest challenge is finding time and sustaining MLCs. In some MLCs, teachers felt intimidated by teachers of higher grades. Additionally, some teachers would find only one or two ways to do a problem and not go further. Working with many teachers in a large district posed logistical challenges in running the MLC sessions effectively. Finally, at times, teachers were not sure of the next steps to take with their students after examining the student work.

MEETING THE CHALLENGES

With time being one of the most precious resources in schools today, it is sometimes challenging to find time for teachers to meet regularly as a learning community. Using available time effectively and not spacing meetings too far apart are important to consider. More often than not, MLCs meet after school hours, which allows for easier participation among teachers who do not want to be pulled from classrooms or who are coming from different schools within the same district. However, this schedule creates the need for another resource—compensation for time. Many school administrators have said that teachers need incentives in addition to professional development credit hours to participate in afterschool professional development. Possible incentives include graduate credits at a reduced rate or a stipend.

Districts have addressed working with large groups of teachers in several ways. One district chose to create an MLC with twenty-five participants facilitated by two math coaches in order to include as many teachers as possible, while another offered MLC participation to forty-eight teachers who meet for a common introduction as a whole group and then split up into four smaller learning communities of twelve people each.

The challenge of determining how best to support teachers who feel that they have now developed their ability to LASW in order to know what individual students understand but who do not know what to do next provides a district with an opportunity to improve. Often teachers request help with resources and instructional strategies to address newly uncovered student needs. This is an ideal situation to bring in appropriate professional development that teachers incorporate into their practice immediately.

LESSONS LEARNED

The three most important lessons learned throughout the initial implementation of the MLC focus on facilitators, administrative support, and MLC facilitator training. Appointing team leaders, math specialists, and/or math coaches as MLC facilitators has been very effective, as people in these positions usually have the necessary pedagogical math content knowledge to facilitate conversations involving math teaching and learning. If the MLC facilitators need more content knowledge to be effective, it is important for them to take a content course prior to the training. The learning community conversations are much richer and deeper with a strong facilitator. Cofacilitation is also highly recommended for many reasons, including sharing of the workload, greater depth of knowledge, continuity in cases of absence, and the ability to listen more attentively to the voices of the MLC members. Attending MLC facilitator training provides the support a facilitator needs to create an effective learning community.

Administrator support and participation have also been central to the success of MLC implementation. Administrators help to make the learning community a priority in the school or district by including it in professional development plans and school improvement plans, by helping to avoid competing priorities, and by connecting MLC to current initiatives. Administrators can also provide time and resources for the MLC meetings themselves. It is important to provide the administrators with information about the value of the MLC and to encourage them to participate at some level, either by attending an overview of the MLC, sitting in on some sessions, or attending part of an MLC facilitator training.

Finally, the MLC facilitator training, which is critically important, needs to model an MLC in action and effectively becomes an MLC for the facilitators. Without that modeling, the facilitators tend to instruct instead of enabling conversations and learning in their MLC sessions.

NEXT STEPS

In the last year, we prepared for expansion of our work both in Massachusetts and across the country by training three more MLC facilitator training instructors and updating the materials to align with the Common Core State Standards in Mathematics. In Massachusetts, the MLC project, in collaboration with the Massachusetts Department of Elementary and Secondary Education, has focused on urban districts for the past four years. During that time, 44 MLCs with 705 teachers led by trained MLC facilitators have been established in five large urban districts and three small districts. Now we are expanding and are included in the state's District School Assistance Centers' menu of endorsed professional development opportunities. We provided two weeklong training sessions during the summer of 2011. Massachusetts' high-needs schools and districts will be offered MLC facilitator training as an avenue for ultimately increasing student achievement in mathematics though teacher professional development. Although most of the initial MLCs were in urban districts, they are now established in schools with a variety of student populations. In addition to the MLCs led by trained facilitators, seventy-five Massachusetts districts have downloaded the MLC curriculum materials for in-district use.[2]

Nationally, we are collaborating with K–12 Math Progressions (formerly Intel Math) at the Institute for Mathematics and Education at the University of Arizona. The MLC materials, which are aligned to this eighty-hour math content course, connect the content that teachers learn in the course to their daily practice in the classroom. As a result of this partnership, many districts across the country have downloaded the MLC materials. Recently, school districts in both California and Illinois have used the MLC facilitator training to develop math personnel to lead MLC sessions in their schools.

To date, our primary focus has been on teachers, administrators, and school districts as the MLCs take shape in schools. We have captured the impact of the MLCs on teachers' practices and professional mathematics discussions. What we have not yet had the opportunity to do is to focus directly on the impact that an MLC has on student achievement. Our next major goal is to systematically follow the impact that the MLCs have on student learning.

CONCLUSION

A district-level administrator once commented on how the school as a whole must be aware of the need for a collaborative community such as an MLC, otherwise its success will be short-lived. Beth D., a math support specialist, New Bedford, Massachusetts, shared advice for districts thinking about beginning this process: "The most important thing is to have people in place who believe in the process and are willing to be committed to it and follow through. Often, there are so many initiatives [occurring simultaneously], that it is important to tie it into other work."

The end goal of math education is for students to know, understand, and be able to do quality mathematics—to solve problems, reason, communicate, and make connections—about important mathematical concepts, skills, and ideas. In order to teach students so that they can learn best, teachers need to know what students already know. It is through this process of connecting new information to prior knowledge that the human brain is able to learn. Understanding what students already know is a vital skill that can help support teachers in their quest to best teach their students who in turn can learn their best.

Within an MLC, colleagues work collaboratively to enhance their understanding of mathematics and teaching and to effectively use student work as the vehicle for this learning. We envision that participation in an MLC will enhance teachers' understanding of student thinking about mathematics, develop school-based structures for doing and talking about math with fellow teachers, and advance the practice of teaching to improve student achievement in mathematics.

CHAPTER 3

How Did You Get That Answer?

Computer Assessments of Young Children's Mathematical Minds in mCLASS Math

HERBERT P. GINSBURG, SANDRA PAPPAS,
YOUNG-SUN LEE, AND CYNTHIA CHIONG

Formative assessment is a promising method that teachers can use to improve instruction. mCLASS Math (mCM) is a computer-based system that helps teachers conduct formative assessments of early mathematical knowledge, from kindergarten through grade three. mCM draws on three diverse and even seemingly contradictory approaches: (1) curriculum-based measurement (CBM) is popular in special education and stresses frequent monitoring of student performance; (2) contemporary cognitive research illuminates the development of children's mathematical minds; and (3) the clinical interview, originally developed by Piaget, is used in cognitive developmental research and education to investigate the thinking that underlies performance.

The blending of these three traditions is perhaps unusual, but we think the combination is more valuable than any one alone. The CBM approach focuses our attention on monitoring everyday classroom performance; cognitive science research identifies the underlying mental processes that are important to measure; and the clinical interview is the inspiration for flexible questioning that can bring children's thinking to the surface.

THE ROLE OF CBM IN FORMATIVE ASSESSMENT

One important component of formative assessment is the monitoring of *performance*, the student's overt behavior and achievement. The goal of CBM measurement is to provide a quick reading of basic skills in mathematics. The common analogy is a thermometer, which serves as an *indicator* of an illness and monitors the treatment's success.[1] The indicator should be sensitive to changes over time in the individual student and, of course, to differences between groups. CBM scores can be used first to identify students at risk and then to monitor their progress over the course of instruction. Sometimes CBM scores are used to create tiers of students in a Response to Intervention (RTI) approach in which some students receive standard instruction, some extra help, and some intensive remediation.

CBM tests aim at brevity and simplicity. Typically, they require the student to solve a series of similar problems in a short time, often a minute or two. Usually there are multiple, equivalent forms of the tests that can be given repeatedly, even daily. The scores are basically the number of correct responses, which can be graphed so that the teacher can follow the individual student's progress over weeks of instruction. The scores can also create benchmarks for adequate performance.

CBM mathematics performance assessments typically focus on *written computation* (like column addition) and *number facts* (like 5 + 3 or 9 − 4). In recent years, several CBM tests have been designed to measure *number sense*, a kind of mathematical street smarts that involve intuitive and meaningful ideas about numbers. For example, one type of number sense is appreciating how much bigger some numbers are than others (7 is a little bigger than 5 but 100 is way bigger, which means that the answer to 5 + 7 cannot be anywhere close to 100).

In this age of accountability, the CBM approach is popular. It offers the promise of helping teachers to stay "on top of" student performance, to learn on a daily basis whether students are keeping up with their work and "getting it." Moreover, there is some evidence showing that frequent use of formative assessments can improve achievement, particularly when the results are used to adjust instruction.[2]

At the same time, the CBM approach suffers from several possible disadvantages. One is a narrowing of educational focus: to get children to meet the benchmark, teachers may encourage the kind of performance that the CBM requires, namely, a large number of fast, accurate responses. Although accuracy is of course desirable, speed may not be: we don't want children and teachers to acquire the belief that mathematics is a subject in which one produces quick responses without thinking. Moreover, the pressures of speed and accuracy may produce anxiety in some children, which in turn may serve to dampen the enthusiasm of those who enjoyed mathematics before entering school. And some children, knowing that the test lasts only a minute or two, may not try very hard, may guess, or may just wait for the not-so-happy experience to end.

At the same time, the aspirations of CBM measurement make sense: of course, it is important for the teacher to become aware of student performance during the year, as often as possible, and not just at the end of the year, as is the case with many achievement tests. And it is also important for teachers to aim at meeting benchmarks—to expect students to achieve at an adequate level.

Therefore, our development goal was to create a CBM test that provides sound measures of number facts, written mathematics, and number sense. Our research goal was to evaluate the CBM approach in the context of a cognitive framework. We were particularly interested in whether those students whom the CBM classifies as low performers are as incompetent as they appear to be and, conversely, whether students classified as high performance are as competent as the test results suggest.

FORMATIVE ASSESSMENT FROM A COGNITIVE POINT OF VIEW

How can you teach well if you do not understand how your students think and learn? All of our assessment and teaching efforts must start with a deep understanding of children's behavior and minds. Fortunately, cognitive, developmental, and educational researchers have made remarkable advances in understanding the development of children's mathematical knowledge.[3] This body of research offers several important contributions to the formative assessment of mathematics: the central concept of cognitive process; detailed knowledge of the development of mathematical thinking; the idea of everyday mathematics; the notion of understanding as the synthesis of the formal and everyday; and a focus on metacognition and language. These foundational ideas can be used to create effective formative assessments and to evaluate the CBM approach to formative assessment.

Cognitive Process

The central tenet of the cognitive approach is that overt behavior results from underlying processes that can be specified in detail. For example, a student's failure to solve the problem 3 + 5 may result from various underlying processes such as miscounting, subtracting instead of adding, or lack of memory for the "fact." An explanation that relies on general (and vague) concepts like poor math ability or skill is not as helpful as is a rich description of current cognitive process.

Detailed Knowledge of Development of Mathematical Thinking

Any assessment system is only as good as the ideas that generate it. If your only idea about mathematics learning is that it results from "mathematical aptitude," then your formative assessment system must reflect that not particularly useful approach. Tests reflect and entail ideas about psychological functioning. All other things being equal, the better the ideas, the better the test. Cognitive research on mathematical thinking can provide those basic ideas from which an assessment can be constructed. Cognitive research has produced comprehensive accounts of mathematical development, from basic understanding of arithmetic to rational number. The research examines the everyday mathematics that students bring to school or develop even when they do not attend school; the mathematics that they develop in school, for example, their invented strategies ("I know that 5 and 6 is 11 because it's just one more than 5 + 5, which I know is 10"); their "bugs" ("12 – 4 is 12 because you can't take 4 from 2 so you have to take away 2 from 4, which gives you 12"); and their understanding and self-awareness (ability to identify and express their solution strategies) with respect to mathematics. The research deals with individual differences as well as the ways in which all people show common elements of mathematical thinking. Cognitive research also provides detailed developmental trajectories—accounts of how children's mathematical ideas and skills develop over time, not only in number, but in the other areas as well.

Everyday Mathematics

A major contribution of the research is the idea of everyday mathematics: on entering school, children already possess a great deal of informal mathematical knowledge, some surprisingly powerful and some incorrect. They have intuitive ideas of small and large, how to count, adding and taking away, and division (creating fair shares). Moreover, young children generally begin schooling well motivated to learn mathematics.

They are self-confident and have positive attitudes toward school. But their motivation decreases within the first few years of school, most likely because of boring textbooks and inappropriate teaching.

The importance of understanding what children bring to school cannot be overstated. To succeed, instruction needs to take into account children's current knowledge—sometimes building on it and sometimes counteracting it.

Understanding as Synthesis

Lev Vygotsky's theory provides a useful framework for thinking about the relations among basic aspects of the child's mathematical knowledge.[4] He proposed that children enter school with various everyday concepts that are very different from "scientific" or academic concepts, like the mathematics taught in school. This everyday knowledge may contain within it important ideas that can serve as the basis for understanding more formal and general notions. Hence, one important educational strategy is to relate the spontaneous and scientific, the everyday and the academic. For example, the student needs to see that his reasonable informal strategies and ideas about adding are related to the formal addition taught in school. Yet many students do not connect their informal ideas with what they are supposed to learn in the classroom. They feel that what they learn in school is merely "academic," in the pejorative sense of being unrelated to anything personal and sensible. They have particular difficulties in relating their everyday mathematics to the special written symbolism of mathematics. A child may be able to do mental addition of 5 and 3 but may have no clue as to the meaning of the written symbols 5, +, 3, and especially =. Formative assessment needs to be sensitive to the possible synthesis between the everyday and the academic, particularly the formal symbols of mathematics.

Metacognition and Language

Learning mathematics requires learning several kinds of language. From the age of two or so, children learn the language and grammar of counting. They memorize the first ten or so counting words (which are essentially nonsense syllables with no underlying structure or meaning) and then learn a set of rules to generate the higher numbers. For example, once you figure out that forty comes after thirty-nine, it's easy to add on the well-memorized sequence from one to nine. Young children also learn other kinds of mathematical language, like the names of shapes ("square") and words for quantity ("bigger" "less"). Indeed, some of these words (like "more") are among the first spoken by many babies. But more importantly, language is required to express and justify mathematical thinking. With development, children become increasingly aware of their own thinking and begin to express it in words. The child needs to be able to say, for example, "I know that 5 and 5 is 10 because I counted the fingers on this hand and then the other." These kinds of metacognitive skills begin to develop in children as young as four or five years of age and are increasingly important as schooling progresses.

So learning mathematics includes being aware of thinking and expressing it in words. In this sense, learning mathematics is partly a literacy activity.

CLINICAL INTERVIEW

Piaget's experience with the development of Binet's IQ test taught him that tests are not particularly effective in uncovering cognitive processes. He felt that answers to IQ test items were ambiguous and required further examination in the form of a clinical interview. His preferred method begins with a task chosen by the adult. In this sense, the adult's point of view dominates, at least at the outset. Then the interviewer observes the child's response, behavior, affect, and anything else that might be relevant, and develops an interpretation of the processes underlying the child's behavior. To check the hypothesis, the interviewer develops new tasks as appropriate, follows up with questions designed to elicit thinking, and in general follows the child's thought process to where it leads. In this sense, the interviewer makes every effort to be child-centered—to see the issues from the child's point of view. The interviewer sometimes challenges the child's response ("But Johnny said that 2 and 2 is really 5") to assess its stability and the child's confidence in it. The interviewer may sometimes employ gentle hints to help the child overcome a difficulty ("Can you use your fingers to help you figure it out?"). The interviewer continues these nonstandardized interview maneuvers, which must be constructed on the spot, in real time, until enough evidence has been obtained to support a reasonable interpretation of the child's behavior. In its purest form, the procedure deliberately does not employ standard administration; rather, the procedure is customized to motivate the individual child and measure her cognitive processes.

Like any other form of assessment, the clinical interview can be only as good as the theoretical ideas on which it is based. The interviewer must make interpretations of what the child says and does. Again, the interpretation is based on a theory—explicit or intuitive—about children's thinking. The interview is not a mechanical process. It can succeed only if the interviewer produces sensible hypotheses and interpretations that can guide the search for evidence. What makes the interview extremely difficult is that these interpretations must be produced quickly as the interviewer works with the child.

Here is an example of a very short and simple interview sequence with a first grader, Joe.

> *Interviewer (I):* How much is 8 plus 7?
> *Joe (J):* 8 plus 7 equals . . . *[pause]* 15.
> *I:* OK. I have some questions for you. When you did 8 plus 7, how did you do that?
> *J:* Because 8 plus 8 equals 16 and 7 plus 7 equals 14 and if I add one more to that 7 it would make, it would make 15. If I add one less on the 8, then it would make, then it would still make 15.

Despite its brevity, several features of the interview stand out. One is that Joe's initial pause suggested that his first response, 15, was not simply memorized but was the product of some thought. Second, a simple "How did you do it?" type question, elicited a very interesting result. The child's line of reasoning about 7 + 7 can be considered a "derived" or "invented strategy," a method that Joe might have developed himself to solve a simple "number fact" problem. This kind of invented strategy typically employs something the child already knows (presumably he had memorized 7 plus 7) along with a little adjustment (adding 1) to solve the new problem. Third, that his method was invented and not simply taught is suggested by the second half of his response where he claimed that he could get the same result if he were to "add one less" to an 8 in the double resulting in 16. This is remarkable because he appears intuitively to add a negative number rather than subtract a positive one. It would be highly unlikely that negative integers were taught at his grade level. And finally, it is of great interest to learn that Joe was able to express his methods of solution so clearly.

If done well and guided by appropriate theory, the clinical interview can both motivate children and provide deep insight into their thinking, revealing strengths and weaknesses that otherwise may go undetected.[5] The interview can help the teacher uncover thought processes of which she was previously unaware and realize that her students may not in fact be learning what she is attempting to teach. And, finally, it can convey the value that understanding thinking is important; indeed, it should be the heart of the curriculum.

There is also some evidence that asking children to explain their understanding of material can promote learning.[6] When talking about mathematics in the interview setting, students become actively engaged in the learning process, gain awareness of their own thinking, learn new mathematical ideas, develop skills of expression, and learn that adults value their thinking and learning. From the child's point of view as much as the teacher's, clinical interviewing should be a fundamental educational activity.

At the same time, the clinical interview is hard to implement. It depends on human skill, may not produce reliable results, and, if done badly, can distort student thinking and elicit only what the student thinks the interviewer wants to hear. Its demands are considerable: the interviewer must employ appropriate theoretical ideas about thinking and must possess the mental agility to develop useful questions on the spot. It is subject to examiner bias, the possibility of which was a major impetus for the development and use of standard tests. But the existence of serious difficulties does not necessarily imply that the method should not be used.

MCM SYSTEM OF FORMATIVE ASSESSMENT

These theoretical foundations and educational needs inspired our development of mCM. Our goals were several. First, we wanted to design a CBM instrument to help educators, primarily teachers, to identify students at risk of failure and to monitor student progress in learning mathematics, specifically number, from kindergarten through grade three. Second, we wanted create a system that would enable educators to probe the thought processes, both everyday and school learned, that underlie overt performance in fundamental aspects of number. Third, we wanted teachers to learn to understand children's thinking, revise their views of mathematics education, and incorporate the clinical interview method into their daily practice.

The Technology

Because we wanted the system to be widely usable, not by only a minority of skilled teachers, we joined with Wireless Generation, an educational technology firm, to develop mCM as a computer-based system that could both guide teachers' formative assessment and record the results. Wireless Generation has shown that technology can be used effectively in the service of formative assessment. The company has produced a computer-based reading assessment system that is used in more than 100,000 classrooms, with more than 2 million students around the country. Teachers report that use of the system to identify struggling readers, group students for instruction, and monitor their progress is central to their reading instruction. Evaluations of the literacy assessments show that using handheld assessments can save teachers between twelve and thirty minutes per student, including setup, administration, data transfer, and analysis, compared to the paper version.

The mCM computer system is designed to operate on computers of several types, handheld (like smart phones or the old Palm Pilot), laptop, or desktop. mCM is *software*—a set of programs that guides the individual teacher's assessment and records the individual student's responses. The student does not see the screen and does not use the computer.

Imagine a teacher who begins by opening a screen that shows her a list of students in her class, as well as their location in a series of assessments (see figure 3.1). The teacher selects Luisa P. The tabs show, from left to right, a thermometer, which stands for the CBM screening (on track, emerging, or at risk); a graph, which indicates progress monitoring; a magnifying glass, which indicates the interview; and finally the ACT, or activities tab that recommends useful teaching methods for the child in question. The thermometer shows that Luisa has completed CBM screening. (Clicking on the thermometer reveals her status.) Progress monitoring is optional and an interview is recommended.

After tapping on the magnifying glass, the teacher sees several screens that guide her through a series of interview questions. As we shall see later, an interview on early number is complex and involves many screens and many student responses. But suppose the interview has been completed. The computer stores the results until the teacher uploads them to a server. In some schools using the Wireless Generation technology,

FIGURE 3:1   Student screen

Note: This is what the software looks like on a handheld Palm Pilot.

teachers go to a special "sync" room where they wirelessly upload the latest results from their day's assessment and also download reports on the students. The reports might include records of an individual student's performance on every single task that he did over the past year; graphs describing the class's performance over the course of the year; and suggestions for instructional activities suitable for an individual student. In principle, the reports could include tables comparing the performance of this class with that of other classes in the school, the state, or indeed the nation.

In brief, the computer guides the teacher's questions, provides tasks suitable for individual children, allows her to record the responses, saves the data, and provides reports of various types. This is the context in which we developed our CBM and interview methods.

The Content

According to an array of professional and governmental organizations, number should be at the core of the Early Mathematics Education curriculum. We therefore deliberately focused on fundamental topics like counting, enumeration, addition, subtraction, and multiplication from kindergarten through grade three. But there is another reason for our content choice: we wanted to start where the teachers are. Most teachers and textbooks pay an inordinate amount of attention to the simplest and often most boring aspects of number, specifically number facts or combinations. Textbooks contain pages and pages of number-fact drills, and many teachers spend more time on stuffing these facts into what become children's passive minds than on stimulating mathematical thought. It is no wonder then that many children come to believe that mathematics is a wasteland of dreary, meaningless bits of information that must be memorized without understanding.

Yet the analysis of number-fact learning may be rewarding both for formative assessment and professional development. Research shows that children may use their number sense to solve number-fact problems in an inventive fashion. Not only do they memorize number facts, but children also draw on their everyday mathematics to *think* about them. They assimilate number facts into what they already know, for example, by employing "invented strategies." Thus, a child may reason that 5 + 7 is 12 because she already knows that 7 + 5 is 12, or she may get that answer because she knows that 5 + 5 is 10 and then because 7 is just 2 more than 5, the answer must be 12. The assessment of apparently trivial number-fact learning may indeed shine a spotlight on children's mathematical thinking to reveal more (or less) competence than initially assumed. From this, the teacher may learn the value of mathematical *thinking*.

In brief, the content of mCM involves basic aspects of number partly because it is important for children to learn the subject and partly because assessment of number can reveal children's inventive mathematical reasoning.

CBM

Our CBM assessment evaluates three broad categories of mathematics learning: quick retrieval, written computation, and number sense. We believe that these three measures cover what is essential about student mathematics: the ability to retrieve information quickly, to compute, and to have a good feel for the meaning of the material. First, we present the content of the measures and then the method of administration.

Quick Retrieval

Not all mathematics learning involves higher-order thinking. It is often useful to achieve mastery of key facts, symbols, or procedures. For example, it is easier to remember the sum of 9 + 7 than to reason about it or calculate it all the time. Reasoning and calculation are important, but eventually the child should achieve fluency in number facts so that she does not have to expend mental energy on them and can instead think about more interesting mathematical problems. Further, it is important to measure number-fact fluency because it predicts academic achievement and because children having difficulty with mathematics often have intractable problems with number combinations.[7]

For these reasons, we included, for all grades except kindergarten, where it is inappropriate, a measure of quick retrieval of number facts such as 6 + 8 or 5 x 7. Students in grades one through three receive addition and subtraction fact problems; students in grades two and three receive multiplication fact problems.

Written Computation

Children need to learn to compute problems involving double digits and higher. They can quickly retrieve smaller facts, but cannot be expected to do the same for larger numbers like 19 + 8 or 36 + 17. Students need to know how to read numbers and to execute the common algorithms involving "regrouping," more commonly known as "borrowing" or "carrying."

Hence, our CBM measure includes reading written numbers and calculating multi-digit problems such as 12 + 7 (two-digit number plus a one-digit number without carrying), and 36 – 19 (two-digit number minus two-digit number with borrowing). The type and difficulty of the problems is adjusted appropriately for different grade levels. For example, kindergarten children are asked to read numbers but not to calculate. Grade one students receive written addition problems, and children in grade three are given calculation problems in addition, subtraction, and multiplication.

Number Sense

Number sense involves basic intuitions and ideas about numbers, including concepts that make computation easier or eliminate the need for it. Number sense includes such components as the ability to compare the magnitude of numbers (5 is less than 7); to understand the relative effect of arithmetical operations on numbers (addition makes whole numbers bigger and subtraction smaller, excluding the use of zero); to know whether certain numbers are plausible answers to certain problems (knowing without any calculation that the sum of 57 + 38 must be larger than 57); and to break numbers into convenient parts that make calculation easier (88 + 12 can be solved as 88 + 2 is 90 and then 10 more).

Our number-sense measure varies by grade. For example, in kindergarten, our problems include quantity discrimination (children's ability to determine which of two numbers, like 9 and 7, is larger) and missing number (the ability to identify the missing number from a pattern of three numbers, like 5, 6, 7). In grade three, the problem type categories increase in difficulty. So, for quantity discrimination, instead of comparing single digits, students now compare sums of digits ("Which is larger, 9 + 6 or 5 + 6?"), and for missing number, they now solve more complex series (like 6, 12, 18, 24).

Administration

Teachers use the computer to administer four one-minute measures to individual kindergarten students and six one-minute measures to individual first-grade students. All problems are presented verbally or visually. For example, for the numerical identification task, students are shown a sheet with a series of written numbers and asked to say the name of the numbers. Total testing time is about five to ten minutes per student.

For second and third grades, the five CBM measures are administered in groups, each for two minutes, so that each session lasts approximately twenty minutes. The paper measures are passed out individually, and the students are asked to turn them over after their names have been written on the top of the form. The teacher then reads the instructions and asks students to turn the papers over and begin working. The students are expected to solve as many problems as possible within two minutes. After two minutes, the teacher asks the students to put their pencils down and pass the measures forward. The teacher then distributes the next measure. These procedures are followed until all measures have been completed.

DIAGNOSTIC INTERVIEW

We use the term *diagnostic interview* instead of *clinical interview* for two reasons. One is that educators tend to be squeamish about clinical interview because they misinterpret *clinical* as referring to *pathological*. A second reason is that the mCM interview method is not as flexible as Piaget's. Our computer-based interview involves only a baby step toward a mature clinical interview. Hence, we term our nonpathological guided approach a diagnostic interview (DI).

How It Works

We developed the DI by creating flow charts that specify a sequence of interview questions, possible student answers, and then questions contingent on those answers. Our development drew heavily on the research literature and on our own experience in interviewing children and learning about the range of their responses. For example, research shows that children tend to use any of five or six specific strategies at various points in the developmental sequence and that these strategies evolve over time. Consequently, we created icons that allow the examiner to note the occurrence of particular strategies likely to be used at a given age level. The icons are research-based embodiments of a cognitive theory intended to capture key processes underlying number-fact solutions. Learning to use the icons is learning about the possibilities for children's mathematical thinking.

Because research shows that backup strategies are useful when memory fails or when it is important to check a result, we included a probe to elicit possible backup strategies. Our interviews also include some contingent questioning in which the child's response to one question determines the next, although not as much as an authentic clinical interview would entail. Of course, preliminary explorations showed that we were not always right in our choice of possible questions and responses. If we found that to be the case, we changed the flow chart and software.

Figure 3.2 gives an example beginning with the left screen. Taking into account the child's level and previous performance, "Mr. Say" on the top left suggests that the interviewer ask the child, "How much is seven plus eight?" The child may choose to use paper and pencil, chips, or fingers to solve the problem. Or he may perform the solution entirely on a mental level. Or he may give no answer at all. Suppose that the child says 15. The teacher then taps on the green 15 (green because it is the correct answer), and the computer then records and saves that response. The teacher also notices that the child used chips to solve the problem and taps on the appropriate icon to record the response. Of course, if the child exhibited no overt behavior, the teacher would not tap any icon at this point.

Next, as shown on the right screen, the program guides the teacher to ask the child how he got that answer ("How did you know that?"). This fundamental question is important for three reasons. One is that the child may not have shown any overt behavior that could be observed. A second is that the *expressed* strategy may be different from the observed. And a third is that we are interested in learning how well the child expresses what he does (later, the teacher is asked to rate the child's mathematics language proficiency). Next, on a subsequent screen not shown here, the program directs the teacher to ask the child for another method—a backup strategy—that could be used to solve the problem. If none is offered, the program guides the teacher to ask, "Is there another way to figure it out?" The computer saves all information that the teacher enters—numerical responses and strategies—in response to all of the screens.

The Content

The content, of course, varies by grade level. We will consider an example from grade two. The system examines three key areas: *small numbers, mental calculation,* and *written number.*

Small numbers. At this level, small-number problems include addition, subtraction, and multiplication (a topic not covered in kindergarten and grade one). In each case,

FIGURE 3.2   Sequence of small number screens

Note: This is what the software looks like on a handheld Palm Pilot.

questions examine not only accuracy of solution, but also basic strategies, backup strategies, and relevant principles like the commutative property, namely, that the order of adding or multiplying numbers does not matter (5 x 3 *must* give the same answer as 3 x 5). These probes enable us to learn whether the child simply memorizes answers or has sensible strategies for getting them; whether the child has the flexibility and knowledge to employ backup strategies; and whether the child understands basic principles underlying the basic operations of arithmetic. The child's responses also form the basis for the teacher's overall rating of verbal expression.

Mental calculation. The next section involves mental calculation of relatively large numbers. Because written calculation is not permitted, and because the numbers are too large to be remembered, solution requires some kind of invented, nonstandard procedure—that is, some degree of creativity and thought on the part of the child. Research shows that by second grade, children can simplify larger problems by decomposing or partitioning them into the addition of tens and ones. Thus, the child may solve a problem like 24 + 15 by converting it into the easier problems 20 + 10 and 4 + 5. The DI leads the interviewer through a series of questions designed to identify interesting strategies like these. The topic is important because children on their own may generate strategies that are very important for instruction. In the example of decomposing earlier, the child solves the problem by breaking it up into tens and ones and then adds essentially from left to right (first the tens and then the ones). This approach is essentially the same as the standard algorithm, except that the latter always begins by adding units, not tens or multiples of ten. Teachers need to understand that a child who has not mastered the algorithm may nevertheless have a sound mental addition strategy, which then can be used as a foundation on which to build the algorithm in a meaningful way.

Written number. This section involves use and understanding of written numbers and standard computation methods. Successful reading and writing of numerals containing two or more digits require an understanding of the relationship among the various digits. That is, children must be able to understand that the 2 in 23 refers to 2 tens, whereas the 3 refers to 3 ones. From this point of view, 2 is larger than 3. Our DI probes for this understanding.

The DI also focuses on use and understanding of standard computation methods that build on a base ten–place value system. For example, the child must understand that lining up numbers as in

$$
\begin{array}{r}
23 \\
+\ 5 \\
\hline
\end{array}
$$

is important because doing so facilitates adding the unit digits first (3 and 5) and then the tens (in this case, only 2). Students who misalign by putting the 5 under the 2 get an incorrect answer of 73.

Place value ideas are also critical in cases of carrying and borrowing. In this connection, the DI investigates common "bugs," systematic errors like

$$
\begin{array}{r}
42 \\
-\ 6 \\
\hline
44 \\
\end{array}
$$

This absurd result occurs because the child, having no sound conception of place value, believes that you cannot subtract a smaller number from a larger and therefore takes away the 2 from the 6, instead of borrowing a 10 from the 4.

Putting It All Together

The DI provides a huge amount of data for each child. It can yield many different measures of accuracy, strategy, and concepts. To make sense of all this, it is important to understand how the different pieces of the child's knowledge fit together, in particular, the child's memory for facts, use of procedures, and understanding of mathematical ideas. The DI therefore groups children into *profiles* that attempt to capture important patterns of their mathematics learning. For example, some children may perform well and at the same time not really understand the basic ideas. Others may understand the ideas but not perform so well.

WHAT WE HAVE LEARNED

It took us many years to develop and explore mCM. After the initial formative work, we received support from the Institute of Education Sciences to undertake a large study to examine mCM's reliability and validity, and to learn about development of mathematical thinking in the context of gender, ethnicity, and socioeconomic status (SES).

We are in the process of administering the mCM and also a standardized test, the Woodcock-Johnson, to approximately 1,200 students in kindergarten through grade three, from seven school districts in the New York State and in Missouri. Each grade level has about three hundred students, roughly half boys and half girls. Our plan is to assess these children over a course of several years, so that we can observe their development. In this chapter, we present a slice of the results from assessments given in the middle of the first year of the study.

Reliability and Validity of the CBM

How reliable and valid are CBM screening measures? We learned that the CBM scores are reliable in the sense that the various tests are internally consistent and that children get similar scores when tested on several different occasions. We also learned that the CBM measures are generally correlated with an independent measure of student achievement (the Woodcock-Johnson). This means that the CBM tests are valid in the sense that they adequately predict performance on standard achievement tests. Yet this is only the first step: the more important question is whether the CBM measures provide information useful for formative assessment.

Reliability and Validity of the DI

First, we investigated whether different assessors can agree on interpretations of children's DI behavior (inter-rater reliability). Do they make the same judgments about a specific interview? We investigated this issue by asking two independent and well-trained observers to score the same DI sessions (on video). We found that they did indeed substantially agree on the scoring of both performance and strategy. So use of the DI can produce reliably observed results. Of course, this does not mean that poorly trained assessors will do a good job using the DI, just as poorly trained microscope users will perform badly using their instrument. Adequate training is necessary for reliable use of any tool that relies on human judgment.

Second, we attempted to determine whether the DI measures what it was designed to measure (its construct validity). The common practice is to establish the validity of a test by comparing its results with those of another test. But the DI is not a test, and available tests do not provide adequate measures of the processes that cognitive research shows are essential for understanding children's mathematical behavior. Therefore, to determine the validity of the DI, we compared our students' performance with what the research shows is the typical course of development.

The results showed that the children we studied used the same strategies as those described in the research literature. And the developmental sequence in both cases was substantially the same. For example, in accordance with established research findings, our second- and third-grade students were more likely than younger children to use partitioning and base ten ideas (like $21 + 32 = 20 + 30 = 50$ and then just 3 more) to mentally solve large addition problems.[8]

In sum, different observers can agree on how they interpret and score the DI, and the DI measures the same developmental trajectory of processes that research has identified. The DI can reliably provide teachers with insight into children's thinking; most tests do not.

Profiles

The profiles were created to present a portrait of the "whole mathematical child" that can then be used to guide instruction. We used both developmental theory and statistical analyses to develop profiles that capture the relations between performance and understanding across all of our DI tasks. For example, for the small-numbers task, we categorized the students' performance as falling into five different categories.

Expert. Experts are skilled in procedures, remember what is necessary, and understand what they are doing. This, of course, is what we aim for: students who have mastery over facts and procedures, but also understand basic mathematical ideas.

Proficient. These students are making progress and perform reasonably well but make mistakes in spite of understanding many of the basic ideas and having good strategies available. The mistakes tend to conceal sound underlying knowledge.

Memory. These students recall facts but do not understand *what* they are doing. They cannot use sensible strategies when it would be useful to do so. Memory students may seem to perform at a high level, but they are on very shaky ground when memory fails.

Struggling. These students are usually incorrect but show some glimmer of hope: they can use some sensible strategies.

Lost. These lost mathematical souls seem to have neither skill nor understanding. They get wrong answers and don't remember and can't use sensible strategies. Much must be done to help them.

We believe that these profiles not only describe significant groups of students, but also offer ways to help them. *Experts* should be given more challenging problems (and maybe extra recess). Teachers need to help the apparently successful *memory* students to deepen their understanding of the real basics—the mathematical ideas. By contrast, teachers need to help the *proficient* students to become more careful about their work so as to improve accuracy. Teachers can help *struggling* students by strengthening all aspects of their work: memory, strategies, and careful work. And teachers need to provide intensive instruction of all kinds for the *lost*. One way to begin is to search for the rudiments of skill and intuition that are likely to be buried beneath mounds of failure.

One interesting, albeit obvious, fact is that profiles are related to the type and difficulty of problem at different age levels. For example, about 83 percent of third graders are expert in small-number addition. This should come as no surprise, and the profile system is of no great value at this age level. But in kindergarten, all profile categories capture substantial percentages of children: about 40 percent are already *expert* by the middle of the year; about 18 percent are proficient; about 16 percent are *memorizers*; about 15 percent are *struggling*; and almost 12 percent are *lost*. The kindergarten profile presents teachers with a sound basis for differentiated instruction. For example, the *proficient* (those making mistakes despite understanding) students may benefit from drill, whereas the *memory* students may benefit from meaningful work with manipulatives (concrete or virtual objects used to promote learning).

One goal of CBM measurement is to identify at-risk children in order to provide them with effective instructional support, sometimes above and beyond typical classroom instruction. Although this goal is admirable, we wanted to examine how well CBM measures achieve it. Are the CBM measures valid when they sort children into several categories—*on track, emerging,* and *at risk*? To answer this question, we compared student performance as shown by our CBM measures with what the DI reveals about the strategies underlying performance.

This approach assumes that the DI, based as it is in cognitive research, provides a deeper view of children's abilities than does the CBM. The DI examines not only children's performance, but also their strategies, concepts, and understanding. By contrast, the CBM is limited to quick behavior samples—two-minute-long tests of such content as number facts. Our strategy then is to examine the validity of the CBM by contrasting it with the more comprehensive, research-based information provided by the DI. To do this, we used a key subset of DI measures, such as small numbers and mental calculation, that captured not only accuracy of response but also strategy use.

We evaluated on-track, emerging, and at-risk children, as measured by the CBM, in terms of four key profiles of mathematics learners (as measured by DI). We wanted to determine, for example, whether children classified as at risk would be classified as lost by the DI profile system, and whether children considered to be on track would be considered expert or proficient by the DI.

Our findings are that in general, the CBM and DI results are roughly correlated. Children who do poorly on one tend to do poorly on the other. But these correlations are small, and a closer look yields some interesting results.

One pattern is that the CBM is a good predictor of performance on the DI, as in the case of grade one addition mental calculation. Children at risk on the CBM are lost on the DI; and children who are on track on the CBM are expert on the DI. This pattern suggests sound CBM validity.

A second pattern is that the CBM overrates student performance, as when on-track students are lost on the DI, as in the case of grade-three multiplication mental calculation. In this case, the CBM produces false successes, students who may actually need extensive help.

The third pattern is that the CBM underrates student performance. Students at risk nevertheless are considered experts on the DI, as in the case of grade one small-number addition. In this case, the CBM produced false failures.

The fourth pattern involves a situation in which performance on the CBM did not predict performance on the DI.

While the CBM was a good predictor of about a third of the DI profiles, it also frequently (in about 45 percent of the cases) tended to underrate children's competence and to a lesser extent (about a fifth of the time) overrated children's abilities. These results suggest that the CBM's identification of successes is generally accurate. In other words, a child whom the CBM identifies as on track does have adequate cognitive resources, as measured by the DI. But a child whom the CBM identifies as at risk may be more competent than that label implies. The DI shows that many children who perform poorly on CBM performance measures nevertheless have sound cognitive strategies. These false failures have a good deal of intellectual potential that teachers can tap.

Overall, CBM measures can make a contribution to identifying successful children and those with sub-par performance, but should at the very least be used in conjunction with the DI, which provides in-depth information about students' mathematical knowledge and is especially useful in identifying false failures.

Group Differences

In the early grades, girls and boys perform at roughly equivalent levels, with the possible exception that boys may employ more "abstract solution strategies that reflected conceptual understanding" than do girls.[9] Our results show that as expected, differences between boys and girls are minimal: there were differences on only six out of the sixty-four submeasures. When there was a difference, boys tended to perform better than girls on problem types that were just being taught. For example, figure 3.3 shows that on the subtraction identity principle (i.e., any number subtracted from itself equals zero), there was no difference between boys and girls in kindergarten when the concept was hard. But in first grade, when students are learning the principle, 60 percent of the boys used it to solve the problems, where as only 45 percent of the girls did. By second grade, the performance differences between boys and girls have evened out, with most students consistently using the principle.

If there is any fact certain in American education, it is that low-SES children perform at lower levels than middle-SES children. From the very beginning, the achievement gap between disadvantaged and advantaged children is wide: in the fall of the kindergarten year, about 47 percent of low-income children are in the lowest performance group, and only 8 percent of low-income children perform at the top level (compared with 30 percent of the more affluent children) on the Early Childhood Longitudinal Study Math Test.[10] Yet results like these derive from standard test performance

FIGURE 3.3   Subtraction identity principle by gender

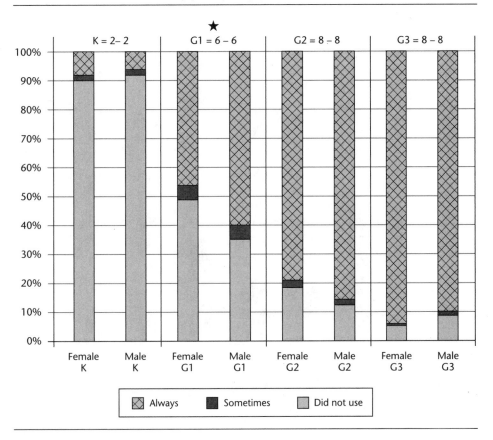

measures that are not particularly sensitive to motivational and cognitive processes. By contrast, our DI profile data can illuminate possible differences in both performance on the one hand, and strategies and concepts on the other.

Our results show that in most cases, the performance of low-SES students (as determined by student participation in a free or reduced lunch program) was roughly equivalent to their middle- and upper-income counterparts. There were differences in fifteen out of the sixty-four submeasures. Similar to the gender differences, the major SES differences that emerged were on new concepts that the students were just being taught. When problems were familiar or of high difficulty, the SES groups performed at roughly equivalent levels. For example, in the first and second grades, there were SES differences for the challenging mental calculation subtraction problems but no differences by third grade (see figure 3.4).

Why do we find few SES differences? One possibility is that the DI does a better job of uncovering children's competence than do traditional standard tests. The DI motivates children effectively and uncovers their underlying potential. Standard tests may do a poor job of identifying children's competence. The moral for the classroom is clear: teachers should use flexible formative assessment to uncover children's underlying

FIGURE 3.4   Mental subtraction calculation by SES

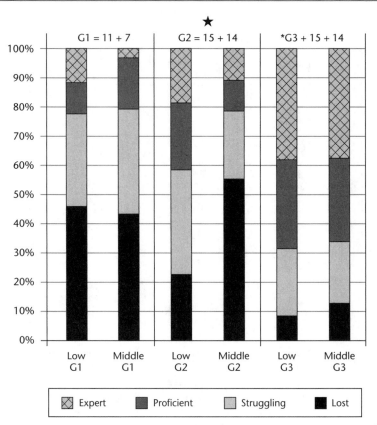

abilities as the first step in helping them to learn. Low-SES children may know more and be able to learn more than many teachers expect.

CONCLUSIONS

We found that our CBM measures are reliable and valid in the traditional sense of being stable across multiple administrations and being predictive of performance on other standard tests. A particularly promising finding is that a computer-driven variant of the clinical interview, the DI, is also reliable and valid. We found too that profiles contrasting performance and underlying knowledge as assessed by the DI are an effective way to categorize students and point the way to effective instruction. Teachers need to understand that some children who seem to know something really don't, and that others who seem not to know something really do. Understanding both performance and underlying processes is the key.

Our research shows that although they can help identify successful children, CBM measures tend to misclassify at-risk students, many of whom possess important cognitive strengths revealed by the DI. One way to improve the measurement power of the

CBM, so as to enable it to identify truly at-risk students who need special attention, may be to allow students extra time to complete the problems. Eliminating or reducing time constraints may lessen anxiety and motivate students to try harder. Another option may be to include an adaptive feature so that problem difficulty may increase or decrease, depending on student performance. Lastly, the use of the CBM may be replaced entirely with a short version of the DI that might do a better job of identifying at-risk students and even shed some light on their underlying competence.

Our results concerning gender and SES are encouraging. Gender differences in early mathematics are virtually nonexistent. Teachers should expect as much mathematical competence from girls as from boys. Similarly, SES differences as measured by the DI are less extensive than usually reported. Our interpretation is that the DI provides more motivating and more sensitive assessment than do most standard tests. Teachers should expect that low-SES children can achieve a great deal in mathematics.

Although our development efforts have produced a productive system of formative assessment, we are still faced with two important unanswered questions. Can mCM help teachers to reduce their own preconceptions to see their children's mathematical learning in a new light? And can mCM lead to useful changes in instruction that ultimately will benefit children? These are not simple questions; answering them will take a long time and much effort.

The research reported here was supported by the Institute of Education Sciences, U.S. Department of Education, through Grant R305B070325 to Teachers College, Columbia University. The opinions expressed are those of the authors and do not represent views of the institute or the U.S. Department of Education. We also wish to thank the students who took part in the study and the many principals, teachers, and parents who supported it.

CHAPTER 4

Customizing and Capture

Online Assessment Tools for Secondary Mathematics

KATHI COOK, CATHY SEELEY, AND LINDA CHAPUT

In its comprehensive picture of professional mathematics teaching, *Professional Standards for Teaching Mathematics*, the National Council of Teachers of Mathematics (NCTM) describes a classroom in which students are continually expected to demonstrate and explain their thinking and interact with engaging mathematical tasks—and in which teachers make decisions about instructional next steps based on student responses.[1] The picture is both exhilarating in its possibilities and daunting in the prospect of its implementation.

In the two decades since NCTM's powerful vision of the act of mathematics teaching, practitioners and developers have considered possible ways to support this vision. New applications of technology make this kind of classroom more attainable than ever before, with resources and systems emerging that can be tapped to give teachers access to information on mathematics learning. The Charles A. Dana Center at the University of Texas at Austin, working with applications of technology pioneered by Agile Mind, Inc., is asking: *Is it possible to build a technology-supported assessment system that truly enables and enhances mathematics teaching and learning, and that is experienced by students as part of their learning, not something separate?*

An objective of the instructional support system for secondary mathematics developed by the Dana Center and Agile Mind is to assemble and, through experience, optimize a range and variety of resources, tools, and methods that support teachers in orchestrating discourse in the kind of classroom NCTM envisioned. In such a classroom, the critical elements of formative assessment and instruction should weave seamlessly together. Experience has taught us that effectively integrating ongoing formative assessment with purposeful classroom instruction requires teacher expertise, a suite of flexible assessment tools, and administrative leadership focused on comprehensive learning outcomes rather than on single test scores.

Since its founding, Agile Mind, a young education company, has engaged in intensive research and development of technology-supported instructional systems. One of its key goals is to support teachers and other educators in implementing an expanded set of formative assessment resources in a way that changes what happens between teachers and learners in the classroom. An additional goal is to create online environments that engage students in *assessment as learning* by increasing both interactivity in problem solving and the difficulty of problems students can solve. This chapter will describe these assessment efforts and some of the challenges and insights that might be helpful to others with similar objectives.

Over a period of eight years, the Dana Center–Agile Mind collaboration has developed both instructional resources and technology supports for teachers and learners, primarily in middle and secondary mathematics, and now also in science. The technology is used in support of, rather than as a replacement for, teachers' interactions with students. This, in our view, is a critical feature of the system we describe, as many computer-based systems, regardless of the intentions of their designers, have been misused as electronic worksheets or poor substitute teachers.

We believe that two features of technology-based tools can save time for educators at several levels, while giving them more and better information for making instructional decisions in real time. By *letting students visualize concepts* and by *gathering instant information* about individual students and groups of students, technology can help teachers focus their attention where each student needs it most.

In this chapter, we focus not on the whole learning system but on resources educators can use in formative assessment in mathematics. We take a broad view of formative assessment, considering any resource that sheds light on student work to inform instruction as a potential formative tool. We will explore this notion of formative assessment through the assessment tools thus far developed and embedded within one particular engineered system. We will then describe teacher professional supports for implementing those tools, discuss how to deal with possible barriers to their widespread use, and look closely at how school districts are using these resources. We will conclude by examining the future outlook for incorporating these kinds of online resources into instructional programs.

As a basis for this discussion, we rely on experience with twenty thousand teachers and two million students of mathematics in twelve states—more than 80 percent of them in underserved areas. And we keep firmly in mind what we learned in the initial, and continuing, participatory design process undertaken by the founders of the initiative that became Agile Mind. They began with a question to teachers of mathematics, science, and language arts, first in Texas and California and then expanding throughout the United States: "To dramatically increase the number and diversity of the students you serve who are engaged in mathematics and science and who succeed at high levels, what are the tools and resources that would most benefit you and them?"

ASSESSMENT TOOLS WITHIN COURSE PROGRAMS

Agile Mind's course programs are designed to be comprehensive resources that incorporate—in a sequence of topics that support each week of instruction—curriculum, homework, formative assessment, test preparation, professional development and support, and an array of real-time reports to inform teaching and learning. Data captured from the company's data-mining system, as well as observation of classrooms, indicate that, among the resources provided in these course programs, the embedded assessments are the first or second most popular features among teachers who use the programs—and equally as popular with students.

Knowledgeable teachers seamlessly blend the components of the system, weaving formative assessment with instruction throughout a topic, sometimes using formal assessments and sometimes informally monitoring what a student or group of students is learning, fine-tuning instruction based on the information gleaned. New teachers or teachers new to teaching mathematics use the system differently and, as must be expected, with less fluency. They often rely on the program assessments to help them in ways experienced teachers may have moved beyond: to understand the standards by which they and their students will be assessed, to measure progress toward external measures of learning, and to help them grasp what formative assessment can look like in practice. All teachers, especially novice teachers, can benefit from a range of assessment resources that support and enhance instruction, rather than sidetracking it with special practice tests or test preparation materials, too often found in mathematics, where teaching is burdened with pressure to produce results on high-stakes assessments.

Each topic in one of our course programs includes many informal assessments and four types of formal assessments.

Formal Assessments

Formal assessments for each topic include *guided assessments* (that give students hints and feedback for each item), *self-test* questions (that offer students a private online space to solve problems related to a concept they have just encountered and to receive hints and feedback for each item), and topic tests that include both online, automatically graded *multiple-choice* items and *constructed response* items (where students are expected to respond in writing, on paper, to open-ended items, and to explain their thinking in answers to questions more complex than those that could be presented in multiple-choice format). Typically, students solve the guided assessment, self-test, and multiple-choice items on a computer connected to the Internet, although all are printable. When students complete the assessments online, they and their teachers receive instant feedback, because the items are automatically graded and reported to both (except for the self-tests, for which assessment results are reported only to students).

Reliable access to bandwidth and technical support problems continue to challenge the goal of ubiquitous computing for learning. As has been amply noted in the nation's most recent technology plan, the United States has fallen behind both industrialized and developing countries in its technology infrastructure for all purposes— and particularly for education.[2] Because of this, Agile Mind has adapted its tools to function well at the low bandwidth that is typically available in classrooms (28.8Kbps– 56Kbps). Participating students can use a computer at home, in a library, or in a school's learning lab before or after school. A growing number of schools are providing classroom sets of computers so that all students can work online at the same time. As of 2005, more than 90 percent of middle and high schools in the United States report having computer access for students at a ratio of at least 1:4.

Guided assessments like the one shown in figure 4.1 are particularly useful as formative assessments, because of the instant feedback they allow.

Figure 4.2 shows a portion of a sample guided assessment report, with students' names disguised. This report reveals information that may otherwise be hidden in the simple reporting of percentages of correct answers. For example, the report indicates

FIGURE 4.1   Guided assessment item

Fill in the blanks to complete the statement about the graph of Natalie's and Raul's data.

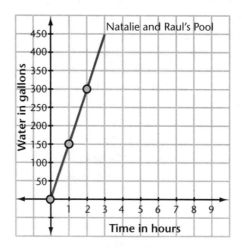

The [A   ] of the line that represents filling the pool with water is [B   ] gallons per hour.

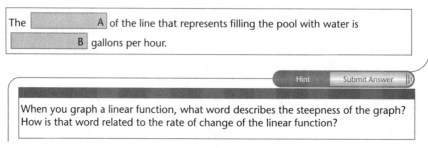

When you graph a linear function, what word describes the steepness of the graph? How is that word related to the rate of change of the linear function?

that over half the class failed to answer any of the first three questions correctly on the first try. Even though most students were able to determine the correct answer within three tries, the fact that such a high percentage experienced some difficulty indicates to the teacher using the program that students' understanding of the relevant concept is not robust. We observed teachers deciding, based on these data, to take time during the next class period to discuss these three items with the class to make sure students understand the concepts they address and, if need be, to step back and reteach.

Aside from identifying items for possible class discussion, the teacher can also analyze answer patterns for individual students and plan appropriate interventions. For example, Harley Hill was able to complete all nine items correctly, even though some items required more than one try. On the other hand, Manuela De Maria may have a tendency to "give up" after one incorrect answer, as evidenced by the data for questions 3, 7, and 8. The teacher can have conversations with both students about the value of persistence; in the case of Harley, the conversation may be a simple acknowledgement that the student's persistence was noted and valued. In the case of Manuela, the teacher will want to talk about the reasons why the student did not try and offer support and

FIGURE 4.2   Teacher report on student usage of the guided assessment

Student	Effort hh:mm:ss	9 assessment questions		Q1	Q2	Q3	Q4	Q5	Q6	Q7	Q8	Q9
		Score	% Tried									
Caldwell, Ursula	00:10:36	100%	100%	✓1	✓1	✓2	✓1	✓2	✓1	✓1	✓2	✓1
De Maria, Manuela	00:07:49	67%	100%	✓1	✓3	✗1	✓1	✓1	✓1	✗1	✗1	✓2
Gilmore, Allen	00:07:14	100%	100%	✓2	✓1	✓2	✓2	✓1	✓1	✓1	✓1	✓2
Hill, Harley	00:05:17	100%	100%	✓1	✓2	✓3	✓1	✓1	✓2	✓1	✓2	✓2
Jacobson, Cyrus	00:19:32	89%	100%	✗3	✓1	✓2	✓1	✓1	✓1	✓2	✓1	✓1
Lizarraga, Roderigo	00:05:57	100%	100%	✓3	✓1	✓2	✓1	✓2	✓1	✓1	✓1	✓1
Maynard, Carroll	00:09:02	89%	100%	✓2	✗3	✓3	✓1	✓2	✓1	✓1	✓3	✓1
Menendez, Desmond	00:30:55	78%	89%	✓3	✓1	✗3	✓1	✓1	✓1	—	✓1	✓1
Norman, Ben	00:15:56	89%	100%	✗3	✓1	✓1	✓1	✓1	✓1	✓1	✓1	✓1
Palacios, Lucio	00:13:02	89%	100%	✗3	✓2	✓1	✓2	✓2	✓1	✓1	✓1	✓3
Raymond, Marty	00:08:32	100%	100%	✓2	✓1	✓1	✓1	✓2	✓1	✓1	✓2	✓1
Roth, Dwayne	00:08:07	11%	11%	—	—	—	—	—	—	—	—	✓1
Salazar, Armena	00:25:08	89%	100%	✓1	✓1	✓2	✓2	✓1	✓1	✓2	✗3	✓2
Schwartz, Lara	00:32:10	89%	100%	✓1	✓2	✗1	✓1	✓1	✓1	✓2	✓1	✓2

encouragement to build that student's desire to persist. The teacher will want to have a different kind of conversation with Dwayne Roth in an attempt to discover why that student did not even attempt the first eight questions on the assignment.

Flexible reporting by student, item, and group enables students to find out how they are doing right away, while teachers can choose reports in various formats according to what they want to know at the time. For example, by looking at how many times a student or group of students attempted to solve a problem before reaching a correct response, teachers can decide whether to provide additional instruction on one or more concepts or whether students are ready for new learning.

Self-tests are formative tools in that students find out whether they have learned key skills and concepts related to the topic being taught. The students themselves can then inform their learning by spending more time on the instructional materials associated with assessments, by requesting additional practice, or by clarifying misunderstandings with their teacher. While students see self-tests as a safe place in which they can practice and see how they are doing without direct connection to the teacher, teachers can receive reports about how much time students invested in making use of this type of assessment question.

Figure 4.3 shows a portion of a report on a self-test from a different topic, assigned for homework after students have received instruction and after they completed and discussed the guided assessment for the topic. Here, the teacher can see immediately how many students in this class have begun the assignment. Student 2 spent some time with the assignment, yet never answered a question. Student 3 spent almost twenty minutes with the assignment, yet answered only two questions. The teacher now is equipped with data to talk with both students to determine whether they were having difficulty with the concepts being assessed, or whether there was some other reason for their lack of responses. Remembering that the self-test is designed as a private space in which only students see their own scores, the teacher can reinforce that notion of privacy while talking about effective effort.

FIGURE 4.3   Teacher report on student use of self-test

Student	Effort (minutes)	7 self-test questions % tried	Q1	Q2	Q3	Q4	Q5	Q6	Q7
1, Student	0:06:55	100%	•	•	•	•	•	•	•
2, Student	0:02:08		—	—	—	—	—	—	—
3, Student	0:19:59	29%	•	•	—	—	—	—	—

Legend:

If there is no information to display, the report field is blank.

Effort is the amount of time a student spent on the assignment.

% Tried is the percentage of assigned items a student tried to answer.

• = Self test question answered.

— = Self test question not answered.

Topic tests composed of multiple-choice and constructed response items are designed to mimic high-stakes assessments and can be considered either formative or summative assessments, depending on how the teacher chooses to use them. They could be used as short-term summative tools, providing information on how well students learned the intended content within the topic. But if teachers choose to modify instruction based on results—either revisiting part or all of the topic or adjusting the approach in a future topic—these assessments become a useful addition to the teacher's suite of formative tools. Our studies of teacher use show novel and, we think, healthy approaches by teachers, in which they administer assessments and then revisit items that proved problematic for some students—enlisting the help in class of students who achieved success with them.

Assessing as Part of Instruction

Dana Center–Agile Mind programs use a variety of online teacher resources to provide additional guidance on formatively assessing students. As we envision it, whenever the teacher orchestrates and manages classroom discourse, the resulting interactions among students and between students and the teacher provide an opportunity for ongoing formative assessment. In our model, online "Advice for Instruction" for each topic, viewable only by teachers and not seen by their students, offers teachers suggestions on what questions they might ask to frame discussions, what to look for to make sure students understand both previous content and the intended point of the learning activities at hand, and how to adapt their teaching approach based on possible student misconceptions or gaps. It also includes clear advice on how to make productive use of assessment strategies to support and enhance instruction.

Also embedded throughout lessons are additional technology-supported animations used as interactive self-checks, including "check-reveal" types of questions, in which students are asked a question, select a response through any of a number of possible interactive formats, and receive immediate feedback on whether they are correct. Teachers have access to customized reports that aggregate student data on time spent on tasks for such pages as selected by teachers.

Thus, twenty years after NCTM articulated a vision of a mathematics classroom rich in discourse, technology is making such a classroom a more attainable goal for more teachers. By giving the teacher a variety of ways to look at students' learning throughout the learning process, the kinds of resources described here can enhance the teacher's ability to effectively facilitate discourse and manage the classroom. Whether students are working individually, in small groups, or as a class, such resources allow students to adjust their thinking and the teacher to adjust instruction in ways that enhance student learning.

THE AGILE ASSESSMENT SYSTEM

Useful as these tools are, we have learned that teachers want yet more flexibility. For example, we have learned that teachers want to be able to assess learning without the cues created by placement within a topic. They also want to be able to assess differentially—for different levels of difficulty, and for different reading levels among the students they serve. A versatile technology platform, in our view, must create the potential for additional assessment tools that teachers can customize based on their understanding of their students' learning needs—for a single standard, a group of concepts, or a complete course.

Based on this feedback from educators, we embarked on a new phase of work to create an assessment application called Agile Assessment. Through Agile Assessment, we have been able to expand our e-learning assessment technologies to provide educators the ability to construct and administer high-quality assessments—from weekly quizzes to benchmark assessments—containing varied and gamelike "assessment as learning" interactions that are highly functional at low bandwidth. These Internet technologies support dynamic test construction by enabling educators to choose among items authored by nationally respected experts and aligned to standards, concept strands, reading level, and level of difficulty. Agile Assessment is now fully prototyped and in early use in 2010–2011 with 34,601 students in 113 schools in 41 school districts across 8 states.

With Agile Assessment, teachers can construct assessments that encompass not just multiple-choice, single-answer items and fill-in-the-blank items, but also novel items, such as puzzlelike questions with multiple correct answers, partially correct answers, and multiple incorrect answers (see figure 4.4). The goal is to provide varied, interesting, and even gamelike learning interactions that increase student motivation and support the use of more cognitively demanding tasks to better assess higher-order learning. These include drag-and-drop problems in which the learner matches labeled tiles to labeled slots and short-answer, fill-in-the-blank problems in which the student provides input on a real or virtual keyboard. Because students cannot simply guess the answer from a fixed set of alternatives, these kinds of problems are believed to be more meaningful indicators of understanding than multiple-choice or other single-answer questions. Teachers can choose to use this system in formative and summative ways to either inform instruction or measure learning outcomes. Early studies indicate positive migration trends, as teachers seem to continue to grow in their sophistication of use of the tools. Specifically, data thus far show that teachers using the system for the second and third years make significantly greater use of the more challenging items than in their first year. We hope to secure research and development funds to study this change more deeply and also to further develop and test items.

To support flexibility in construction and use of assessments for different purposes, Agile Assessment provides a variety of online tools—for teachers to construct, schedule, and deliver tests; for students to take the tests; and for teachers and administrators to obtain real-time reports on student scores and responses, test analysis, and item analysis. During test taking, Agile Assessment captures student responses and reports them in real time. Current reports display both graphical and tabular data summaries of item coverage by standards, objective, key concept, or instructional topic so that educators can easily track their students' learning and progress. Three types of reports—test analysis, scores and responses, and item analysis—present data on individual students and also aggregated at the class, teacher, school, or district level and offer varying levels of detail depending on the role of the viewer.

Figure 4.5 shows a sample student test analysis report for a six-question quiz in geometry, focused on a particular standard related to right triangles. The quiz includes

FIGURE 4.4   Sample puzzlelike fill-in-the-blank and drag-and-drop problems

Anthony creates a table to find the number of tiles in the border for a rectangular swimming pool that is two feet longer than it is wide. fill in the blanks below in order to extent his table for the values shown.

Borders for rectangular pools

Width of pool in feet	Tiles in border
1	12
2	16
3	20
5	28
10	48
16	72

Place the correct label on each circle to identify each group of numbers.

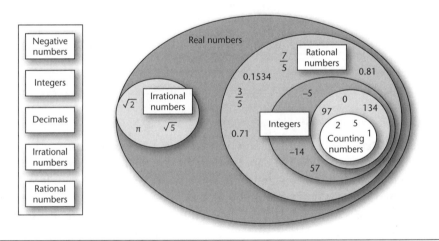

not only single answer multiple choice items (MCSA, questions 4 and 6) but also fill-in-the-blank (FIB), drag-and-drop (DND), and multiple-choice multiple-answer (MCMA), in which students must select all correct responses. In the case of incorrect responses, analysis is provided to highlight possible student mistakes or misconceptions that might have led to the student's errors. With this information, the teacher can plan appropriate interventions to address the mistake or misconception and get the student back on track. Additionally, the relevant topic in the instructional program is cited below the statement of the learning standard so that the teacher can easily find appropriate materials for reteaching.

Agile Mind and the Dana Center, with other independent experts in both mathematics assessment and report design, have also designed and implemented an expanded

FIGURE 4.5   Sample of student test analysis report

Standard G.11.C

The student is expected to develop, apply, and justify triangle similarity relationships, such as right triangle ratios, trigonometric ratios, and Pythagorean triples using a variety of methods.
See Agile Mind: Geometry: 16

Item	Item type	% Students answered correctly	Student response, with available analysis
1	DND	75%	✗ The student may have chosen the shortest length available to be the short leg of the triangle, or may have determined that 55.1 is the hypotenuse and divided by 2 to get the short leg.
2	FIB	56%	✗ The student used inverse cosine rather than inverse sine.
3	MCMA	87%	✓
4	MCSA	47%	✗ D: Volumes of solids cannot be found directly using sine and cosine values. They require the use of other formulas.
5	DND	94%	✓
6	MCSA	63%	✗ A: The student may have found the difference between Chuck's height and the length of ground between him and the end of the cable, 1 foot. The student then might have assumed the difference would be the same for the telephone pole, so 12 − 1 = 11 feet.

Student mean: 33%
Class mean: 70%

set of reports that enable administrators overseeing groups of schools spanning multiple districts to aggregate student data for their groups. Student test-taking behaviors are captured, stored in databases, and represented as anonymous data for internal analysis to support the developers' continuous process of test-item improvement. The system currently stores historical data on student use of more than four thousand items. Researchers and developers study student data in order to continually improve assessment items based on empirical evidence of their utility. It is our hope that by continuously refining items and item clusters, we will be able to describe for both educators and learners clear trajectories toward mastery of concepts. This aspect of the work is a major focus of our research and development efforts, with significant time dedicated by Dana Center program development and research staff, external researchers at leading institutions, and Agile Mind program development, instructional design, and engineering staff; we hope, over time, to create a repository for assessment as learning backed by a powerful research base.

ONE DISTRICT'S ASSESSMENT JOURNEY

The following story—of a real district that we will call Mountain Rock Consolidated School District (CSD) (not its real name) for confidentiality reasons—reflects the experience of districts choosing to use the tools described in this chapter to support student learning at the district, school, teacher, and student levels.

District Sets and Monitors Teaching and Learning Goals

After many efforts to improve achievement in secondary mathematics, and an examination of their various outcomes, leaders in Mountain Rock CSD decided to establish a transparent set of learning goals for the middle- and high-school mathematics programs for all of their schools. They chose to use Agile Assessment to create a series of interim assessments linked to the state standards to be given by all algebra teachers in the district. They determined that, in this way, they could support teams at each school in their analysis of comparable data and in their use of them to measure and respond to student progress throughout the year.

One School Makes the Most of Teacher Collaboration Time

Susan Jones, a math coach in the district, will be meeting with the algebra teachers at one high school on Wednesday. She has been analyzing data from the most recent interim assessment the algebra students at this school took online last week. Agile Assessment's teacher test analysis report shows that Daniel Ortiz, one of the district's Algebra I teachers, has had success in improving his students' performance on items related to rate and speed since the last interim assessment. Jones makes a note to ask Ortiz to share with the department what worked for him and his students, and then to have the group develop ideas other teachers can try. It is also clear from the data that the department should discuss ways to improve learning of concepts with which students still appear to be struggling. Jones would like to spend time at the meeting developing a plan for how the teachers will use upcoming topics in the Algebra I program to ensure more students master these skills—and how they will motivate students to work on mathematics outside the classroom.

A Teacher Develops a Plan to Modify Instruction

Ortiz is collecting lots of data about his class; he has data from the annual state assessment and data from the course-based assessments (such as guided assessments and multiple-choice items). He also has student work from the program's activity sheets and constructed response items, as well as other projects he has created for the class. Today, Ortiz is reviewing data from the latest interim assessment created by his district using Agile Assessment.

The class scores and responses report highlights areas in which most of his students appear to be on track for success. This knowledge frees him to focus on areas in this assessment in which students in his class struggled. Ortiz sees that many of those students did not do well on questions related to interpreting the y intercept of a function. He plans to ask his colleagues at the upcoming department meeting how they help their students master this concept. By looking closely at the questions and student responses with his fellow teachers, he hopes to develop ideas about the types of instruction that will make a difference for his students.

Based on his students' performance on the last interim assessment, Ortiz had made a point to spend more instructional time on rate of change, developing deeper understanding of this concept through exploratory, interactive lessons and visualizations. Based on his students' work on topic-level assessments, Ortiz thinks his approach is making a difference. He is pleased to see that the interim assessment data confirm that his students' understanding has improved in this area. For those students who are still having trouble, he looks at the most common incorrect responses to see whether there is a pattern that might suggest ways he can help them.

A Student Sets and Monitors Educational Goals

Desmond's Algebra I teacher, Mr. Ortiz, passed back Desmond's student test analysis report on the latest interim assessment (see figure 4.6).

Based on his past performance on class assessments, Desmond had set some goals for improvement. While he has met his goals overall, he still missed some questions, and the report highlights possible misunderstandings. Ortiz encourages Desmond to review the mathematics concepts that were most challenging to him. He offers to set a time to talk with Desmond to discuss his results.

Today Ortiz reviewed the assessment with the entire class, projecting the class item analysis report. Desmond saw that other classmates made mistakes similar to his. The ensuing class discussion helped him understand his mistakes.

Desmond also described the strategies he had used to answer some items correctly. At the beginning of the year, this was awkward for him, and some of his fellow students scoffed because they were unaccustomed to perceiving him as a leader in communication. But his teacher has maintained the practice of sharing outcomes and of challenging classmates to help one another succeed academically by learning from both productive and unproductive strategies. As a result, Desmond's confidence has grown.

FIGURE 4.6   Portion of student test analysis report

Standard A.08.B

The student is expected to solve systems of linear equations using concrete models, graphs, tables, and algebraic methods.
See Agile Mind: Algebra I: 17, 18

Item	Item type	% Students answered correctly	Student response, with available analysis
9	MCSA	60%	✗C: The student mixed up which value was the sum of the numbers, and which was the difference. The different is 14 (not 142), and the sum is 142 (not 14).
10	MCSA	80%	✓
11	MCSA	66%	✗ A: The student substituted the y + 3 for 2x instead of just x
12	MCSA	53%	✓

Student mean: 50%
Class mean: 77%

IMPACT ON TEACHERS AND STUDENTS

What do we know about the effects of the assessments on their users? As with many such innovations, it is impossible, in classroom contexts, to isolate the specific effect of the assessment piece of these programs, because so many of the formative assessments are embedded in text and visualizations used for instruction. Among the information we are sure of is how much teachers use the tools and which tools they use: (1) the Fall 2010 use data indicate that more than 50 percent of teacher participants use the online resources sixty to ninety minutes each week for instruction and that 25 percent use the resources two to four hours per week; (2) the components of the programs that both teachers and students use most intensively are the visualizations and assessments of all types; and (3) as indicated by internal studies and confirmed in independent analysis by researchers Brian Rowan and Richard Correnti at the University of Michigan and Carnegie Mellon University, teachers who use the programs for more than a year increase both their instructional use of the assessments and the amount of the algebra curriculum that they are able to complete with students.[3] This last finding is important, because it shows that assessments don't improve outcomes merely by requiring more instructional time. In our internal studies of schools that use these programs beyond a threshold of two hours each week for instruction, public school leaders in San Antonio, Dallas, Chicago, Corpus Christi, Los Angeles, and Cleveland, as well as in a single charter network, report that their students are scoring statistically significant (and educationally meaningful) gains compared to performance in prior years.

We now consider the programs and implementation models to be sufficiently stable to permit more systematic and controlled study of their effects. We will continue our research to potentially refine the models and tools for effective use in increasingly complex contexts in support of our goal to increase student engagement and achievement.

PUTTING THE SYSTEM INTO ACTION:
IMPLEMENTATION SUCCESSES AND CHALLENGES

From the point of view of developers and implementers, the experiences in implementing formative assessment have ranged from exciting to humbling. We have been both gratified and sobered by how hungry educators are for well-designed formative assessments in secondary mathematics. It appears that, although exemplary assessments in mathematics do exist, many of those that are most broadly available do not reflect the quality that educators seek. Teachers and administrators also complain that many test items are not truly aligned to the standards against which their students are measured, even when they claim to be.

Early Successes

Teachers make broad use of the assessment tools described here, and they particularly value the ability to use their professional judgment to customize assessments based on their particular instructional needs. We believe that developers should be encouraged by administrators' interest in formative assessment, even during a period of dramatic downward pressure on budgets. We are optimistic about the apparent trend toward teachers' improved use of assessments embedded in instruction, especially when they are provided with high-quality resources.

We feared that, in an environment in which so much emphasis is placed on high-stakes testing that relies on multiple-choice and fill-in-the-blank formats, some educators might not be willing to employ puzzlelike items with their students. But we have found the opposite to be the case. Teachers have been more adventurous than we anticipated, and once items were shared with their students, they were excited by the increases in student engagement that emerged during the assessment process.

Infrastructure Challenges

Nonetheless, many educators, particularly those at the district level who feel direct pressure related to student achievement, continue to miss the opportunity to use the full range of possible formative assessment resources. Teachers in many schools lack access to powerful tools they could use to help significant numbers of their students tackle challenging problems and correct their misconceptions. In many settings, infrastructure problems inhibit the systemic use of online assessments: districts and schools simply are not organized to accommodate an equity agenda that includes access for every student to the full set of instructional and assessment resources.

Our observation, having worked with more than a thousand schools (most serving high-need populations), is that many schools and districts in the United States are ten or more years behind even small businesses in their use of technologies for the true business of education—teaching and learning—even where they may be more up to date in their use of administrative technologies. Many are unaware of simple, inexpensive adjustments that could make their technologies function optimally.

What, specifically, do we mean by infrastructure problems? Several representative examples will perhaps illustrate best. In one urban district serving 600,000 students, because of a lack of understanding by technical administrators of how to manage bandwidth to accommodate instruction as well as administration, classroom computers routinely freeze during the period of the day in which attendance is recorded on the administrative software. This problem, if unaddressed, renders first-period teaching with computers—as well as use of the school's learning lab—impossible. The technical fix for this problem costs between $1,000 and $3,000, depending on the size of the school and the available staff.

In another urban district serving a million students, the central office at one point determined that city schools would not be allowed to update their browser configurations, setting the standards for browsers introduced three years earlier. Because free browser updates now occur from most major providers twice each year, and software applications are adapted to conform, schools discover that many of the software applications they had purchased under mandate will no longer run. Large corporations routinely upgrade browsers for all employees in several hours' time; smaller corporations, individually, with instructions for each computer user. This district could protect the value of its investments in hardware and software, and the usability of these investments in support of student learning, with attention to such necessary routine maintenance.

In many other settings, the number of computers is adequate, but the bandwidth is not sufficient to support simultaneous use by the number of users. The technical fix for this problem costs about $1,000.

Despite a national technology plan to update educational infrastructure, in these challenging economic times, some administrators argue that there simply are not enough funds to support technology investments. However, given comparative data on technology infrastructure in the United States versus other countries and the potential for technology to improve the efficiency of teaching and learning, that argument demands serious scrutiny. We should note that administrators also face the challenge of trying to manage young people's creative, often inappropriate uses of technology. As schools implement firewalls and other restrictions to control what may not, in the end, be controllable, they can unintentionally restrict teachers' use of the kinds of powerful technological resources we have described here.

Challenges of Practice

Also, as authoritative research makes clear, few practitioners can be expected to fall into the category of "early adopter" with respect to technology-based resources.[4] The adoption of any innovation takes time and requires the use of differing strategies if it is to become robust. Given the escalating turnover during the past decade of district administrators, school administrators, and even teachers in science, technology, engineering, and mathematics (STEM) fields, this poses a serious design challenge for managing the adoption of innovation at the school or district level, including the particular innovations we describe in this chapter. We have learned a great deal over the past eight years about the differences in implementation between the secondary level and the elementary level. Specifically, elementary educators experience less turnover and they more readily and consistently adopt innovations selected by their administrations than do secondary educators. Consistent with the conclusions of the RAND studies on secondary practice, we have worked with school administrators to develop strategies to encourage participation in programs rather than attempting to impose it.[5]

Helping teachers continue to grow in their knowledge about and use of a wide range of formal and informal assessments must be central in schools' decisions about using any instructional or assessment system. With or without the use of technology, most teachers can benefit from continued learning about appropriate forms and uses of assessment to improve teaching and learning. In our work, this emphasis on teacher learning and support is central to the implementation of any systematic improvement program. We have found that, in implementing a technology-based system, teachers need face-to-face professional development as part of their support. Our experience is that most teachers need a minimum of twenty hours of professional development to gain the confidence and knowledge to put such a system to effective, comprehensive use. Without this amount of preparation, teachers are likely to use only one or two components. We have found that professional development should focus not on mechanics but on mathematical content knowledge and on pedagogical knowledge—how to use the program to maximize student learning of the content. In our program, we also provide teachers with online access to professional resources to enhance and continue that learning, as well as providing support from a professional development advisor throughout the school year.

Educators themselves sometimes identify challenges that inhibit them from fully tapping into the power of this kind of comprehensive technology support for instruction and assessment. Such barriers, either perceived or real, include the continued lack in some districts of the equipment or modest technical support required to take advantage of online delivery, grading, and reporting; districts' consolidated purchase of instructional resources or assessments (purchases of English language arts, history, mathematics, and science together); and teacher uncertainty about how to incorporate informal assessment in day-to-day teaching.

We have described earlier some examples of relatively economical and straightforward ways to address the first of these teacher-identified barriers related to technology infrastructure. Leaders at the school or district level can address the second teacher-identified barrier—central purchases of resources across disciplines—by more closely considering the advantages and disadvantages of a centralized system. Some may simply be unaware that systems that meet district needs in language arts may be deficient in mathematics and science. Many districts have solved this problem by instituting rigorous content-specific selection criteria for all instructional materials and systems. Such a shift can liberate schools to make decisions based on what will most help students and their teachers in each field of study. In terms of the third barrier, teachers' sophistication in appropriate uses of informal assessment continues to be a high-priority target for professional development, regardless of the particular type of informal assessment tool(s) being considered.

Further, district leaders continue to be challenged by the mantra of using data to inform instruction. Most educators intuitively see the sense of basing instructional decisions on data, but they may not have a good sense of what data-driven decisions look like in practice. In our work with schools, we have seen enormous gains over the past five years in the sophistication with which educators approach the uses of a wide variety of data, not just test scores, to shape instruction. But there remains much work to do. We still see, even in districts committed to examining and using data effectively, a lack of understanding of the nature and limits of statistical data and very unproductive uses of these data to shape teacher practice. And we continue to see little attention to data beyond individual and group scores on large-scale tests.

LOOKING BACK AND LOOKING AHEAD

Today, as in the early days of computer-aided instruction, it remains common to find schools that have chosen to invest in expensive computer-delivered instruction and assessment programs that involve students sitting alone at computers, engaged in tasks that are little more than electronic worksheets. Clearly, the kinds of formative assessment resources described here represent a new generation of technology support for teachers and students. Tools can be flexible, engaging, and varied, drawing in students with interesting and novel problems and formats and providing real-time data for teachers. The use of such tools demonstrates a commitment to rigorous instruction and supports teachers as key decision makers in classrooms where students' interactions with each other and with the teacher are valued.

Agile Mind's current technologies support rapid, iterative, research-based development and allow districts an economical way to make powerful tools available to teachers for the improvement of learning. As we look to the future, we and other researchers and developers will continue to explore, develop, and test new formats and forms of student interactions for formal and informal assessments, because the interest in this work is intensifying.

At the same time, current resources already foreshadow the next generation of mathematics and science assessments now being envisioned, designed, and tested for future large-scale exams, including those administered through the National Assessment of Educational Progress, the Educational Testing Service, the College Board, and, we hope, the national assessments under development in support of the Common Core State Standards for Mathematics and English Language Arts. Specifically, the assessment forms and structures described here support measures of critical thinking and flexible problem-solving skills that are essential for the contemporary workplace and for success in a global economy. And we believe they represent an example of the kind of work that can be done in the United States to build on and broaden the exciting array of assessment work done over the past several years in other nations, such as the rich instructional and assessment resources developed by the Freudenthal Institute for Science and Mathematics Education (the Netherlands) and the Shell Centre for Mathematical Education (England). Further, we continue to refine ways to exploit the current technological platform as an economical and expeditious vehicle that could be used in large-scale assessments, even when the types of assessment items and tasks are as diverse as those described here or those under consideration for the future.

In response to the coming changes in large-scale assessment, we will continue to gather teacher and student feedback, use, and performance data to determine the effectiveness of the current suite of assessment tools, as well as to support external researchers in their study of our work. Planned future initiatives include development of assessments customized to support the Common Core State Standards for Mathematics as well as the development of expanded support for assessing open-ended student work, such as long-term projects.[6] The latter effort could support the incorporation of elements of project-based learning into selected courses.

The use of these many tools also enables us to more closely examine philosophical questions related to the abundance of information becoming available to teachers. Is it realistic to think that teachers will be willing and able to process so much information and target instructional adjustments based on what each student needs? How much information is too much? Should we work to simplify reports to make them easier for teachers to digest? It will be important over the next few years to examine the costs and benefits of increasingly detailed student information systems to determine how to optimize teachers' effectiveness toward actual results. Meanwhile, there is no question that technology-based formative assessment tools can help teachers help students learn mathematics. Desmond and his classmates would surely agree.

PART II

Literacy and Language Arts

CHAPTER 5

Identifying Craft Moves

Close Observation of Elementary Student Writing

AUDREY E. POPPERS

Close observation is virtually a lost art in education. Pre-service teacher training programs focus on instructional delivery, with little or no emphasis on differentiation of instruction and even less attention to diagnosis of individual needs. The dominant use of prescriptive texts as a way of standardizing teaching, at least in California—presumably to overcome the impact of less than adequate teacher training programs—also works against the practice of close observation. Although a well-developed text can provide helpful guidance, too often the text is used as a one-size-fits-all recipe, and varied student responses are viewed solely as a measure of individual student capacity rather than an indicator of the effectiveness of the instruction. Interim assessments and similar benchmark measures are often touted as tools to support differentiation. Typically, these exams provide broad indications of knowledge within topic areas, but fail to provide sufficient insight into individual students' thinking to support differentiated instruction. As a result, citing a lack of time and the need to manage the class as a whole, many teachers target instruction to the average for the class, leaving some students behind and failing to challenge others.

Effective differentiation requires:

- Good knowledge of the content to be taught.
- The ability and inclination to observe individual students closely to ascertain their needs.
- A varied repertoire of pedagogical approaches.
- A classroom structure or routine to manage differentiation.

The Every Child a Reader and Writer (ECRW) initiative, sponsored by the Noyce Foundation, of which I was a director, was designed to address these needs. In this chapter, I will describe the initiative, the assessment practices utilized in the initiative, and what we learned.

EVERY CHILD A READER AND WRITER

In 2000, the Noyce Foundation invited five Bay Area school districts to participate in the ECRW program. Although the initiative was initially intended as a program to support improved instruction in both reading and writing, the focus was soon narrowed to the improvement of writing instruction in grades K–6 in five school districts in California's Silicon Valley.

Why the focus on writing? The participating districts had been working to improve literacy for some time, with limited evidence of success. Although reading results weren't satisfactory, most teachers felt that they knew how to teach reading. In addition, districts had adopted state-mandated reading texts and were hopeful that these prescriptive programs would lead to improved results in reading. By contrast, writing difficulties seemed like a good place to begin, since most teachers willingly admitted that they lacked strategies for teaching writing effectively. Reading and writing are reciprocal skills—the two complement and reinforce one another. With these facts in mind, we decided to focus initial professional development efforts in the area of writing. Although the project did eventually turn attention to reading as well as writing, this chapter will focus on our efforts in the area of writing.

A writing workshop model comprised the core pedagogical strategy to address rigorous grade-level writing standards. Initially, we adopted the Primary Literacy Standards developed and published by the National Center for Education and the Economy as the project's defined writing standards.[1] Eventually, coaches and exemplary teachers elaborated and modified these standards. (For an overview of the writing standards ultimately used in ECRW, see the Noyce Foundation Web site at www.noycefdn.org.)

In the model, the sixty-minute daily workshop opens with a mini-lesson focused on a specific instructional objective, followed by an independent writing time in which students pursue their writing individually and participate in response groups with other students, conferences with the teacher, and small group strategy lessons. The workshop hour closes with some type of whole-group activity, typically revisiting the instructional objective of the mini-lesson.

The workshop format promises a structured model for meeting the needs of the diverse population of students within a typical classroom. Once the workshop routines are in place, students should work with minimal supervision during the independent writing time, allowing the teacher to provide instruction to address the specific needs of individuals and small groups. During this time, the teacher should use his or her observations of each student's daily work to plan and provide differentiated learning opportunities and to determine the focus of the mini-lesson for the next day.

PROFESSIONAL DEVELOPMENT

Recognizing that a knowledgeable, skillful teacher is the most powerful determinant of student achievement, ECRW relied heavily on professional development for classroom teachers. These efforts targeted the workshop structure, genre and craft knowledge, grade-level writing standards, and pedagogy. Before long, we realized that these focus areas were necessary but not sufficient.

In initial ECRW professional development sessions, teachers were taught to implement a writing workshop model in their daily classroom routine. Teachers and students enjoyed the predictability and flexibility provided by the workshop format and felt fairly successful by the end of the first year. Students reported enjoying the writing workshop, and teachers observed that students were writing more and seemed more engaged in their writing. As implementation of the workshop structure eased the necessity for teachers to engage in constant student management, teachers felt free to teach more—to the whole class, to individuals, and to small groups. However, it soon became apparent that many teachers were confused and unsure about what to teach.

Each month, coaches, principals, and professional developers visited selected classrooms as a group to observe the workshop hour. After each observation, they gathered to review and provide feedback to the teacher. In addition, coaches videotaped lessons, as well as pre- and post-lesson conferences with the teacher.

We observed that most teachers actually knew little about writing and how to teach it. They tended to teach lessons they had seen demonstrated or found in a publication or teacher's guide. Often the lesson did not match student needs and couldn't be utilized by the student(s) during the independent writing time. Teachers were following old habits developed from using prescriptive programs—looking for formulaic lessons and activities. They demonstrated little inclination to investigate what a student was thinking and trying to do, and what skills or understandings he needed to be successful.

During summer institutes, teachers participated in training and scoring of student work. Although some teachers were able to identify high-quality pieces of student writing, they were much less able to discern the specific elements that comprised good pieces. Many teachers identified mechanically correct writing as being of high quality, regardless of the substance of the piece. For example, teachers initially judged papers like "Drowning" as meeting the standard for narrative in third grade, since it contains few errors in mechanics. After working through anchor papers using scoring rubrics tied to the standards, teachers could see beyond the mechanical correctness to discern the reasons that the paper falls short of meeting the grade-level standard.

Drowning

I am a very good swimmer. When I got to the pool, a kid was already there. We started playing together. Then I went in the big end of the pool. He chased me, but he didn't know how to swim in the deep end yet. So he got out. So did I.

I went to the really deep end and we both jumped in. He forgot that he couldn't swim in the deep end, because we were having so much fun. He started to drown.

I was the only one who could swim in the deep end, because my brother Max didn't know how to swim. My grandma was getting ready in her house, and my mom had clothes on. The boy's mom and dad weren't there. He panicked, and panicked. It was my job to save him. So, I swam over to him and I got him to the side of me. Then I swam to the stairs of the pool, and walked him out of the humongous pool. Then his mom and dad saw and said "Thank you, kid" to me, and I've never seen them since.

Specifically, the narrator of "Drowning":

- Attempts to develop an interesting beginning, although there is a need for a transition between the two opening sentences.
- Establishes the main character at the start of the piece.
- Creates a sequence of events.
- Contains some details and concrete language.
- Offers a conclusion.
- Has lapses in coherence and pacing (i.e., "we were having so much fun. He started to drown.") that prevent the piece from meeting the grade-level standard.

Although teachers had access to the grade-level standards and thought they understood them, they were less able to identify the existence or absence of important elements in a given piece of writing, and lacked strategies for teaching these elements. Teachers easily recognized that the third-grade narrative excerpted next, "Lady," was a superior piece of writing, but before receiving scoring training, teachers had difficulty identifying and describing the effective elements of the writing.

Lady

Lady came bounding up to us, licking us and sniffing us and jumping on us, her stubby tail waving back and forth faster than you can wave your hand. Grandpa trailed behind, walking up to us to help us with our luggage. Lady followed tight on our heels, more excited than a little boy at a baseball game. We dropped our bags in his unusual garage, then walked up to his porch.

Staring straight ahead there are groves of trees on both sides of the lake, which was rippling, in a slight breeze. Rattlesnake Island is inbetween the groves of trees, emerald green as always.

Grandpa looked at me and asked "So, how's school going?"

[. . .]

I was very sorry when I had to leave. I knew this was the last visit this summer. I wouldn't get to see Grandpa for almost a year.

When I walked to the truck, Lady followed tight on my heels, more excited than a little boy at a baseball game. I thought I knew why. She was feeling we wouldn't see each other for a long time. And she was right. She died that winter. I will never forget those large, brown, unblinking eyes, her black fur with brown patches, the stubby tail that wave back and forth faster than you can wave your hand, and most importantly, all of the things we did together. I still miss her very much. Maybe even too much.

The scoring rubric includes five score points: 1—needs substantial support; 2—needs instruction; 3—approaching standard; 4—meets standard; 5—exceeds standard. This outstanding score-point 5 paper exceeds the standard by employing a range of appropriate strategies in an unusually mature way for a third grader. One of the most striking devices, clearly a conscious choice, is the repetition of the opening description of Lady in the conclusion. In addition, the narrative:

- Orients and engages the reader with use of metaphorical descriptions of the grandfather's home, and more importantly, the dog Lady, who becomes the focus of the story.
- Creates a sequence of events that unfolds naturally.
- Provides good pacing.
- Develops characters by describing their actions, dialogue, and internal dialogue.
- Is brought to a satisfying conclusion through the use of repetition and reflective comments.

DEVELOPMENT OF THE ASSESSMENT MODEL

ECRW teachers were asked to teach units of study focused on four writing genres—narrative, informational, response to literature, and procedural—to implement a complementary skills block, and to gather samples of each student's work into a portfolio. Each year, a student's completed portfolio consisted of the following written pieces gathered throughout the year: rough and final drafts for each of the genres; responses to two on-demand prompts for narrative writing; a piece demonstrating knowledge of conventions; and a student self-assessment of progress. In the spring of each year, The Noyce Foundation contracted with Educational Data Systems to identify and gather a stratified random sample of portfolios from classrooms across the five districts. During a weeklong institute each summer, coaches and trained teachers scored the portfolios.

Previously scoring tools had been developed by a team of consultants, ECRW coaches, and foundation staff, based on the grade-level standards. The team used student papers collected by teachers at each grade level to inform the development of the scoring rubrics. The team developed anchor papers and wrote supporting commentary. Procedures for training and anchoring scorers were also developed by the team.

Scoring sessions were focused on building teachers' knowledge and inclination to anchor their judgments to specific elements in the student work. The training process was detailed. Each scorer was required to demonstrate the ability to score a series of anchor papers reliably and to justify their scores with evidence from the paper being scored. Led by a knowledgeable trainer, small groups of teachers discussed each training paper, comparing it to the scoring rubric and anchor papers until all members were able to reliably score the paper and state the justification.

Educational Data Systems disaggregated and analyzed the resulting data by a number of demographic factors, and ECRW provided reports to indicate progress within the initiative, districts, schools, and classrooms. We encouraged districts and schools to organize additional scoring opportunities so that some or all of the remaining portfolios could be scored and the resulting information could provide a fuller picture of progress and areas of need.

Levels of teacher willingness and ability to engage in close observation could be observed during the scoring training and anchoring sessions held in the summer institute. Initially, readers tended to settle on a score point based on a gut feeling about the quality of the paper. Teachers would make statements like, "I just like it," or "I just know it is better than most kids at this level can produce," or, "This is a really interesting, good paper." When pressed for evidence, many teachers were initially unable to point to specifics. Frequently, they were able to identify a section that was particularly skillful, but lacked the language to describe the craft move or attribute that made the section effective. We use the term "craft move" to describe the strategy the writer employed to incorporate a particular writing element or attribute. At times, teachers seemed annoyed and dismissed the need for evidence with statements like, "Well, it's obvious to everyone who has a sense of good writing that this is a superior (or poor) piece of writing."

We were gratified by teachers' responses subsequent to participation in the scoring process. When first introduced to the standards used in ECRW, many teachers objected to the rigor of the standards. Frequently voiced opinions included "My students can't do this" and "These standards are not developmentally appropriate for children of this age." Scoring writing from other classrooms at their grade level caused teachers to reexamine their beliefs about what students could achieve. In addition, the scoring experience helped them gain a deeper understanding of the elements of good writing, the subsets of skills involved, and what a novice attempt at a particular writing element might look like. Following is a typical comment from a participant at the close of the 2003 summer scoring institute.

> *In my school there was a lot of resentment and resistance around the standards. People felt that they were unreasonable and they were way too hard . . . now I think the teachers are a lot more accepting of the standards and they're a lot more willing to look at them and strive for them . . . there's been some pretty deep thinking or re-thinking.[2]*

We had high hopes that teachers would be able to incorporate these insights to improve their planning and teaching. To a certain extent, this was true. Study of the anchor papers and the commentary helped to bring the standards to life. Summer institute participants demonstrated a deeper understanding of the standards and what they look like in written work. Additionally, this work helped them to appreciate how their teaching could change what their students were able to do. However, we observed few teachers who used this knowledge back in their classrooms to differentiate instruction for individual students or small groups.

Our observations indicated a need for changes in the professional development efforts. Initially, we had focused our attention on designing and implementing a portfolio assessment system as a means of tracking progress within the initiative. Over time, we realized that the assessment system could provide more than an annual indication of student progress; the scoring practices could be elaborated into a powerful vehicle for teaching the teacher and informing daily instruction.

FORMATIVE ASSESSMENT TO PROMOTE CLOSE OBSERVATION

In Noyce Foundation programs, we subscribe to the definition of formative assessment offered by Marnie Thompson and Dylan Wiliam, "The central idea of formative assessment, or assessment for learning, is that evidence of student learning is used to adjust instruction to better meet student learning needs."[3] They go on to describe formative assessment as the teacher's continuous practice of assessing, planning, and adjusting instruction on a daily and minute-by-minute basis. We wanted teachers to regard student work as evidence of the effectiveness of their teaching and to use this feedback to revise and plan their daily instruction.

A majority of teachers were unprepared to utilize the diagnostic information revealed in each student's daily work. Although participation in scoring activities helped teachers to learn more about the elements of good writing, more scaffolding would be required to enable teachers to move these understandings into the context of their own classrooms.

Reasoning that one can't effectively teach what one can't identify and describe, we had made study of writing craft an important element in ECRW professional development from the outset. As a first step, teachers studied craft moves in a number of professional publications such as *Wondrous Words* by Katie Wood Ray and *Craft Lessons* and *Nonfiction Craft Lessons* by Ralph Fletcher and Joann Portalupi.[4] Whole faculties and grade-level teams studied these works, and we redoubled our efforts to incorporate explicit study of craft moves into professional development sessions. Noyce also provided a Saturday Speakers Series for all ECRW participants—eight sessions per year in which nationally known professional developers in the field of writing presented six-hour sessions focused on the teaching of writing to elementary school students.

As teachers became more familiar with craft moves and the attributes of good writing, they were more successful in identifying these moves in actual student writing. Here, support was also needed; craft moves look different at various developmental levels, and it takes some experience to identify a novice attempt at a particular move. The third-grade narrative, "The Loved One Dead," provides examples of novice attempts at various craft moves. For example, the opening description of Nell's happiness at the author's birth foreshadows their future bonding; however, the lack of a coherent transition from the birth to the time of Nell's sickness and death interferes with the impact of the opening sentences.

Grade 3 Narrative, Score Point 2:

The Loved One Dead

It was a cold spring night when I was born. My great grandma Nell sat rubbing my cheek as if I were a magic lamp and her wish had just come true.

As she carried me into the house I felt protected. My mom put me in my crib and Nell left. Over the next few weeks Nell cancelled appointments and made time to come and see me. I felt like she knew something was wrong.

One day I heard the phone ring. I heard my mom drop my meal. I heard my mom scream her scared scream. We rushed into the car so fast that my mom just put me on her lap and said," GO GO GO" to my dad. In the hospital room my mom was holding me, trying to make me stop crying. But her tears dripped down on me. Nell rubbing my *cheek again. Then slowly drifted to her death. I was crying like babies do but this was not a normal baby cry, I was crying for Nell.*

Years passed and I know that her body is dead but not her spirit. It still is inside my heart.

This score point 2 paper shows some attempts at craft, especially in the second sentence of the opening and in the repetition of "Nell rubbing my check"; however, the author skips over the kinds of details that would give it coherence. It is at first unclear if "something is wrong" with the author or with the grandma. These novice attempts show definite potential for some fine writing from this writer. The writing shows sensitivity and "heart." With some work on transitions and elaboration, this writer could progress swiftly. The teacher's coaching for revisions is likely to be effective if she is able to appreciate the intent of the novice attempts.

Most of the teachers in the ECRW program were not writers themselves and had little practical knowledge of the craft of writing. Once they were able to discern a craft move and to describe it, attempting to incorporate the move into some writing of their own gave them a better understanding of how to teach it. We encouraged teachers to write a piece themselves prior to introducing students to the study of a new genre. This practice proved very beneficial in that the teacher not only created a model for her students that could be used to illustrate various writing elements during the course of the study, but also clarified her understanding of the attributes of the genre and the craft moves she planned to teach. Literacy coaches reported that those who wrote and tried out the lessons that they designed for their students were able to observe their students' work more accurately, to discern their instructional needs, and to design better lessons.

Coaches provided critically important support for teachers, especially when working in concert with a knowledgeable and committed principal. At first, the work was difficult and somewhat threatening, since teachers found it hard to admit to a lack of command of subject matter and pedagogy. It took the support of the coach or a partner, as well as the clear expectations of the principal, to keep most teachers engaged in the effort long enough for them to begin to feel more comfortable and to achieve satisfying results that were self-generating.

In some schools, teachers and students made remarkable progress. Periodically, the coach and principal of each school observed and assessed the teacher's level of practice using the Writing Workshop Implementation Scale, developed by coaches and staff developers in the initiative (the scale can be found on the Noyce Web site at www.noycefdn.org). When teachers worked collaboratively over time to consider students' work and discuss their instructional needs, great improvement could be observed in a teacher's instructional practices and in the work their students produced. In the most successful schools, the literacy coaches were knowledgeable and skillful, and the principals knew a lot about literacy and were committed to moving the school community as a whole. Working in tandem, the principal and coach engaged the full staff—usually working with grade-level teams. Teachers agreed on specific elements of a given genre that they wished to address, guided by the standards, scoring rubrics, and anchor papers. They worked together to examine the resulting pieces of student work, using evidence in the work to determine the effectiveness of the teaching and making a new plan. One principal urged teachers to look for "the tracks of their teaching" in their students' work. Each teacher was engaged in such conversations with the principal and coach at least four times during the year.

Teachers in several schools selected three students to act as proxies for the rest of the class: a special education student, a second language student, and a gifted or regular education student. Supported by the principal and the coach, the teacher critiqued the effectiveness of her own lessons, looking through the lens of student work from these three students. In this manner, it was possible to estimate the degree to which the lesson had provided sufficient differentiation for the various learning needs of students within the class. Using the proxy students made the analysis more manageable, since it was easier to look at the work of three students rather than a whole class's papers.

EXAMPLES OF ECRW STUDENT WRITING

During the first year of ECRW, we did not see obvious improvement in student writing; however, over time, students in some classrooms produced more competent and interesting written pieces. Some teachers learned to diagnose student needs from their written work and to present effective lessons designed to improve each child's writing skills.

Following are excerpts from pieces written by ECRW students. A small percentage of students—those who read widely and enjoy literature—can produce good writing without instruction. When provided with effective and targeted instruction, many more students can learn to produce competent and engaging writing. Formative assessment practices can prepare the teacher to observe student work closely and design lessons that help students move their writing to the next level.

Growth over Time

Table 5.1 shows a transcription of three pieces of writing produced over time by one kindergarten student. Joshua's work clearly shows the "tracks of teaching" from September through January, providing a powerful example of the impressive growth a student can make in a short time when instruction is focused on the child's specific developmental needs.

Joshua drew an elaborate picture to accompany each written piece. For reasons of space, the student's drawings are not included here; however, we have included a description of the drawings that accompany each written piece since they provide a window into the student's writing development. For beginning readers and writers, pictures are an important vehicle for conveying ideas and stories. At first, the picture conveys most of the story. As children learn more written language, they begin to label the pictures and then to describe the story represented by the picture. Over time, the balance shifts, with growing emphasis on the text and less reliance on the pictures.

In the September sample, Joshua's work demonstrates knowledge that:

- Words, including his name, are made up of letters.
- Words are used to label things.
- The letters in words move from left to right on the page.
- Pictures have meaning and are not just scribbles.

TABLE 5.1   Work exhibiting growth over time

Student writing	Corrected for readability	Picture
September 15, 2001 " JOsHuA"	"Joshua" (the student's name)	The picture appears to be a landscape with the sun in the sky and grass and water below.
October 15, 2001 " i ws FEDing Mi SNAK. Joshua"	"I was feeding my snake. Joshua"	The picture shows a person with an arm extended to a snake.
January 21, 2001 "I am a expit an trex. He is the danjrus animl in the world. He ets Dinusars. They run and hit trees. Wene he gets cold he pots levs and drt They skar Brds. They la eggs. Trex is the kiing"	"I am an expert on T-Rex. He is the danger-ous animal in the world. He eats dinosaurs. They run and hit trees. When he gets cold he puts leaves and dirt. They scare birds. They lay eggs. T-Rex is the king."	The picture depicts a large, bird-like crea-ture waving its 'arms' over an apparently slain creature lying on the ground.

By October, we see that Joshua understands that the story should match the picture. His one sentence, "I was feeding my snake," demonstrates new knowledge. He knows:

- That letters match the sounds in words.
- That letters can be used to make words that can be read by others.
- Many letters, but does not yet distinguish between upper- and lowercase letters.
- There are spaces between words, but he does not consistently apply that knowledge.

The third sample, written in January and reproduced in table 5.1, is a coherent, factual piece of informational writing. Joshua demonstrates knowledge of the elements of the informational genre and the conventions of print by:

- Establishing a controlling idea, elaborated by supporting detail.
- Declaring himself to be an expert on the topic.
- Closing with a conclusion.
- Using phonetic spelling throughout.
- Separating all words with spaces.
- Using upper- and lowercase letters appropriately.
- Ending sentences with periods.

This piece exceeds the standard for the end of kindergarten. It is clear that Joshua has been taught both the characteristics of the informational genre and the conventions of print appropriate for his grade.

Excerpts from Student Work

These additional excerpts from work produced by students in the initiative demonstrate some of the elements that students learned to employ in their writing.

Engaging Opening, Grade 3 Informational:

> Flags. I love flags. I have loved them for as long as I can remember. I notice them everywhere, outside my school on a flagpole, in my classroom, in stores, on cars, at ball games and even in my Nana's and Papa's front yard. I am a flag collector!

Engaging Opening, Grade 5 Narrative:

> The car pulled in the driveway like a topper dropping sail. Just kidding. Jack and George, both of them short, blond, and freckly, hopped out of the car and ran around the yard as if they'd been burned. Shouting Hello to a wall and then rushing back for hugs, these boys were bent on making their visit a lively one.

Pacing to Create Suspense, Grade 4 Narrative:

> We lit the candle and put some water in the cauldron. Then we started sprinkling little bits of glitter into the water (all with the lights off). Before we knew it we were dangling little pieces of rough white toilet paper over the candle, closer and closer to the reaching flame until finally what was bound to happen happened. The toilet paper caught on fire. We both screamed!

Literary Language, Grade 4 Informational:

> Hopping from tree to tree, climbing up unbelievable heights, hanging on thin branches, leaps the coolest, the greatest animal of them all . . . the chimpanzee.

Use of Internal Dialogue, Grade 4 Narrative:

> While I watched my mommy and daddy pack, I thought a lot about how America would be like. Who would spoil me? Who will take me to the park? Who will wear a smile for me? I had so many questions to ask and think about! At dinner I couldn't eat anything. All I thought about was America. America. The word got stuck in my mind.

Conclusion, Grade 5 Narrative:

> Mason. I'm so excited and proud you believed in Grandma and even made a wish for the world, just like she would. You are so much like your grandma!"
>
> He smiled to himself: I am. I am like my grandma. A dreamer.

IMPACT ON STUDENT PERFORMANCE AND TEACHER PRACTICE

Student performance on the ECRW-designed assessments was used to judge program effectiveness and progress over time. Each year, we identified and collected a stratified random sample of portfolios to be scored during the summer institute. The sample was constructed to match the overall population of students in the program, reflecting grade-level, gender, ethnicity, parents' education level, language proficiency, and program exposure. Each year, a significant number of teachers and students joined the program and were included in the sample. The number grew from 600 portfolios scored in 2002, representing 3,300 students and 165 teachers, to 2,322 portfolios scored in 2005, representing a pool of 11,717 students and 536 teachers. Approximately 50 percent of teachers and students were new program participants in 2002 and 2003, 30 percent in 2004, and 12 percent in 2005.

Narrative and informational writing received the most instructional attention and professional development in the first few years. Genre entries were scored using the five-point scoring rubric specific to each genre (see ECRW scoring rubrics on the Noyce Foundation Web site at www.noycefdn.org).

As a measure of each student's progress within an instructional year, students wrote three narrative pieces in response to on-demand prompts; the pieces were administered in the early fall, midwinter, and spring. The fall and spring pieces were submitted in the portfolio and scored during the summer institute. As one measure of program effectiveness, we tracked the percentage of students who gained one or more score points or levels on the rubric. On the whole, a high percentage of students at most grades demonstrated significant progress by gaining one or more levels when their fall and spring scores were compared, with an average of 69 percent across all the grades ranging between a low of 39 percent in grade four and 95 percent in kindergarten.

Despite the high percentage of students showing good progress each year, a disappointing number of students actually demonstrated the ability to meet the grade-level standard by attaining a rubric score of 4 or 5. Only 13 percent met the grade-level standard in 2002 and 22 percent in 2005. We felt that this slow rate of progress was not commensurate with the level of effort invested.

We were interested to learn if the level of teacher implementation had a positive impact on student scores. From classroom observation, it was clear that there was considerable variation in the level of teacher implementation of writing workshop elements. We created a scale describing writing workshop practices across a range of developmental levels. Initially, this scale was developed to facilitate teacher self-assessment and goal setting, as well as to identify professional development needs. We subsequently used this instrument to consider teacher implementation levels in our analysis of student achievement.

In order to assess a teacher's level of implementation at a given time, the coach and principal for each school observed the classroom teachers and estimated their level of implementation using the Writing Workshop Implementation Scale (the full scale, available at www.noycefoundation.org, addresses the following components: mini-lessons; conferring; assessments; environment; independent writing time; response groups; and closings).

In 2004, student portfolio scores were analyzed through the dual lens of teacher implementation level and program exposure, comparing scores of students who had been exposed to the initiative for two or more years and who were in high-implementation classrooms—about one-quarter of the total group—to the scores of all other students in ECRW. Overall, a higher percentage of students in the high-implementation–high-exposure group met or exceeded the grade-level standard for narrative (23.2 percent compared to 11.1 percent). In addition, a higher percentage of the high-implementation–high-exposure group gained one or more levels on the fall to spring on-demand narrative entries (68.1 percent compared to 62.6 percent). This suggests that exposure to the initiative had a positive effect on student performance.

We also tracked fourth-grade students' scores on the California Fourth-Grade Writing Test, STAR (Standardized Testing and Reporting) Program. This writing test was administered each spring and required students to produce a written piece in response to an on-demand prompt. Although we attempted to design the ECRW prompts to resemble state prompts, there were some significant differences in the prompts, in the format for administration, and in the scoring rubrics. In addition, ECRW students spent most of their time writing from their own experience rather than writing to a prompt. We were aware of these differences, but hoped that student genre and craft knowledge, along with increased confidence in their writing skills, would have a positive impact on their ability to respond to the state prompts.

An independent evaluation conducted by Educational Data Systems (EDS) compared the performance of ECRW and non-ECRW students from all ECRW districts on STAR, and found that, on average, there was no difference between the performance of ECRW and non-ECRW students. Both groups earned a mean score of 4.26 (possible scores ranged from a low of 0 to a high of 8). While these results were disappointing, they were not entirely surprising. The evaluation included all teachers who had participated in the ECRW initiative, regardless of the extent to which they implemented these practices in their classroom.

EDS also analyzed student STAR test results by teachers' levels of implementation. Based on a random sample of fourth-grade ECRW students, the data suggested that students in classrooms in which teachers had more effectively implemented writing workshop earned higher scores on the state's STAR writing test (see table 5.2).

In addition, longer program exposure was generally associated with higher STAR writing test scores, ranging from a mean score of 4.2 for one year of exposure to 4.51 for students who had participated for five years.

We planned to benchmark ECRW portfolio results to this state-mandated test. Since each subsequent cohort of fourth graders had participated longer in ECRW, we hoped to detect an increase in scores on the STAR test. Although increases were noted for some groups, as previously described, the results weren't compelling enough to make a convincing case for the efficacy of the ECRW approach.

It should be noted that the California Fourth-Grade Writing Test scores remained flat across the entire state for the four years the test was in use, from 2001 to 2004, and parents and school districts raised questions about the validity of the test. It appears that the four-point rubric was insufficiently sensitive to discriminate between more than the gross differences in writing performance. At the request of the California

TABLE 5.2   2002 results of California State 4th grade writing test (STAR)

Mean scores for ECRW students by teacher implementation score

Teacher implementation score	N[1]	Mean[2]
1	67	4.17
2	137	4.23
3	94	4.26
4	35	4.49

[1] The Ns represent the sample size.

[2] Means are adjusted to match overall ECRW population demographics; therefore, statistical significance could not be tested.

Notes: Writing assessment score range: low 0–high 8.
         Teacher Implementation score range: low 1–high 4.

Source: Educational Data Systems, Inc., *ECRW Technical Report 2005*, 10.

Department of Education and the State Board of Education, Educational Testing Service convened a task force to review and recommend changes. Subsequently, the task force recommended extensive revisions, and test administrations were suspended pending the changes.

LIMITED EVIDENCE OF SUSTAINED EFFECTS

Since 2006, when formal Noyce Foundation support for ECRW was withdrawn, we have talked with numerous teachers, coaches, principals, and district leaders. We were interested to learn what degree of practice had been sustained despite staffing changes, the reduction of district support due to the ongoing state fiscal crisis, and the withdrawal of all Noyce support. The following observations are based on informal conversations; we have not gathered objective data regarding implementation or student achievement.

We estimate that schoolwide practices have been maintained in only seven or eight schools out of the thirty-five that participated in the project. Three schools in particular seem quite committed to writing workshops and formative practices; teachers in these schools feel that their instructional practices are stronger as a result. As one teacher said, "I'm more confident as a teacher. I can look at my students and their work and have a good idea of their needs . . . and my kids are better at self-assessing their work." In addition to diagnosing needs for the majority of the class, these teachers attempt to differentiate their support for students through teacher-student conferences and by providing additional, targeted instruction for individuals and small groups.

These small groups are flexible and based on need, which is determined by looking for evidence of the teaching point in the student work. In the words of another teacher, "I look for the teaching points to show up in their work after the mini-lesson. It helps me to see who is struggling and needs to be pulled into a small group." Numerous teachers stated that participation in the initiative had transformed their approach to teaching.

As has been found in many other reform efforts, the principal's role has been key to maintaining schoolwide practice of these strategies. Without a strong focus by the principal, only the most committed ECRW teacher participants continue to implement writing workshops and to use formative assessment practices in their daily instruction. Three schools reporting high enthusiasm for these practices are led by principals who played a key role during the ECRW initiative. Prior to ECRW, all three had a keen interest in literacy and committed time to learn about writing workshops and formative assessment practices through reading, study, and participation in ECRW professional development sessions. These principals require writing workshops and formative assessment throughout the school, and employ specific strategies for training new teachers and supporting schoolwide practices. In a few other schools, implementation is encouraged and continues in the classrooms of some teachers. In the rest of the schools, formative assessment practices exist only in isolated classrooms where there is a committed teacher.

Our data gathering regarding sustainability was anecdotal and not comprehensive; however, it is our impression that these practices are sustained on a schoolwide basis in only a handful of schools, at best, and in the individual classrooms of committed teachers scattered across the initiative.

LESSONS LEARNED

In the ECRW program, we learned that formative assessment practices offer the possibility of better achievement for all students, the gifted as well as typically underachieving groups; however, effective implementation requires a fundamentally changed orientation to teaching. Few schools were able to manage this shift in thinking across the entire school, and even fewer were able to maintain it when a key leader moved on and outside support was withdrawn.

Our experiences in ECRW led us to conclude that prevailing beliefs about student capacity and the nature of learning and teaching are a significant barrier to making fundamental changes in teachers' approach to instruction. Much current practice demonstrates the belief that good teaching is a series of activities that, when done well, will result in student achievement along a normal curve distribution. In this paradigm, the teacher's role is to enact and manage a series of well-orchestrated steps in a linear process, with the expectation that the resulting student achievement will fall along an inevitable continuum, solely as a result of student intelligence and motivation. Successful implementation of formative assessment practices requires that the teacher instead regard the student work as evidence of how well the teaching matched the needs of the learner. Such a shift in thinking is difficult to realize and maintain given the current focus on prescriptive approaches.

Creating Favorable Conditions

We concluded that the following conditions support the establishment of effective formative assessment practices and an instructional culture in which student work is the driving influence.

An uncompromising focus on student work. The teacher must regard the student work as essential feedback regarding the effectiveness of his or her teaching and as an important indicator of each student's needs. Close analysis of student work should precede attention to "teacher moves." Planning pedagogical teacher moves outside of this context of need is pointless, driving instruction that is accidental and haphazard rather than intentional and powerful.

Teacher preparation. Professional development programs should provide a primary focus on content knowledge and close observation of student work. This orientation to using student work to inform lesson planning should continue throughout the year. Teachers need the support of coaches or mentors to scaffold their learning as they work to integrate new practices into the classroom. School funding priorities need to be reordered to provide in-service sessions during paid time so that programs are inclusive, not voluntary.

High-quality assessment tools. Use of high-quality formative assessment tools is critical to the process. The formative assessments must be tightly aligned to the curriculum and constructed to reveal student thinking. Benchmarking these assessments to whatever standardized assessments are mandated in the system can aid these efforts, building the credibility of the formative assessments and motivating teachers to believe that their use is worth the effort. However, the success of benchmarking will be limited by the quality of the standardized measure and its alignment with the curriculum.

A collaborative environment energized by a common vision. The ECRW schools with the most success developed a common vision that targeted student outcomes in daily work. The vision was made tangible by developing a common understanding of the content and performance standards, along with common vocabulary to describe evidence in student work.

Sustained effort. Sustained effort over several years is required to realize any deep-level change in beliefs and practice. The high mobility of teachers and principals, as well as the press of competing initiatives, seriously inhibits efforts to change schoolwide practices and beliefs, and must be mitigated to some extent.

Skillful, purposeful leadership. The leadership of the principal was key in setting and maintaining expectations and support for the work, providing time to collaborate, and motivating teachers to work together toward shared goals. Each of the schools that made significant progress was led by a strong principal who remained at the site for a significant period of time. Inspired by their leadership practices, we developed the Principal's Instructional Leadership Profile, outlining the beliefs and practices that contributed to their success (the document can be viewed at www. noycefdn.org\ecrwresources\).

CONCLUSION

Our experiences in ECRW suggest that formative assessment practices have the potential to transform teacher beliefs, practices, and student achievement by focusing the teacher's attention on student work. Through formative assessment practices, teachers can gain a deeper understanding of the standards and the content to be taught. They come to understand that student work is a good indicator of the effectiveness of their instruction and to rely on close observation of the work as guidance for daily instructional planning.

Given these potentially powerful outcomes, fostering widespread use of formative assessment in public schools seems like a logical and desirable path to pursue; however, in the current high-stakes accountability environment, it is difficult for formative assessment practices to gain enough traction in public school settings to actually promote widespread gains. Using the analysis of daily work to drive instructional planning flies in the face of the habits and beliefs associated with the current system, which relies heavily on prescriptive approaches—classrooms in which one lesson follows another in a faithful sequence, regardless of the outcomes evident in the student work. Overcoming current beliefs and practices may require the creation and maintenance of conditions that are at odds with most of current classroom practice, as well as the structure and culture of most schools.

I wish to express my appreciation to Jane Danbold, Alicia Heneghan, and Mary Elsea for their contributions to my thinking in the preparation of this chapter, and to the National Center on Education and the Economy (NCEE) for permission to use samples of student work generated in the ECRW initiative and now owned by NCEE.

CHAPTER 6

Homing in on Key Skills

*Formative Assessments of Student Thinking
in Reading (FAST-R)*

LISA LINEWEAVER

During the 2002–2003 school year, the demand from Boston Public School (BPS) teachers and principals for assessments that could guide Readers' Workshop instruction was growing, at the same time as the school and student-level accountability for performance on the state's rigorous MCAS exams was ratcheting up. Many teachers perceived these two pressures to be in conflict: what could be more different from *The Joy of Teaching Reading* than a standardized multiple-choice reading exam? The Boston Plan for Excellence (BPE), a local education foundation whose mission is working to ensure that every child in Boston receives an excellent education, was spurred by schools it worked with to try to bridge that gap. Superintendent Thomas Payzant authorized BPE to purchase or develop an assessment to test in a network of volunteer BPS schools.

At this time in Boston there was a huge gulf between the uniform district benchmark reading assessments (which were administered to all students three times per year at the primary grades, and as midyear and final exams at the intermediate and upper grades) and the highly variable day-to-day formative assessment practices of individual teachers. Many teachers attempting to plan reading instruction without the structure of a textbook or anthology for the first time realized that while existing assessments helped to gauge their students' *reading* skills, they lacked a way to assess students' comprehension and to get insight into students' *thinking as they read*. Principals also were clamoring for periodic common assessments because, unlike informal classroom assessment methods, they depended less on teachers' instructional skill (which varied considerably in the first years of workshop instruction), and because the results can be analyzed to identify class-, grade-, and school-level patterns of strength and need. The Formative Assessments of Student Thinking in Reading, known as FAST-R, were created to meet these needs.

DEVELOPMENT OF FAST-R

Around the same time, John Yun, a doctoral student at the Harvard Graduate School of Education, was examining the reading skills assessed on the English language arts (ELA) MCAS exams. His analysis revealed that the vast majority of the multiple-choice questions required students to apply one of two important reading skills: finding evidence explicitly stated in the text, or making inferences about ideas that are implicit in the text.[1]

When Yun approached BPE with his findings, Executive Director Ellen Guiney realized the possibilities: the two skills that were highly valued on the state test were also widely recognized by BPS teachers as ones that their students needed to improve. Having recent evidence from evaluations of BPE and BPS's new coaching approach—Collaborative Coaching and Learning (CCL)—that teachers collectively analyzing instruction led to changes in teacher understanding and practice, Guiney began to wonder: could a well-designed assessment, structured to ensure collaborative analysis of and planning with the data, help teachers understand their students' development of key reading skills and actually catalyze changed instruction?[2]

The prospect of developing an assessment based on MCAS-tested skills sparked spirited debate among BPE staff and focus groups of teachers and principals. Given nationwide concerns about the narrowing of curricula due to testing, some feared that focusing on skills that are heavily assessed on the state's test could prove too narrow or low level to promote good reading. Further, while Paul Black and Dylan Wiliam made a strong case that teachers' use of in-the-moment formative assessment *practices* results in significant gains in students' learning, there was less evidence that interim assessments—even collaboratively analyzed—typically result in improved instruction.[3]

However, because MCAS is a rigorous and well-designed test, rated highly by Achieve, Inc., for assessing both basic and high-level skills, and because BPE was willing to provide instructional data coaches who would carefully introduce FAST-R and help them use the assessments formatively, BPE concluded that those risks were offset by the potential.[4] Principals and teachers quickly endorsed this conclusion; as one principal reported in the pilot year, "it clearly is instructional, because those are the two main concepts [finding evidence and drawing inferences] that are tested in MCAS, but those are the things that good readers need to do, and those are the things that, obviously, students struggle with."[5]

Since literacy coaches were already promoting in-the-moment formative assessment as part of responsive workshop instruction and BPS teachers were already analyzing student work together, the goal became to complement those classroom assessment practices with a periodic common assessment intentionally designed so every feature would increase its likelihood of being used formatively to guide reading comprehension instruction. Put colloquially, the team would aim for something that would "look like an interim but work like a formative."

With that goal in mind, BPE contracted with Yun and one of his colleagues, who with a small team of BPE staff began designing and drafting assessments, teacher support materials, and data analyses. The guiding design principles aimed to incorporate the consistency and alignment to standards of an interim assessment but promote formative use:

- The assessments would be short enough to be completed in a single class period, and data would be returned to teachers in user-friendly form within a week.
- A framework describing the levels and types of thinking demanded by each question would keep the focus on important reading skills and encourage classroom questioning.

- All materials would code questions by type of thinking required and annotate each answer choice to permit analysis of patterns of error types.
- Teacher support materials would help teachers choose and use the texts and assessments in ways that link to their reading instruction, and would illuminate possible teaching points to help students improve.
- The only requirements were that teacher teams have an intentional plan for when and how they would use FAST-R, and that they would meet as a team to analyze and plan with the data. All other implementation details could be decided by the teacher teams themselves.

Interim assessments are typically used for three possible purposes: instructional, evaluative, and predictive.[6] Agreeing with Margaret Goertz, Leslie Nabors Oláh, and Matthew Riggan that "if interim assessments are to be used formatively, they must be designed for instructional purposes," BPE intended FAST-R to serve only an instructional purpose.[7] To maintain the low-stakes "safety" for teachers using FAST-R as part of inquiry and instructional experimentation, the design team made quite deliberate choices to ensure that FAST-R would not be used to evaluate or compare students, teachers, or schools. That firm boundary was maintained by having the data entry and analysis housed at BPE, totally independent from the district and its supervisory structure. The district was willing to tolerate the impossibility of aggregating FAST-R data because FAST-R was only used in addition to—not instead of—other district assessments. Since no ten-question test would ever meet gold-standard psychometric criteria for validity or reliability, it was easy to ensure that teachers and principals would not use FAST-R as a basis for high-stakes decisions about students' course grades or promotion. Rather, the assessment design decisions clearly situated FAST-R as an aid to making low-stakes, midstream instructional adjustments. With evaluative and predictive uses off the table, teachers and principals understood FAST-R's purpose as giving teachers entry points to examine the limits of their students' skills so they could design opportunities for focused instruction in particular skills needed by their whole class, small groups, and individuals.

Skill Areas Assessed on FAST-R

The developers of FAST-R were not psychometricians but current and former teachers and literacy coaches with a keen vision of what teachers needed to know about their students' reading skills and a pragmatic understanding of what it would take for teachers to actually turn assessment data into targeted instruction. Over a period of four years, BPE's FAST-R team created more than seventy assessments (known as "question sets") available for use in grades two through ten.

FAST-R question sets assess two primary ways that readers construct understanding as they read: *finding evidence* to determine explicit meaning in the text, and *making inferences* to determine implicit meaning in the text. Students must develop these two essential skills for every type of reading, at every grade level, and in every content area; these skills are heavily assessed on MCAS and other reading tests.

In FAST-R's pilot year, questions were coded using only the broad "finding evidence" (FE) and "making inferences" (MI) categories. Realizing that those categories encompassed several distinct, more specific reading and thinking skills, the second-stage FAST-R development team—then composed of skilled and knowledgeable teachers, special educators, and literacy coaches—scoured the research literature for existing taxonomies of thinking and questioning frameworks. The team closely examined Bloom's Taxonomy and Robert Marzano's hierarchy of educational objectives, but neither those nor others uncovered in the research were specific to the thinking that readers do as they attempt to make meaning of a text and therefore would not yield the fine-grained learning targets that teachers needed to match their instruction more directly to students' gaps in comprehension.[8]

In the end, the team took a descriptive rather than a prescriptive approach, undertaking detailed task analysis of the cognitive demand of the various types of questions that appear on the MCAS reading tests.[9] By analyzing what a reader actually has to think and do to understand texts in various important ways, and to correctly answer particular types of questions based on that understanding, the team developed a framework of the levels and types of thinking that dissected the broad FE and MI categories into more nuanced skills. This "levels and types of thinking" framework organizes all the assessments and teacher materials, and it remains one of the unique features distinguishing FAST-R from other available assessments.

Finding evidence. Readers find and use evidence when they determine the author's explicit meaning from details that are stated in the text. There are two types of FAST-R FE questions. They assess students' ability to determine explicit meaning:

- By identifying evidence explicitly stated at *one location* in the text (type 1 FE questions).
- By recognizing evidence explicitly stated at *multiple locations* or with *varied wording* in the text (type 2 FE questions).

Making inferences. Readers make inferences when they determine *implicit* meaning that is implied but not directly stated in the text. FAST-R MI questions ask readers to fill gaps based on knowledge gleaned from a close reading of the text. This close reading can help students avoid basing inferences on incorrect or irrelevant prior knowledge. There are five types of FAST-R MI questions. They assess students' ability to determine implicit meaning:

- From particular words, phrases, or ideas in context (type 1 MI).
- From the total text (type 2 MI).
- By understanding the organization of information in the text (type 3 MI).
- From the text, then apply that implicit meaning *beyond* the passage context (type 4 MI).
- By incorporating literary knowledge (type 5 MI).

Figure 6.1 represents how these skills build on one another as readers answer questions of increasing sophistication. To successfully answer a type 3 MI question about the organization of ideas in a text, for instance, readers rely on having understood the explicit meaning of details throughout the passage and having correctly interpreted implicit meaning of particular phrases and the text as a whole. FAST-R teacher guides annotate each question with a miniature version of this graphic to signal the level of thinking it assesses.[10]

FIGURE 6.1   FAST-R "levels and types of thinking" framework

Finding evidence

Readers find and use evidence when they determine the author's explicit meaning:

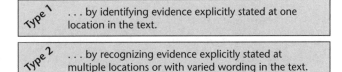

Type 1 . . . by identifying evidence explicitly stated at one location in the text.

Type 2 . . . by recognizing evidence explicitly stated at multiple locations or with varied wording in the text.

Making inferences

Readers make inferences when they determine implicit meaning that is implied but not directly stated in the text:

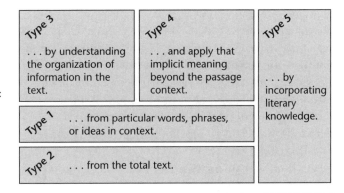

Type 3 . . . by understanding the organization of information in the text.

Type 4 . . . and apply that implicit meaning beyond the passage context.

Type 5 . . . by incorporating literary knowledge.

Type 1 . . . from particular words, phrases, or ideas in context.

Type 2 . . . from the total text.

The way in which FAST-R codes the levels and types of thinking required of readers is different from the "strand" or "skill" analysis that is becoming common among state and commercial reading assessments because it focuses less on what a question is ostensibly *asking* and more on what the reader has *to do to answer* it. This difference seems subtle, but it is important because the lens through which we examine data frames the problem that we see and the solution we seek. For instance, some other commercially available assessments identify some questions as "vocabulary" questions. Teachers seeing low performance on those questions might reasonably conclude that students "didn't know that word" or "don't have a strong vocabulary"—which might reinforce stereotypes about the capacity of English language learners and students raised in poverty, or frustrate teachers with the futility of trying to anticipate and teach all the words students might encounter on a future exam.

The same type of questions on FAST-R would be categorized as MI type 1 questions, which ask students to "determine *implicit* meaning . . . from particular words, phrases, or ideas in context." A logical conclusion when the data are analyzed in that frame is that "we need to teach our students strategies to figure out the meaning of unknown words they may encounter." These strategies—which typically include use of context, syntax, morphology, and subtle connotations of other words in the sentence or paragraph—are flexible, powerful things that good readers (not just good test-takers) do.

The "Levels and Types of Thinking" Framework serves as the bridge between assessments (FAST-R and MCAS) and classroom instruction. FAST-R coaches take some care to refer to the framework as describing not "the FAST-R question types," but "the levels and types of thinking assessed by FAST-R" because such thinking is what good readers do and what good instruction will help them learn to do.

Systematic Error Classification

Every answer—right or wrong—can give clues to a student's thinking. On FAST-R, wrong answer choices are coded either as *"out of place" (OOP)* or *"out of bounds" (OOB)*, depending on whether they are based in the text.

OOP1 ("near miss") answers are true statements from or about the text, but they do not answer the question because they're too general, too specific, or irrelevant to answer what the question is asking. Dramatic events or interesting phrases that stick in readers' memories are common OOP1 answers. Students choosing many OOP1 answers probably comprehend the text at a literal level, but may not recognize implied layers of meaning. A pattern of OOP1s may be a sign the student is not reading questions closely or referring to the text to distinguish the best answer.

OOP2 ("misread") answers are also based in the text, but they reflect a significant misunderstanding of it or of the question. Students who choose many OOP2 answers may be reading the text or questions too quickly and may not be monitoring their understanding while they read, or may be finding the text too difficult to derive much meaning from.

OOB answers are not based in the text at all, but may seem plausible to readers with some prior knowledge or a personal connection to the text. "Commonsense" statements, misconceptions that students may have about a topic from prior instruction, and emotion-based statements that students might agree with are all common OOB answers. Students choosing many OOB answers may tend to rely on text-to-self connections rather than close reading to help them understand a text. Sometimes, fairly sophisticated reasoning processes may lead students to pick OOB answers. Listening as students articulate their reasoning may suggest ways to honor and encourage the thinking they *are* doing while helping them understand when, why, and how to base their interpretations more closely on the text.

A simple "traffic-signal" color scheme (green/yellow/orange/red) highlights each student's answer to each question on the data reports, enabling at-a-glance error analysis. Many teachers report finding this very useful; as one teacher put it, "it gave us an insight into why the kids would select A as opposed to B; it would tell us a lot more about their thinking . . . [and help us] to get inside their brains!"[11] Many students show patterns of error types, so knowing each student's tendencies—and hypothesizing that those tendencies likely also affect their comprehension when reading in other settings—can help teachers identify *which* students to pull together into small groups and *what* targeted coaching or skill/strategy instruction each group needs.

For many teachers, nuanced exploration of the thinking behind students' wrong answers was new and gave them newfound insight about their students' thinking: "We had a discussion as to why students may answer a question a certain way . . . [or choose] an answer that seemed totally off the wall . . . I would not have even considered that in looking at why the students did not do well, but that was useful."[12]

Teachers quickly adopted the "OOP and OOB" language for use with students, as one shared: "[O]ut of bounds, out of place . . . [i]t was good, it gave [kinds of errors] a label. I think [we should] start right away in the earlier grades . . . so there's a common terminology across the grade levels."[13]

Many teachers used that terminology to engage students in reflecting on their own thinking as they read, as this teacher describes:

> *[FAST-R is] a way that both myself and the students can look at a reading and the response and actually think about our answers and be better able to understand some of our weaknesses . . . I just read some of the explanation as to why they may have chosen certain answers, and they gave me some feedback as to some things they were thinking. So they started thinking about the answers that they wrote . . . The students are now taking it seriously because they see . . . . clear and detailed feedback coming back from their answers.*[14]

The Levels and Types of Thinking Framework is often used by teachers and coaches to code released MCAS questions, other multiple-choice assessments, and even teacher-generated question prompts, building common language about the reading skills students need to develop. Even more important, some teachers report that its emphasis on understanding student thinking has affected their own thinking: as one teacher put it, "I just learned that I've become stagnant—you know, 'if it's wrong, it's wrong; if it's right, it's right!' Looking at the [FAST-R] data just allowed me to go back to where I was when I first started teaching, looking at the *why*."[15]

FAST-R TOOLS

The FAST-R framework for question and error analysis serves as the skeleton for four distinct forms of FAST-R reading assessments, each of which fills different needs for teachers in grades one through twelve:

- Classic ten-question "dipstick" assessments represent seventy different question sets in a variety of genres for grades three through twelve. (See figure 6.2 for an example.)
- Longer and more psychometrically rigorous start-of-year Anchor Assessments give teachers at entry grades (sixth and ninth grade) a robust start-of-year data set and anchor future analysis of the ten-question sets.
- Midyear assessments developed with the BPS literacy department help teachers get more from analysis of performance on the district's midyear exams; these also give a robust point of comparison for ten-question sets.
- Informal primary-grade assessments designed to be integrated with guided-reading instruction help generate instructionally relevant data for primary-grade students or those who are reading below grade level in third grade.

This build-out occurred over the course of several years: as use of the "classic" ten-question FAST-R assessments became widespread throughout Boston, teachers and the district literacy department each suggested ways to widen the usability of the framework they found so helpful by adapting it to meet both more and less formal assessment needs.

FIGURE 6.2   Sample FAST-R question set

"Sonnet 116" and "Sonnet 43" (Grade 10 poetry set)

Sonnets are 14-line poems, traditionally about love, that follow particular rhythm and rhyme schemes. The word "sonnet" comes from the Italian "sonnetto," which means "little song." These two sonnets are by writers of different genders from different centuries, but they express similar ideas about love.

Read these two poems (William Shakespeare's "Sonnet 116" and Elizabeth Barrett Browning's "Sonnet 43") and answer the questions that follow.

Directions: On your answer sheet, fill in the circle for the correct answer.

"Sonnet 116" by William Shakespeare

1. **According to "Sonnet 116," love is**

    A. an impediment

    B. an ever-fixed mark

    C. a tempest

    D. Time's fool

2. **In line 2 of "Sonnet 116," what does the word impediments mean?**

    A. inconsistencies

    B. obstacles

    C. impertinence

    D. virtues

3. **What is the theme of "Sonnet 116"?**

    A. True love remains steady.

    B. Even the strongest love is temporary.

    C. Love changes as life changes.

    D. Age and time alter love.

Data Analyses Designed by Teachers for Teachers

FAST-R data tools are designed to help teachers quickly move from data to actionable insight. After watching a FAST-R user in the pilot year shuffle back and forth between a spreadsheet, test questions, and her own notes when trying to make sense of patterns in her students' performance, the design team realized that applying Edward Tufte's principles of "data density" could produce a meaningful improvement in the data-analysis experience—decreasing frustration and increasing the percentage of time when the teacher's mind is making inferences and hypotheses that will guide her teaching.[16]

BPE produced—and now has enabled teacher users to easily produce—individualized, color-coded data packets so that teachers' limited common-planning time can be spent analyzing and reflecting together on their data. Data reports are designed to prompt the following types of analysis:

Integrated item, error, and question analysis. This simple three-page report replaces several other documents by lining up the graph directly next to the question (as shown in figure 6.3), so that after reading an answer choice, the user's eyes travel directly to the right to see how many of her students selected that choice. The bar is also color-coded to signify if the answer was correct, OOP1, OOP2, or OOB, and the question type is labeled above the graph. To our knowledge, this user-friendly format remains unique to FAST-R reports.

Student-level item and error analysis. This grid, which is sorted by students' percent correct (rather than alphabetically) again increases the data density of the typical spreadsheet by color-coding the distractors. As shown in figure 6.4, a teacher can look down a column to see whether her higher performers tend toward different types of wrong answers, or distractors, than the lower performers, or whether certain students start off strong but pick more OOP2 and OOB answers toward the end, perhaps signaling fatigue. Analysis templates in the FAST-R teacher resource binder help teachers identify teaching points targeted to the whole class, small groups, and individual students.

Cumulative performance by question type over time. After students have answered a total of at least thirty FAST-R questions (through any combination of anchor assessments, ten-question sets, or midyear assessments), this report aggregates performance by question type so teachers can observe and address persistent patterns. This aggregation increases the reliability of analysis because what may be a fluke response to one question becomes a pattern if it recurs over four or five similar questions on different assessments at different times.

Individual student reports. A single-page report summing up students' cumulative performance on FE and MI questions across the various tests is popular as the basis for parent-teacher conferences and for adding to students' cumulative portfolios. Teachers' feedback to program evaluators has consistently confirmed that the information-rich design and usability of the data reports is unique and sets FAST-R apart from other data-analysis experiences, streamlining the process of turning that data into insight that can guide instruction.

Teacher Support Materials

One inherent tension in promulgating a framework for reading and thinking skills is that at times it focuses attention on those skills to the exclusion of other factors critical to a student's comprehension, such as attributes of the text itself. A reader who quite ably infers main ideas of paragraphs in a supportive expository text may stumble when doing the same thing in a narrative text, or with a less straightforward nonfiction passage. So, FAST-R teacher guides contain substantial support to familiarize teachers with the various dimensions of each text, calling out points of cognitive demand for readers so that if students miss a particular question, their teachers can quickly identify several possible reasons why and search for corroborating patterns.

FIGURE 6.3   FAST-R student performance summary

These graphs show how many students selected each answer choice, while the annotated answer key highlights types of wrong answers, where answers were found in the text, and what thinking may have led to that answer choice.

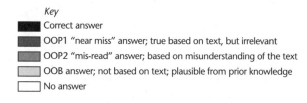

Key
■ Correct answer
■ OOP1 "near miss" answer; true based on text, but irrelevant
■ OOP2 "mis-read" answer; based on misunderstanding of the text
□ OOB answer; not based on text; plausible from prior knowledge
□ No answer

This analysis represents the performance of:

Question Set: **HP2**

School: New Mission HS   Grade: *   Class/Sec: *   **Sonnets #116 & #43**

---

1. **According to "Sonnet 116," love is**

    A. an impediment—(OOP2, line 1-2) students may not equate "the marriage of true minds" with "love," or may be looking for clues surrounding the first reference to "love" in line 2

    ✔ B. an ever-fixed mark—(line 5)

    C. a tempest—(OOP2) line 6, love "looks on tempests" but is not one

    D. Time's fool—(OOP2, line 9) "Love's not Time's fool"

    1. Finding evidence (Recog)

    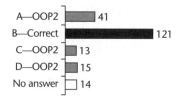

    A—OOP2 ▮ 41
    B—Correct ▮ 121
    C—OOP2 ▮ 13
    D—OOP2 ▮ 15
    No answer □ 14

---

2. **In line 2 of "Sonnet 116," what does the word impediments mean?**

    A. inconsistencies—(OOP1) plausible using a "substitute in another word" strategy, since Shakespeare would not wish to "admit inconsistencies" in love

    ✔ B. obstacles

    C. impertinence—(OOB) same beginning letters and similar ending sound, but unrelated meaning

    D. virtues—(OOB) student may not have tested meaning in context

    2. Making inferences (Type 1)

    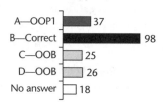

    A—OOP1 ▮ 37
    B—Correct ▮ 98
    C—OOB □ 25
    D—OOB □ 26
    No answer □ 18

---

3. **What is the theme of "Sonnet 116"?**

    ✔ A. True love remains steady—can be inferred from phrases describing love as "never shaken" and "alters not"

    B. Even the strongest love is temporary—(OOP2) may be plausible from students' own experiences, but the text suggests the opposite

    C. Love changes as life changes—(OOP2) text suggests the opposite

    D. Age and time alter love—(OOP2)"alters," is used in lines 3, 11

    3. Making inferences (Type 2)

    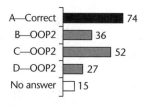

    A—Correct ▮ 74
    B—OOP2 ▮ 36
    C—OOP2 ▮ 52
    D—OOP2 ▮ 27
    No answer □ 15

FIGURE 6.4   Student-level data summary

Admin Date: 4/5/2010
School: Tremont HS
Total Students: 10

Question Set: HP2
*Class/Sec: ***

Skill Summaries:

Student	Q1 FE2	Q2 MI1	Q3 MI2	Q4 MI4	Q5 FE2	Q6 FE2	...Q10 MI2	FE # ✓	MI # ✓	FE % ✓	MI % ✓	Total ✓	Race	Gender	ELL	SPED
Bill	B	B	D	C	A	A	B	4	4	100%	66%	8	Hispanic	Male	-	R2
Anna	B	D	C	D	A	A	B	4	3	100%	50%	7	Hispanic	Female	-	-
Christine	B	B	C	D	B	C	B	2	4	50%	66%	6	Black	Female	-	-
Charles	B	B	A	D	D	C	B	1	5	25%	83%	6	Black	Male	-	-
Mary	B	B	D	A	A	D	N	3	1	75%	16%	4	Black	Female	-	R3
Elizabeth	B	D	C	C	D	A	B	2	2	50%	33%	4	-	Female	-	-
Susan	A	C	B	A	C	C	B	1	2	25%	33%	3	Black	Female	-	R2
James	D	C	B	C	A	A	C	2	0	50%	0%	2	Black	Male	-	-
John	B	D	C	C	D	A	C	2	0	50%	0%	2	Hispanic	Male	-	-
Karen	A	C	B	A	D	C	D	0	1	0%	16%	1	Hispanic	Female	-	R2

Key to shading:

Correct

OOP1   "near miss"

OOP2

OOB   "out of bounds"

"mis-read"

In order to give teachers a snapshot of the complexity of the texts used on FAST-R question sets, the teacher guides rate each passage on the six "aspects of text" that the American College Testing Service uses to rate texts for the ACT college-readiness reading test: structure, purpose, richness, relationships, vocabulary, and style.[17]

A difficulty index atop each teacher guide indicates the degree to which the text is "considerate" or "challenging."[18] As shown in figure 6.5, each teacher guide also contains a full copy of the text, with call-out boxes that annotate these aspects of text as they relate to the questions on the assessment, noting, for instance, that a reader must follow a series of pronoun referents in a poem in order to answer a FE type 2 question about the speaker and her mother, or that readers will encounter the secondary usage of several familiar words.

The message—implicit in the focus of the teacher guides and explicit in the FAST-R coaches' work with teachers—is that while a few of the teaching points revealed by the assessments may relate to test-taking skills, the best way to improve students' performance on reading assessments is to methodically identify and teach the skills they need to read a variety of texts more closely and thoughtfully.

PROFESSIONAL DEVELOPMENT

FAST-R is based on the belief that having timely, nuanced, user-friendly data about students' reading and thinking skills is necessary, but not sufficient, to cause gains in student learning: it's not the data itself, but *what teachers actually do with it*, that makes a difference for students' learning. By implication, then, professional development related to FAST-R had to not only move teachers through the predictable stages of learning to use data described by Susan Trimble, Anne Gay, and Jan Matthews, but also identify leverage points for helping them convert their insights from the data analysis into powerful instruction in response.[19]

With support from the Hewlett, Stone, and Noyce foundations, BPE hired skilled, data-savvy former teachers to serve as FAST-R instructional data coaches. These coaches worked with teams of teachers to create a plan; to select and tweak question sets to match their instructional objectives or test their hypotheses about students' skills; to interpret the data after administration; and to plan (and in some cases, codeliver) instruction in response.

However, the staffing ratio (one instructional data coach for every ten to fifteen schools) was deliberately low touch, intended to ensure that after establishing a foundational level of data-analysis skills in each team, the coaches' primary role was to identify and further develop capacity among the staff. Because FAST-R coaches simply couldn't provide all the support schools needed to ensure focused, consistent, data-informed instruction, their challenge was to catalyze instructional response by working with schools' literacy coaches and principals to align the professional development, support, and supervision functions in the school around the instruction that FAST-R and other data suggested would improve students' performance.

The FAST-R coaching team identified a set of necessary skills and dispositions, shown in figure 6.6, and assessed teams' status on these indicators at the start and end of each year, using that information with the principal to plan implementation and

FIGURE 6.5   Teacher guide for FAST-R passage

At a Glance

Recommended for Reading Levels: 2 3 4 5 6 7 8 9 10 11

Genre: Poetry

Topic: One poet uses the sonnet form to write about the idea and the experience of love.

Author: William Shakespeare

Source: "Sonnet 116"

Special Note: "Sonnet 116" used on the G10 MCAS 2001

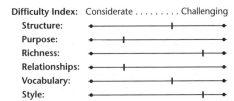

Difficulty Index: Considerate . . . . Challenging

Structure:
Purpose:
Richness:
Relationships:
Vocabulary:
Style:

Lexile Measure: 1000L

Sonnets are 14-line poems, traditionally about love, that follow particular rhythm and rhyme schemes. The word "sonnet" comes from the Italian "sonnetto," which means "little song." These two sonnets are by writers of different genders from different centuries, but they express similar ideas about love.

Read these two poems and answer the questions that follow.

> **Structure:** This is a classic example of the Elizabethan sonnet form, which uses an ABAB CDCD EFEF GG rhyme scheme. Shakespeare used this form so prolifically and with such mastery that it is also known as the Shakespearean form. The fact that each rhyme is used only once gives the poet greater flexibility.

Sonnet 116

1   Let me not to the marriage of true minds

Admit impediments; love is not love

Which alters when it alteration finds,

Or bends with the remover to remove:

5   O, no, it is an ever-fixèd mark,

That looks on tempests and is never shaken;

It is the star to every wand'ring bark,

Whose worth's unknown, although his height be taken.

Love's not Time's fool, though rosy lips and cheeks

10   Within his bending sickle's compass come;

Love alters not with his brief hours and weeks,

But bears it out even to the edge of doom.

If this be error and upon me proved,

I never writ, nor no man ever loved.

— William Shakespeare

> **Relationships:** Unlike the Browning sonnet, which directly addresses a lover, the speaker in this sonnet focuses on the idea of love.
>
> **See especially:** Question 3

> **Style:** Shakespeare uses a series of metaphors and figurative language to define and describe true love.
>
> **See especially:** Questions 1, 4

> **Structure:** Traditionally, poets state their theme in the final couplet of a sonnet, but Shakespeare tends to reflect or comment on the theme instead of merely stating it.
>
> **See especially:** Question 5

FIGURE 6.6   Skills and dispositions for data-based inquiry using FAST-R

FAST-R coaches' goal was that through work with colleagues and coaches, teachers using FAST-R would be able to:

- pose inquiry questions linking students' learning with their own classroom practices.
- analyze the reading and thinking demands required by FAST-R passages and other texts
- use FAST-R tools in intentional ways, and analyze and interpret a variety of data—in addition to FAST-R—to investigate their inquiry questions
- design and deliver instruction, feedback, and guidance in ways that accelerate student learning
- reflect on their teaching practices and learning process in ways that foster collaborative learning and

Over time, teachers and teams would increase their:

- independent practice of inquiry and data analysis
- disposition toward public practice
- focus on students' assets (as opposed to deficits)
- commitment to using assessment to accelerate student learning, rather than merely to measure or audit

---

allocate support. They mapped out objectives, guiding questions, and essential tasks to structure their coaching of teams, and collected key tasks, tools, and resources into a FAST-R teacher resource guide that supports teachers' action research and encourages them to become strategic assessment "consumers."[20]

In many schools, FAST-R coaches worked effectively with school or district literacy coaches, who were facilitating ongoing job-embedded professional development for teachers, known as Collaborative Coaching and Learning (CCL). In CCL cycles, teachers studied an instructional strategy, coplanned a lesson to teach a skill or content using that strategy, observed as one teacher demonstrated, debriefed the lesson, and then tried it themselves.[21] Evaluations of CCL pointed out one weakness in early CCL implementation was that it was too often focused on what teachers wanted to learn about Readers' Workshop, without being grounded in data about what *students* needed to learn.[22]

FAST-R coaches, literacy coaches, and teachers all reported anecdotally that when linked, FAST-R and CCL were each made more powerful than when experienced independently. Instructional data coaches counseled teams as they planned their FAST-R use to ensure that the assessment would help them investigate an authentic question about their students' skills at the current time. Over time, as inquiry became more common in BPS, data coaches stopped promoting a distinct "FAST-R cycle" and now encourage teachers to integrate FAST-R in the assessment phase of *any* evidence-based inquiry cycle.

IMPLEMENTATION

Early on, FAST-R coaches made a counterintuitive observation: the schools where teachers were making the best use of their assessment data were schools where their work wasn't all about the assessment data. Over time, the anecdotal evidence mounted: the schools where students showed consistent—and, in some cases, dramatic—gains almost always had several key conditions in place or developing: they embraced FAST-R not as an isolated initiative but as a tool to improve inquiry or action-research, they had capacity on staff (often in the form of a literacy coach, administrator, or teacher-leader) to facilitate the team's inquiry, and they experimented purposefully with the assessment tools.

Inquiry or Action Research Underway

When teachers are already engaged in inquiry, the assessment is not the entry point, but a tool that teachers put to their use. These teachers are more likely to choose texts purposefully, tweak questions to test a particular hypothesis, and triangulate the data with other information about their students' reading skills—and they are *much* better poised to act immediately and purposefully on what they learn. For example:

> We spent a month and I did different mini-lessons on it everyday, using selections from novels that showed inferencing. Then the students went back to their independent reading, using their think marks for inferencing . . .
>
> Then we'd share and I'd go back and make overheads of those [that they shared] and that would be the mini-lesson for the next day: What's right with this? What's wrong with this? What were you thinking about when you made that inference?
>
> After about a month, from conferencing with my students I felt that the kids were starting to nail it, because instead of 25 percent [of their responses being text-based inferences] they were getting 90 percent.[23]

This leap, away from the test and into real texts, is crucial to realize lasting gains in students' learning, and that happened most frequently when teachers' action research got "on a roll" and FAST-R fed the momentum.

Teams with action research or CCL cycles already underway were often early adopters of FAST-R, and they were also the innovators, asking for changes that would help them glean better data, more nuanced insight, and easier linkage back to their instructional planning. When FAST-R was embedded in an action-research process, it tended to serve less as an interim assessment and much more as a genuinely formative assessment that shaped *what* was taught, *how*, and *to whom*.

A Person to Facilitate Teacher Teams Through the Action-Research Cycle

The light-touch design of the FAST-R staffing model made it simply impossible to work with every team through every phase of the assessment—decide–plan–teach—reassessment cycle. Having a person (e.g., literacy coach, teacher leader, or administrator) responsible for helping the team carry the ball between assessments situated the FAST-R coach as a resource for that person as well as the team; FAST-R coaches would often meet one-to-one with literacy coaches or teacher leaders to link the data to that person's plans to support the team's instructional follow-up.

Purposeful Experimentation with Other Implementation Approaches

The other common implementation approach was to use a FAST-R aligned to a genre study, either as a preassessment of less familiar genres (e.g., myth, drama), a midunit dipstick to help teachers focus and fine-tune their remaining lessons, or an end-unit assessment to see how students applied their Readers' Workshop experience in a testing context. This approach tended to position FAST-R more as a mini-interim assessment, checking on students' current status on key skills as they entered or ended a genre study. Teachers found this approach most useful when they used short question sets in between longer assessments of the same skills, such as the FAST-R anchor assessments at the start of the year, the FAST-R–based midyear assessments, or more recently, the district's commercial interim assessments, so that the assessments "talked to one another" and contextualized each ten-question set in a trend of students' performance on the same skills over time.

Regardless of implementation approach, teachers' follow-up instruction might occur in one-on-one reading conferences, small flexible groups, or a mini-lesson to the whole class—depending on whether one, several, or many students exhibit particular patterns of performance. For instance, a teacher might pull together four students who routinely choose OOP "misread" answers to teach them a strategy for monitoring their comprehension as they read, then coach another student choosing many OOB answers on how to tell when connecting a text to her own life enhances her understanding and when it distracts her from the author's intent.

BARRIERS AND CHALLENGES

FAST-R encountered several challenges to robust, integrated implementation. These predictable challenges included a slippery slope toward test prep when used in a high-stakes testing environment, the need for shared leadership and teacher input into FAST-R use, dilemmas about assessing below-level readers, and the need to support teachers' instructional responses to the data.

Predisposition Toward Test-Prep

The design, explicit messaging, and coaching support helped ensure that most teachers used FAST-R to give students low-stakes experience with MCAS-like multiple-choice and open-response question types *while* focusing their instruction on the reading and thinking skills their students need to learn in order to become proficient readers. As one middle school principal put it, "when teachers first saw [FAST-R], a few thought, 'Oh, more MCAS practice tests.' But after they used the teacher guide and worked with the coach to analyze their data, they said, 'This isn't test prep—this is a tool for our teaching!'" Certainly, in pockets where FAST-R was used without appropriate support (there were a few "bootleg" sites using the materials without support from an instructional data coach), a test-prep mentality may have prevailed, but Education Matters concluded decisively that:

> *Without question, these examples highlight the fact that the focus of the question sets on MCAS skills need not limit what teachers can do with what they learn from the data. These teachers were teaching important reading skills that students would use whenever they read. And, they were aware of how [FAST-R] had influenced their overall instruction while attending to skills that the students would need for MCAS.*[24]

Overall, the gamble to base FAST-R on MCAS resulted in a winning bet.

Need for Shared Leadership

A principal's involvement and engagement of teachers from the beginning of FAST-R use had a direct effect on how teachers viewed and used the tools. Education Matters found that:

> [At schools] in which principals had engaged teachers in FAST-R from the outset . . . teachers asked many questions and they considered what the data might mean for their classes and for individual students. They engaged with each other about how they might use the data . . . [and] sought ideas from [the FAST-R coach] . . . In schools where teachers were not integral to the implementation, such discussions were unlikely to happen.[25]

Principals' district-sponsored professional development at the time unfortunately had little direct connection to the skills and strategies that teachers were using FAST-R to promote, or to the leadership moves that principals could make to support teachers.

Dilemmas When Assessing Below-Level Readers

Most teachers of students with disabilities, English language learners, and other students whose reading level is far below grade level appreciate FAST-R's help homing in on the thinking skills—as opposed to decoding skills—their students need to develop, but many felt concern about using texts they knew would be at students' frustration level. When FAST-R coaches asked, *How would you have to use this assessment in order for it to generate usable data about below-level readers?*, these teachers and their teams tended toward two strategies: (a) using the same passage as grade-level colleagues, but modifying how students accessed the text (e.g., listening as teacher read text out loud, reading text with a partner before answering questions independently); or (b) choosing a different text or question set closer to students' independent or instructional level, including the guided-reading question sets.

So How Do I Teach it?

While many teams were able to plan instruction by drawing on instructional expertise within the team, from colleagues, or from a coach, this challenge was most persistent in schools without a literacy coach and among high school teachers with little prior training in how to teach reading or to differentiate instruction. The optimal means for teams to figure out "now what?" seemed to be using FAST-R in the context of an ongoing action-research or inquiry cycle.

IMPACT ON ACHIEVEMENT AND PRACTICE

With encouragement and financial support from the Hewlett Foundation, BPE contracted with the independent evaluation firm MDRC for a rigorous quantitative study attempting to link the use of FAST-R with student learning outcomes. MDRC conducted a comparative interrupted time series study covering the first two years of FAST-R implementation in a sample of BPS schools.[26] The overall findings were that students in FAST-R schools made positive gains on MCAS, and that teachers in FAST-R schools considered the professional development from FAST-R coaches to have contributed to their understanding of data and their ability to work with their students. However, the student learning gains did not prove statistically significant, nor did the differences from schools not using FAST-R.

There are several plausible reasons, other than a simple lack of effectiveness, that the effects of FAST-R may not have risen to the high bar of statistical significance at the time of the MDRC study. First is simply timing: many would agree that expecting a deliberately low-touch intervention to change instruction enough in its first year to result in measurable changes on the students' state test performance is highly optimistic. When considering only the year two data, Janet Quint et al. found that the estimated impact and effect size of FAST-R on MCAS performance increased on almost every analysis. In the second year of implementation, MDRC's analysis yielded statistically significant effects for:

- Total MCAS scores of third-grade students with disabilities.
- Total SAT-9 reading scores of third-grade students with disabilities.
- Total MCAS scores for fourth-grade regular education students.
- Percent scoring *proficient* and *advanced* among fourth-grade regular education students.[27]

Quint et al. took pains to note that these results should be interpreted cautiously, but the suggestion that impact accelerates in the second year of teams' FAST-R use is corroborated by data beyond the scope of the MDRC evaluation. The FAST-R coaches rated each team's skills and dispositions for instructional data use (using the objectives in figure 6.6) at the start and end of each school year, and schools in their third year of implementation showed notable growth in many teams' capacity.

Second, as Quint et al. pointed out, the purposefully low intensity of the FAST-R coaching model and the concurrent instructional and data initiatives in place in other BPS schools presented challenges in isolating measurable effects on student learning. In other words, in Boston's reform-rich environment at the time of the study, many schools, including those in the control group, had their own efforts underway.

Further, Quint et al. raised an intriguing possibility "that FAST-R may have worked *better* than other training efforts and was, in fact, an 'energy-efficient' and effective form of professional development. In general, teachers at FAST-R schools reported spending less time on professional development than their counterparts at the comparison schools—but students at the two groups of schools nonetheless experienced the same learning gains."[28] Though the sample size did not permit MDRC to disaggregate effects in this way, FAST-R coaches observed this efficiency most in schools that used the results of the assessments to guide and focus their professional development and teacher collaboration. One BPS middle school, for example, received a typical dosage of FAST-R coaching, but its school-based literacy coach (which many schools had at that time in BPS) was quick to use FAST-R to focus the teams' CCL cycles with laserlike intensity on what *teachers* needed to learn to teach in response to evidence of what their *students* needed learn. The percentage of students scoring at the proficient level on MCAS in 2004 rose nearly *thirty percentage points* to 58 percent, with 96 percent passing—results on par with the performance of more affluent suburban districts. Similarly, an elementary school where a cross-grade team and its literacy coach assessed the effects of its cycles of reading intervention with FAST-R and used common-planning and professional development time to help teachers coplan, observe, and debrief instruction in response had *not a single third grader* fail MCAS—for the first time ever!

LESSONS LEARNED AND IMPLICATIONS FOR OTHER ASSESSMENT INITIATIVES

Through independent evaluations of FAST-R, teacher surveys, and careful documentation of implementation, BPE and BPS have learned a great deal about what teachers need in order to use data to guide instruction. Several of FAST-R's innovations are still surprisingly unique among assessment systems, but could applied elsewhere by educators who want to make the formative use of data part of their school and district culture.

Data Defines the Problems You See

BPE's school-based staff has observed a clear correlation between the "grain size" of the data that teachers have access to and the precision of the instruction that teachers are able to plan in response to the data. Grain size refers to the level of data specificity: are you looking at large aggregate data points such as "school percent correct by standard" or smaller, student-level and item-level error patterns? For instructional use, smaller grain size is better. Prior to FAST-R, most of the readily available reading performance data yielded aggregate scores or performance ratings, and teachers' response was correspondingly broad: "Help! My kids can't read!" The first year of FAST-R, when questions were identified only as "finding evidence" or "making inferences," teachers quickly adopted that language and began teaching those skills more intentionally. At that point, coaches heard a lot of "I taught 'inferring' on Tuesday and they still didn't learn it!" that drove the need to explicate, particularly the inferential thinking skills. After the introduction of the more nuanced FAST-R framework, teachers' conversations—and teaching—became dramatically more specific and constructive. For instance, a teacher might now muse: "Six of my students consistently focus on literal details instead of inferring the main idea. I'm going to cut apart sentences from a paragraph and ask them to sort the main ideas from the details, naming the word- and sentence-level clues they used to tell the difference." Providing a common language to name specific reading and thinking skills, and organizing data to highlight performance on those skills are two tangible moves that could help teachers get more out of any reading assessment.

Data Limits the Problems You See

Conversely, a defined framework may also limit what teachers see about their students' performance. A student may do poorly on questions requiring inferential thinking not because he can't infer, but because unknown vocabulary or complex sentence structures undermine his ability to make accurate text-based inferences *about that text*. In that case, considering the thinking skills without also examining the underlying text demands may lead a teacher to make an unsound inference about what she should teach next. Training teachers to ask themselves "the doctor questions" familiarized in Jerome Groopman's *How Doctors Think* can help guard against this overreliance on any one lens: "What else could it be? What other underlying conditions could account for this same 'symptom' in the data?"[29]

Assessment Embedded in Inquiry

The most powerful use of FAST-R we've seen has come when teachers engage in focused, evidence-based action research and seek out FAST-R to help them inform and assess the effects of their interventions. BPE has shifted its efforts over the past four years to support this sort of inquiry.

Thoughtful Data Design Enhances Usability

Many new FAST-R users receiving their data for the first time say, "Wow. For once, patterns really jump out at me!" Simple design principles can make it easier for teachers to grasp patterns quickly and instead spend time discussing instructional implications.

Put data, questions, and interpretive information close together. Putting the annotated test questions side by side with the error-analysis graphs allows teachers to move quickly from analysis to interpretation.

More is not always better. FAST-R data come to teachers in two straightforward, personalized reports printed in a legible font on standard-sized paper. It's a manageable amount of information for a team to analyze deeply in a single planning period and walk away with actionable insights.

Maximize the "data density" of each report and the number of lenses on the performance. FAST-R remains unique in its coding of distractor answers to permit systematic *error* analysis. The color scheme allows teachers to quickly spot common types of errors among a single student's answers or across the whole class or grade.

Order results meaningfully. Data sorted by an element of performance can prompt teachers to notice that getting or missing one particular question is correlated with overall understanding of the text, that one question was missed by both high-performing and low-performing students, or that certain students' performance has changed dramatically from one question set to the next.

The Best "Data Coaches" Know Instruction

In the pilot phase of FAST-R, the data coaches included one of the test designers and a data-savvy former math teacher, because at that point the apparent need was to help teachers learn to analyze data. However, it became quickly and irrefutably clear that the support teachers need is less "what do these data mean?" but "how do I teach this skill more effectively than I have in the past?" BPE found it's far easier to train skilled teachers and literacy coaches in the data skills needed to support other teachers than for data people to become experts in the teaching of reading.

Teachers Can Be "Assessment Consumers"

Because of the many assessments required for state and district accountability purposes, many teachers perceive assessment as something that is done *to* them and their students rather than done *by* and *for* them. The authority to create an assessment plan that works for their school has won over teachers who were initially skeptical about the value of doing one more test. Teachers' sense of ownership is apparent in the way that they talk about FAST-R to their students. One teacher reported: "I told my kids it is an assessment that would not affect what I put on their report card, but [that] they should answer it the best way they know, because it's going to help me figure out what guided reading or literacy groups they should be in, what kinds of books they may need to read more of, and also [is] going to help me to be a better teacher because I'll know exactly what things I need to teach them and what things *I* might just need to practice a little more."[30]

Students Consume Assessment Data Too

As assessment and instruction become more closely linked, many students are also using formative assessment as a source of feedback about themselves as learners: Education Matters noted, "Teachers reported that, as a result of [FAST-R] and the instructional activities that followed, students were giving more thought to why they had chosen certain answers and they were, to varying degrees, interested in gaining insight into their own thinking."[31] Ensuring that coaching helps connect data-based insights into classroom discourse is very powerful. As one teacher reflected, "using FAST-R with my class has been instrumental in providing my students with the strategies [and] skills to become better readers and thinkers. While discussing the results, students use accountable talk in explaining their reasoning. This [accountable talk] is powerful because it clarifies misunderstanding and empowers them to be active learners."[32]

CONCLUSION

Though FAST-R was an experiment of fairly small scale and localized scope, lessons from its implementation in Boston Public Schools carry timely implications for schools and districts investing heavily in assessment systems as a lever for instructional improvement in pursuit of the Common Core State Standards' ambitious reading goals and steady improvement on high-stakes exams. Margaret Goertz et al. concluded from their study of interim mathematics assessments that "interim assessments that are designed for instructional purposes are helpful but not sufficient to inform instructional change. When well-supported by their districts and schools, teachers used interim assessment data to decide what to re-teach and whom, but not necessarily to change the ways in which they taught this content."[33] Our experience with FAST-R leads us to agree: new and finer-grained assessment data alone may help teachers refine the match of *what* they teach, *to whom*.

However, to fully realize the potential of common assessments and to also affect *how* teachers teach, districts and schools must ensure that timely data about students' performance also shapes the focus of teachers' professional development, particularly school-based coaching. A lasting legacy of FAST-R is that it has given teachers a language to talk with each other, and with students, about the complex and dynamic thinking readers must do as they make sense of a text. FAST-R has also driven teachers to learn how to teach their students to become better thinkers as they read. When teaching, learning, and assessing become inextricably linked in teachers' minds, and action-research cycles inform their practice, we have seen reading improve—faster and faster.

(FAST-R materials are available free of charge for educators to use and adapt. Interested schools will find the question sets, teacher support materials, analysis database, and evaluation reports posted on the Web site of the Boston Plan for Excellence: www.bpe.org.)

CHAPTER 7

Becoming Strategic Readers

*Three Cases Using Formative Assessment, UDL, and Technology to
Support Struggling Middle School Readers*

NICOLE COHEN, TRACEY E. HALL,
GE VUE, AND PATTI GANLEY

When middle school students struggle to read, teachers are understandably frustrated and daunted. The challenge of helping children learn to read when they should already be reading content may seem beyond reasonable expectations for middle school teachers. And most teachers do not have a systematic way to recognize barriers and design solutions. Do any of these teachers' statements sound familiar?

- "When you have kids that *can't* read, they *don't* [read]."
- "I can remember sitting at my desk listening to one student read and was just so taken by the fact that there was so much further that she needed to go."
- "They would just keep going without any thought of rereading or responding. In some part of their educational career, they may have been programmed to just finish the work instead of thinking about the work."
- "I was surprised when sixth-grade English teachers would say, 'We read the entire book out loud in class because we can't expect the kids to get it.'"

As these and many teachers know, students encounter many obstacles in their learning experiences, ranging from being unable to read their texts to having insufficient background knowledge to understand the content. For teachers, simply recognizing these barriers is not enough to improve teaching and learning. Such knowledge still leaves teachers laboriously trying to adapt curriculum to address the diversity of students in their classrooms, while at the same time devising creative ways to engage *all* students. To put it bluntly, this is a Herculean task with a handful of students, and a nearly impossible task with an entire class, given current tools available to teachers.

Teachers need innovative supports, strategies, and tools that will make it possible to raise the bar in meeting the educational needs of all students, strong and struggling alike. Educators and researchers agree that data-based decision making is needed to raise the bar for all students to succeed. Formative evaluation procedures provide such data during instruction versus following attempts and failures not recognized until it's too late. The Center for Applied Special Technology (CAST), an educational research and development organization in Wakefield, Massachusetts, recently created a digital tool for proof of concept, the Strategic Reader, to provide teachers with formative evaluation measures with supports and strategies for instructional decision making to move precisely in this direction. More specifically, the Web-based Strategic Reader tool was developed to study if the addition of curriculum-based formative assessment to an existing interactive digital reading environment would lead to better reading instruction and outcomes for all students, especially those with disabilities.

Strategic Reader builds on a prior prototype that exemplified the Universal Design for Learning (UDL) principles[1] by providing a flexible instruction and assessment environment to accommodate individual learning differences. The Strategic Reader then integrates formative assessment into this highly supported, Web-based literacy environment, which includes options to support varied individual needs. The Strategic Reader allows access for all readers to digitized texts and provides scaffolds to support comprehension. One feature of the Strategic Reader is the inclusion of curriculum-based measurements (CBM) to monitor student progress. Thus, this tool explores synergy between two proven effective approaches: UDL and CBM.

FORMATIVE ASSESSMENT USING STRATEGIC READER

The Strategic Reader is a Web-based tool designed to inform teachers of student performance *during* the instructional episode so that teachers may employ interventions *before* students fail. As such, it is designed to provide assessment data to guide not only overall instructional activities for the classroom but also just-in-time adjustments for individual students. There are three main components to the design of the Strategic Reader: (1) a supported and interactive digital reading environment based on UDL principles, (2) a forum for ongoing teacher-to-student and student-to-student topical discussion, and (3) embedded curriculum-based measurement to be used for monitoring student progress. Our focus in this chapter is on the formative assessment components of Strategic Reader. We will also provide background information on the central components of Strategic Reader: UDL and CBM.

The Strategic Reader was created for middle school teachers and students in order to facilitate the reading of novels widely used in English language arts curricula in the state of Massachusetts (and many other states). In this digital reading environment, students' progress is monitored as they work their way through the texts via checks in oral reading fluency, vocabulary, and comprehension. Data are collected, scored, and delivered to the teacher by computer for interpretation and analysis. Strategic Reader provides teachers views of results for individuals as well as the entire class. The Strategic Reader flexibly keeps both cross-sectional data (i.e., across an entire class for a given progress-monitoring test) and time series data (i.e., across time for a given student). These data allow many ways to compare and contrast students' progressions. Strategic Reader also contains graphing tools, which display measurement results over time for each student and a class-wide summary in graphic form.

All of these features combine to provide just-in-time information on student progress for adjusting instructional interventions. Through formative development, pilot tests, and field-test trials, CAST refined the Strategic Reader as an instructional and assessment approach. The Strategic Reader's technology-based system combines UDL and CBM to improve reading comprehension for all students. Although UDL and CBM each have separate bodies of research supporting their individual implementations, Strategic Reader is the first attempt at developing and evaluating them together in a digital environment as an integrated approach to instruction. Doing so creates a tool that links learning standards, strategy instruction, and progress monitoring.

UNIVERSAL DESIGN FOR LEARNING

Universal Design for Learning is an educational framework that has application to instructional methods and effective teaching practices, including formative assessment. Drawing its name from the concept of universal design in architecture, in which structures are designed to accommodate the greatest number of users, UDL helps structure the design of the learning environment to consider from the outset the tremendous variability of individuals in a given classroom. This variability may be physical, intellectual, motivational, cultural, and so forth. UDL asserts that learning, instruction, and assessment are most effective in environments that are flexible enough to accommodate individuals according to their particular strengths and needs. Further, the UDL framework enables the development of educational methods and materials that provide opportunities for all students to participate and progress in the general education curriculum.[2]

UDL is thus a set of principles for curriculum development designed to plan appropriate learning opportunities for all individuals. Applying UDL principles affords more accurate instruction by providing options, tools, and materials that reduce irrelevant barriers that actually interfere with accurate instruction and assessments. The UDL principles call for educators to:

1. Provide multiple means of representation.
2. Provide multiple means of action and expression.
3. Provide multiple means of engagement.

To create a UDL environment in a classroom, teachers need to have instructional goals, materials, methods, and ongoing assessments that incorporate these three principles. As a tool to develop curriculum and instruction, UDL emphasizes the need to build in scaffolds and supports for ongoing progress monitoring so that (1) educators can make data-driven decisions during instructional units or episodes, and (2) learners themselves can develop the capacity to monitor their own progress and make adjustments.

The digital Strategic Reader environment demonstrates the UDL principles of providing scaffolds and supports for the *what* (representation), *how* (action and expression), and *why* (engagement) of learning. Learners climb the stairs of practice and performance, growing from novice learners focused on accessing content to become independent and strategic learners (see figure 7.1). In particular, teachers can increase or decrease scaffolds in the Strategic Reader to reduce anxiety and stress or increase challenge to students within the UDL framework.

FIGURE 7.1   UDL principles

		Independent practice	
			Provide reading strategy resources and background information of novel to deepen comprehension
		Guided practice	
		Provide multimedia links to vocabulary words with definition, example sentence, and image	Provide open-ended reading strategy prompts with minimal supports and scaffolds and an online forum to foster independent practice
UDL principles	**Access**		
Representation	Provide text-to-speech read aloud of passage to support decoding and fluency and graphic or tabular display of progress monitoring results to support meaning making	Provide customizable supports and scaffolds for developing reading strategies—highlighted key ideas in passage, sentence starters and coaches who provide hints and models, and adjustable reading strategy prompts to change the type of strategies embedded in a passage	Provide options for self monitoring of practice and performance; share knowledge and receive feedback in forum and set goals and track progress overtime using progress monitoring results
Action and expression	Provide multiple ways to express comprehension; create responses to reading strategy prompts by typing text or audio recording	Create an optimal learning environment for learners by maximizing supports and scaffolds to reduce challenges or removing them to increase challenges	
Engagement	Offer choice of formats for reading (printed or digital text) and choice of media for expression (text or audio)		

Rose and Meyer developed the UDL framework based on the three neural networks within the brain through which we learn (a network is a specialized group of connections in the brain to perform particular tasks): (1) recognition (the *what* of learning, as in the information), (2) strategic (the *how* of learning, as in the planning and performing of tasks), and (3) affective (the *why* of learning, the engagement and motivation to learn).[3] Although all brains have these learning networks, individual brains can differ substantially in the use and interconnectedness of the networks. Practitioners of UDL aim to take these differences into account in the most flexible manner possible.

Since its development, UDL has received research support demonstrating its effectiveness at presenting information in multiple modalities and customizable formats.[4]

Further, the research shows that flexible formats translate into increased accessibility for learners with diverse abilities (and disabilities).[5] In addition, the UDL framework provides for multiple alternatives for response and expression so that learners with disabilities find an apprentice-learning environment suited to their abilities, while also providing multiple means of engagement.

CURRICULUM-BASED MEASUREMENT

Curriculum-based measurement is a form of ongoing instructional assessment (e.g., progress monitoring) where short, sensitive-to-change measures are administered during the instructional episode to help educators or teachers determine a further course of instruction. Simply stated, CBMs have been developed to function as academic yardsticks to monitor students' growth in basic academic skills. Ideally, CBMs provide teachers with data that may be useful for a number of educational purposes, including curriculum placement (determining the best starting point for a student in the materials), eligibility determination (a measure to assist in identifying the need for special services), screening (to help identify current performance), and decision making.[6]

Additionally, CBMs are meant to support informed instructional decisions. Different from summative evaluations, which are done after instruction is complete, CBM informs teachers of student performance *during* the instructional episode and enables them to implement interventions *before* students fail. Results are often graphically displayed, enabling students, teachers, and parents to literally see a picture of performance over time and to determine whether progress is adequate to meet specific goals and or standards.

The most critical aspect of CBM is obviously that teachers can use the data provided to make better-informed instructional decisions.[7] Research has shown that when teachers use CBM to monitor student growth, evaluate performance, and change their instruction, students make greater achievement gains than students of teachers not using formative evaluation procedures.[8] CBM also improves decision making for teachers of students with disabilities in the general education setting.

Taking a Step Back from UDL and CBM

While the last two sections have expounded the positive aspects of UDL and CBM, it is worth noting that neither is a panacea for student learning issues. For instance, while it is quite easy to claim that designing a generalized framework under UDL will lead to multiple benefits, this claim still leaves open the most important task of, in fact, designing and implementing a viable framework. Even with the best intentions of UDL, a poorly designed curriculum can fall short of a focused, organized program of learning that will flexibly address students' varied needs. Further, even if the program is designed flawlessly, poor or inconsistent implementation of the framework across students and learning situations will result in almost certain failure.

Similar pitfalls plague the application of CBM. For instance, in the application of a CBM program, factors such as: (1) what metric will be used for testing, (2) how often measurement will be taken, and (3) how quickly trends, or patterns, will be diagnosed as "problems," all have critical impacts on the resulting success of the CBM. Choosing even one of these incorrectly could jeopardize the efficiency of the entire CBM tool. In support of this observation, there is research suggesting that teachers often struggle with implementing and interpreting curriculum-based, formative assessment data and using it to modify instructional programs effectively.[9] Realistically, implementation of CBM is a labor-intensive process.

The upshot is that even if UDL and CBM theoretically lead to better learning outcomes for all students, the actual outcomes depend critically on the design and implementation of the tools that utilize their advantageous characteristics. For that reason, in the development of the Strategic Reader, we included (1) oral reading fluency measures to analyze fluency, accuracy, and comprehension; (2) maze reading, a comprehension measure; (3) reciprocal teaching strategies to measure student ability to respond to these specific reading comprehension strategies; (4) a forum for student-to-student and student-to-teacher dialogue about the literature; (5) choice in assessment passages or content; and (6) layers of support for reading, such as text to speech and prompts for strategy responses. The case stories later in the chapter illustrate several means by which formative assessment provides essential teacher information for instruction in diverse middle school settings.

STRATEGIC READER IMPLEMENTATION

An ultimate goal of the Strategic Reader is to inform teachers and students of reading skills and performance. CAST researchers developed and evaluated this technology-based system and then studied its effectiveness with nearly three hundred middle school students in four different schools, including seventy students who were identified as having learning disabilities. Both students and teachers received training in use of the Strategic Reader prior to formal instructional use in classrooms. Researchers provided two four-hour training sessions in which participating English language arts teachers were trained in (1) the reading comprehension strategies of reciprocal teaching and the progress-monitoring procedures of CBM, and (2) the use, components, and features of the Strategic Reader tool.

Students were also trained how to use the Strategic Reader. Training occurred as a part of class instruction, usually with the classroom teacher and researcher teaming up to demonstrate and discuss the tool. Students were first taught how to use the digital books with reading supports, followed by the forum (an online setting for student-to-student and student-to-teacher discussion). They were then introduced to the progress-monitoring measures by way of explanation, demonstration, and use. For all components of the Strategic Reader, students were allowed and encouraged to experience the computer tool prior to formal instruction. Teachers then taught students the classroom expectations for Strategic Reader particular to their class.

To maintain consistency and quality of implementation, researchers visited classrooms on a fairly regular basis. In the classrooms, the researchers observed, coached students and teachers in the use of the tool, demonstrated additional features and functions, assisted in analysis and interpretation of progress monitoring scores, and discussed interventions.

Students used the Strategic Reader for ten to twelve weeks. During this time, they read two novels using the supported digital text environment (selected from the four options of *The Devil's Arithmetic, Maniac Magee, So Far from the Bamboo Grove*, and *Number the Stars*) and responded online to reciprocal teaching prompts during the reading process.[10] Next, they accessed an online forum for peer-to-peer discussion of the novels read and regularly took progress-monitoring measures for reading fluency (oral reading fluency) and reading comprehension (maze and reading strategies).[11]

Preliminary outcomes from the progress-monitoring measures in this study showed that students made steady gains in comprehension and strategy use. Although all participating teachers were working with the same Web-based tool and interpreting the same CBMs, each teacher decided on *different* learning exercises and activities to implement in his or her classes, based on the progress-monitoring information. This aspect was one of the most promising of the study. The built-in flexibility of Strategic Reader allowed each teacher to ultimately create a positive, tailored intervention for individuals in his or her classroom. This variety of effective approaches suggests that there was indeed synergy between the relatively prescriptive principles of CBM and the relatively flexible principles of UDL, as embodied in the design of the Strategic Reader. This finding underscores both the importance and potential power of differentiated implementation of Strategic Reader based on a teacher's own expertise and intuition.

Next are three distinct examples of how teachers designed interventions based on the interaction of student needs and their own strengths, with resultant outcomes making a positive difference for the teacher and the student.[12] We selected these three examples because each shows the flexible adaptation of the Strategic Reader, while illustrating how the various parts work together in the broader measurement-driven approach. The first example is about identifying an unexpected problem and making systemwide change, the second has a focus on individualizing instruction to meet diverse student needs, and the third highlights student engagement and motivation.

Case One. Early Assessment and Attacking the Problem Head On

Ms. Hopkins and Mr. Starbrook teach middle school English language arts (ELA) classes and plan their lessons together. When students walk into class on the first day of school, Hopkins and Starbrook expect that students can read, and read fluently. Middle school is a time of reading to learn, not learning to read. The reality of middle school, as Hopkins and Starbrook were about to find out, can be very different from preconceived notions.

The Strategic Reader tool helped them realize how much their students were struggling. One progress-monitoring metric of the Strategic Reader is the ability to hear audio recordings of students in an oral reading fluency measure. After listening to some of the audio files of their students, Hopkins and Starbrook were shocked at many students' profound lack of reading accuracy and fluency (several students read slowly, had no prosody, hesitated, and made word errors). Even more surprising to them was that it was *not* only the struggling students or students identified with special needs who performed poorly. Students who struggled with reading accuracy and fluency by obvious extension also struggled with reading comprehension. Had it not been for the audio recordings of Strategic Reader, these teachers might never have identified the fluency struggles of their students. In their own words: "This project really opened our eyes to what we needed to do to help students to be more fluent in their reading. We knew students had problems with reading, but we never knew to the extent to [which] we were able to pinpoint where some of the problems were directly. If you can't read with fluency, your understanding is also imperiled."

Hopkins and Starbrook took their newly found knowledge of fluency problems one step further, jumping into action. Together with their principal and teacher committee, they proposed a systemwide response to support those students struggling with reading (decoding, fluency, and accuracy). Based on the data collected using the Strategic Reader with progress-monitoring measures, the school faculty and administration decided to restructure the day and give struggling readers a period of time for direct instruction to address their reading fluency weaknesses. In addition to identifying students struggling in reading, the data recognized some students as fluent readers. During the extra instructional period, these students had opportunities for enrichment in other content area classes. Moreover, the teachers also took steps to improve their general classroom methods to heighten awareness and provide practice of fluent oral reading (prosody, fluency). Hopkins and Starbrook supported their reading instruction with scaffolds for decoding and vocabulary and provided options for students to demonstrate their learning in varied ways. These adjustments resulted from the insights provided by the formative evidence in the Strategic Reader. In summary, the feedback these teachers gained not only helped them to *identify* a problem, but gave them the evidence they needed to make just-in-time instructional *changes* with schoolwide, classroom-wide, and student-specific interventions.

Case Two. One Teacher to Thirty-Five Students. Individualized Instruction?

Imagine thirty-five mixed-grade students from sixth through eighth grades in the same classroom. Now imagine that it's your job to teach this group with diverse backgrounds, strengths, and challenges the standards in English and language arts. You're now imagining the task faced every day by Mr. Chang. Every day proved a seemingly insurmountable challenge of constructing curricula inclusive of the entire class, but flexible enough for their diverse needs.

Chang and others in his school were invited to join CAST's study using Strategic Reader. Given its digitized format and built-in scaffolds, Strategic Reader enabled students in Chang's class to work independently, opening new opportunities for instruction. It provided a platform to change his instructional strategies and address the varied needs of his diverse classes. Chang was well aware of the need to differentiate his instruction for his students' various needs and learning styles; what he lacked were useful tools for doing so.

Once he began using Strategic Reader, Chang started each class with whole-group instruction in the classroom. He then moved the class next door to the computer lab where some students could work independently with the Strategic Reader tool, while he conferred one on one with individual students needing additional support. Chang based his one-on-one instructional sessions on progress-monitoring results provided through Strategic Reader. Chang shared the following about his experience with the tool: "Using Strategic Reader, I could do one-on-one conferencing with kids. When you have 35 or 36 kids in your room . . . work is demanding. So having kids who are self-guided through the Strategic Reader learning allows me to be able to work one-on-one with kids sometimes and pull them over and give them immediate feedback . . ."

Additionally, Chang utilized his own strengths as a teacher when implementing instructional interventions. Having been inspired by his use of the tool's flexibility, Chang employed screenwriting, role playing, and video production as an intervention to engage students with the text and provide alternatives for expression (a direct example of UDL principles). Chang provided templates for creating a script of scenes from the literature and brought in a student expert in video production to film and edit student reenactments of their favorite scenes. This activity was extremely motivating for students but also gave Chang a new perspective on his students' real understanding of the literature they had read.

Case Three. Feedback as a Tool for Engagement

Any teacher knows that student engagement is a necessary piece of the learning experience. This necessity provided a special challenge for Mrs. Cole, who had a broad mix of students in her middle school classroom. Her students' vastly different backgrounds and levels of social maturity made it very difficult to find learning tasks that engaged the entire class. Cole found her invitation to join the Strategic Reader project timely and helpful.

Two features within the tool proved especially powerful for Cole's class: the reciprocal teaching strategies and the forum. The reciprocal teaching strategies of summarizing, predicting, questioning, and clarifying embedded directly in the Strategic Reader not only seemed to aid reading comprehension for Cole's students, but also empowered them to monitor their own learning and thinking processes. Cole had been using a modified version of the reciprocal teaching strategies; however, the impact of the strategies seemed to be magnified when they were reinforced within the Strategic Reader for her students. The tool itself provided an opportunity for interaction and engagement that is supported and structured around reading comprehension—and is measured using the formative evaluation built into it. Here, the UDL emphasis on recruiting and sustaining student engagement, as well as making literature more relevant to individual learners, helped Cole reach instructional goals in her classroom.

Moreover, Cole took great advantage of peer-to-peer communication facilitated by the forums embedded in the Strategic Reader to motivate and engage her students. Using forums, Cole harnessed the power of engagement with her students. More specifically, by using its digitized, interactive environment and flexible platform of scaffolds, Cole addressed engagement in a way that had a commanding impact on her students. In her own words:

> I think it [the Strategic Reader forum] was a big motivator for students; I think they wanted to "hear" what other people had to say and they wanted to be responded to. They wanted to post something and have somebody respond to them and get feedback. I think it was a great experience because I think that it just made the classroom discussion happen at a different level for people to have their voices heard. And also going back to those kids who have social disabilities, I think that it was a good avenue for them to get their opinions heard and receive positive feedback from others where they perceive a lot of negative feedback whether it is present or not.

Cole utilized many of the novel aspects of Strategic Reader. Specifically, she first employed the tool's option allowing student choice of method for reading (the student could read to him- or herself or have a selection read aloud) and responding to the embedded reciprocal-teaching strategies questions in the text (written or oral recording). Second, she set up a forum for student dialogue through peer-to-peer discussions (which the teacher can coordinate and monitor, while also engaging as a participant). Lastly, with the built-in progress monitoring, the Strategic Reader gave her students a choice of reading material for each progress-monitoring task. This enhanced students' interest in the passage, as they could choose whether to take a measure about, for instance, baseball or banana splits.

Broad Summary of Results

These case stories are drawn directly from the sample of teachers using the Strategic Reader. Table 7.1 summarizes the different ways in which teachers in the three case studies responded to the diagnostic feedback they received.

TABLE 7.1   Instructional decisions

Similarities:
Classroom implementation of all three core components of Strategic Reader: • Scaffolded reading environment to develop reading strategy skills and improve reading comprehension   • Curriculum based measurements for monitoring student progress   • Forum for ongoing teacher-to-student and student-to-student discussions   Challenges—how to engage students and improve student reading fluency and comprehension in diverse classrooms with students of different backgrounds and reading ability?

Differences:
Teachers designed intervention based on student needs and teacher strengths

Case 1 solution	Case 2 solutions	Case 3 solutions
• Used CBM (Oral Reading Fluency and Maze) to inform whole class and student specific instruction. • Used CBM to highlight a schoolwide reading fluency problem and advocated successfully for restructuring daily schedule to add more reading instructional time.	• Used both students' reading strategy responses and CBM data for whole class instruction, teacher to student conferencing, and peer to peer mentoring. • Used video production—screen writing, storyboarding, and reenacting scenes from the novel as both a learning activity that encouraged rereading and an avenue to express comprehension.	• Taught and practiced reciprocal teaching strategies across different content areas—English and language arts, social studies, and science. • Taught and practiced reciprocal teaching strategies across different contexts—in the classroom, while reading novel online, and in discussion forum. • Engaged and sustained learner motivation through providing choice of content and context for guided practice and feedback.

However, to provide a more systematic test of the Strategic Reader's impact, an experimental research study was also conducted over a school year. The study was designed with two treatment conditions. Students in both treatment conditions read the novels online, with identical supports, scaffolds, and work logs. The difference between conditions was how teachers and students were presented with and accessed progress-monitoring measures. Treatment 1 had all the progress-monitoring measures online, while treatment 2 monitored progress by using a traditional offline paper-and-pencil structure. In treatment 1, the measures were automatically and semi-automatically administered and scored by the computer, and scores were displayed in graphic and tabular formats for teachers and students on the Strategic Reader Web site. In treatment 2, the progress-monitoring measures were administered, scored, and graphed by teachers and researchers on paper, and paper files were organized for each student in a teacher's class. In addition to administering progress monitoring on a regular schedule during this study, a pre- and post-test of the Gates-MacGinitie standardized reading measure was administered to all subjects.[13]

Preliminary results indicated that students who had *online* progress monitoring in the Strategic Reader showed greater growth on reading measures than those who used the same tool without online measures. Students with disabilities in the online treatment condition demonstrated greater improvements at a statistically significant level than their peers in the offline progress-monitoring condition. Additionally, teachers in the online measures condition also accessed data from the program more frequently, analyzed the information, and in turn made a greater number of instructional interventions or changes for their students than the teachers in the offline measures condition. For example, these "digitized" teachers designed more instructional interventions, individualized student supports and scaffolds in the Strategic Reader program based on student performance, and coached students using data collected. Finally, both teachers and students reported enjoying use of the tool and expressed interest, excitement, and satisfaction in use of the tool.[14]

CONCLUSION

The educational landscape is becoming ever more complex, moving in lockstep with the increasing diversity of needs and challenges students face. Of course, these challenges are passed on to teachers, who must be armed with tools that can adequately address these ever-increasing complexities. Strategic Reader is designed with the diversity of student needs in mind and specifically addresses learning and teaching in English and language arts.

As a tool, it offers digital editions of literature with features for universal access and embedded assessments for monitoring students' progress to enhance instructional decision making. However, the real innovation is hardly the technology. Rather, the tool's power comes from *how* teachers creatively use Strategic Reader to spark interactive and meaningful learning.

There is an old adage that someone who loses his keys should look first under street lamps, as no matter where he lost his keys on the sidewalk, he's most likely to *see* them under the lamps. Combining UDL and CBM creates a new "street lamp" for teaching and learning. While the "keys" to all educational challenges will not be found under this lamp, the initial, very positive response of students, teachers, and, most importantly, student learning to Strategic Reader suggests that the digital combination of UDL and CBM promises an exciting and well-lit space to explore for many years to come.

The authors gratefully acknowledge the generous support of the project described in this chapter provided by the U.S. Department of Education, Office of Special Education Programs, Technology and Media Services for Individuals with Disabilities (Grant #H327B050009-07). The views expressed herein do not necessarily represent the positions or policies of the U.S. Department of Education. No official endorsement of this work by the Department should be inferred.

PART III

Science

CHAPTER 8

I Can Explain

*Academic Language for Science Among Young
English Language Learners*

ALISON L. BAILEY, YICHING D. HUANG,
AND MARYLOU ESCOBAR

In 2007, a group of charter elementary school teachers and their principal approached university researchers asking for assistance in improving instruction and facilitating student engagement in their kindergarten classrooms. The teachers and researchers agreed that, in order to be successful, the intervention should target specific aspects of instruction and particular content areas. We decided to focus our efforts on improving instructional strategies for formatively assessing children's science and academic language learning. In this chapter, we describe our three-year collaborative research study, which coincided with noticeable improvements in teachers' use of formative assessment strategies, specifically, the extent to which they made success criteria explicit for students and evoked evidence of student learning during the course of moment-to-moment instruction.

We begin this chapter with an example that typifies much of the science and language teaching that we observed toward the end of the multiyear collaboration. In the following example, Ms. Beltran is working with a small group of children and giving them an opportunity to explore a plant's root system. She has provided them with plants, paintbrushes (to separate the roots from the surrounding soil), and magnifying glasses.

> *Ms. Beltran:* I need you to find the primary root, secondary root, and the root hairs. You can take it apart using your hands. You can use the paintbrush to take off some of the soil. I really want you to look like a scientist [the way in which scientists observe].
>
> *[As the children work on finding the roots, Ms. Beltran circles the table, observing the children and asking them questions.]*
>
> *Ms. Beltran:* Theresa, what is it that you are pulling there? What is it called?
>
> *Theresa:* The second.
>
> *Ms. Beltran:* The secondary root. Wonderful! Look at that! Beautiful!
>
> *[Ms. Beltran addresses the group.]*
>
> *Ms. Beltran:* Do you see how Theresa is taking apart the roots? That's what you need to be doing—like a scientist. Observing the roots, trying to find the primary, the secondary, and the root hairs. Roberto, have you found any roots yet?

The children in Beltran's kindergarten classroom may be quite young, but they are already learning important science concepts (e.g., aspects of the root system) and authentic scientific processes (e.g., observation and investigation). Additionally, they are being exposed to the specialized academic vocabulary (e.g., *secondary root, root hairs*) and more general academic vocabulary (e.g., *observing*) needed to support that learning. Beltran shows us that science concept and academic language learning goals can be seamlessly and purposefully integrated in a science lesson. She also demonstrates how formative assessment can be used to enhance teaching and learning: by clearly communicating her success criteria for student engagement and asking questions to evoke evidence of student learning during the activity, she is able to assess their understanding of both what they are doing as well as their acquisition of the relevant science terminology.

The children who participated in this teacher-researcher collaborative project all began school as learners of the English language and came from low-income, often new-immigrant Latino families. These families were served by a child development center and an urban charter elementary school run by a nonprofit agency tasked with promoting the development of the whole child. The agency provided not only an education, but also nutrition, child care, and family support services. We focused the project on this population of young students because they are among the most vulnerable children in Los Angeles and possibly the United States in terms of successful academic achievement. Unfortunately, students who come to school with a language other than English are often already behind their English-proficient peers at the start of kindergarten, and disparities in academic achievement between Hispanic students and their white counterparts continue to persist across the grades.[1] The academic needs of the nation's English language learner (ELL) students are an educational concern that has an impact on educators in all content areas, not just those who teach English as a second language. Teachers should ideally be cognizant of both their students' content-area learning needs and their academic language needs. This dual demand on teacher knowledge and pedagogy is particularly vital for the effective instruction of those students who are still acquiring the English language at the point when they must learn new academic content through English as well.

We focused our collaboration on the single content area of science in order to best capture and illustrate the specific linguistic practices associated with content instruction at the earliest stages of formal schooling. Kathleen Metz has established that even very young children are capable of scientific reasoning, particularly when they are provided with quality instructional support.[2] The kindergarten teachers in the collaborative had previously adopted, as part of their teaching philosophy, a strong emphasis on young children as keen observers of the natural world. Specifically, the teachers were already leveraging cognitive capacities such as the ability to identify causes and effects, to make predictions, and to identify patterns in their science instruction. These capacities of the young child can serve as a foundation for more advanced science skills, particularly those associated with "doing science" such as the processes, discourses, and modes of reasoning utilized to generate scientific knowledge.[3] However, the substantial language demands placed on students and teachers to accomplish the explanations, hypothesizing, and so on of such an approach to science necessitates a deliberate attempt to support the academic language of students as well.[4]

The main focus of this chapter is not on the science outcomes of the students; the emphasis is on describing the integration of science and academic language learning and importantly how kindergarten teachers can attend to both in their assessment of the learning that is taking place in their classrooms. Teachers need to be aware of the specific ways in which science-related English can prove challenging for all young learners. This is what we mean by academic English. While many young ELL students acquire sufficient English to engage in social conversations, which might make it seem that they are proficient in English, there are significant differences between the skills needed to engage in informal interactions and the language demands needed to achieve school success. In science, for instance, nouns used to describe processes are derived from verbs of action, and other words may have very different meanings from how they are used in everyday contexts. Sentences are frequently complex in order to avoid ambiguities, and there is engagement in extended talk about persuasion, explanation, hypothesis generation, and so on that can differ from both everyday language and the ways we converse in other academic disciplines.[5]

As we embarked on this study of science and academic language learning, we asked whether a teacher-researcher collaboration could help promote effective formative assessment in these areas. Teachers in the elementary school were already acquainted with formative assessment approaches in general but needed ideas to help them more deliberately use formative assessment strategies at the intersection of science and academic language learning as well as to document their successes. Historically, assessment of the language development of ELL students has focused on initial identification of limited English proficiency, placement in English language development (ELD) services, and annual monitoring of progress toward reclassification as fluent English proficient. Far less attention has been paid to formative assessment—obtaining detailed information on ELL students' learning at the point it occurs and using this information to modify ongoing instruction.

ASSESSING FORMATIVELY:
LEARNING GOALS, SUCCESS CRITERIA, AND EVOKING EVIDENCE

Formative assessment can best be described as an approach to gaining information about student learning rather than as a specific test. Formative assessment is the process of soliciting and using information about students' learning in the course of instruction to make day-to-day teaching decisions to improve learning (see the introduction to the book). More specifically, formative assessment can help teachers to tailor their instruction to students' learning needs by identifying the gap between current levels of student understanding and desired learning goals.[6] Teachers can identify these gaps in many and varied ways, including through their close observations of students as they engage in different tasks and activities, through their questioning of student comprehension and understanding, and even by taking note of the kinds of questions that students are asking them and each other.[7]

Formative assessment can play an important role in instructional improvement efforts, so we felt it was important to document formative assessment practices in the classrooms where we observed and to emphasize those practices in the curricular tools we designed in collaboration with the teachers. We focused on examining three aspects of formative assessment: (1) setting learning goals, (2) making success criteria explicit, and (3) evoking evidence of student learning. These aspects work together to create a continuous feedback loop that informs teaching. The formative assessment process begins when teachers set a learning goal for their students and design a lesson to meet those learning goals. Teachers have an idea of what they want their students to be able to say and do during their engagement in the lesson, and they communicate these success criteria to students explicitly. As students engage in the lesson, teachers continuously support children's learning by evoking evidence of student learning and providing feedback to students about the extent to which they are meeting success criteria. Finally, evidence of student learning is used to inform decisions about future learning goals for students, thus completing the instructional feedback loop.

Setting Learning Goals

Setting learning goals is an important aspect of formative assessment. In this study, we collected teachers' lesson plans at each phase of the project in order to determine whether teachers had clearly articulated learning goals for the children's science concept and academic language learning. Ideally, within the context of science lessons, these goals should be based on state science and ELD standards as well as other documents that describe relevant progressions in science and language learning. For example, when planning a lesson on the root system, a teacher may want children to learn the parts of the root system (science concept), as well as the specific vocabulary, sentence structures, and organization of language (academic language) we need to effectively describe the parts of the root system.

Making Success Criteria Explicit

Making success criteria explicit to students is another important aspect of formative assessment. In this study, we used an observational protocol to document whether teachers made success criteria explicit to students. Within the context of science lessons, teachers should have specific criteria for what successful performance in science and language learning looks like. That is, they should have an idea of what they want students to be able to say and do during their engagement in science activities. Teachers need to be sure that their students actually understand what the success criteria in a lesson are before they can make an accurate assessment regarding the degree to which the students have met those criteria. For example, a teacher may devise an activity in which she provides real roots for children to explore and various materials for the children to use to represent the root system. If the teacher plans to use these representations to assess student knowledge, it is important that students know the criteria for success. The teacher could verbally communicate specific success criteria by saying something like, "I want you to observe the roots carefully and then I want you to represent the root system using the materials at your table. Your representations should show all the different parts of the root system that we have been talking about—the primary root, the secondary root, and the root hairs. I'm going to walk around and talk to each of you about your representations. When we talk, I want you to try and use the new vocabulary we have learned to describe your work." Clear verbal instructions at the beginning of an activity are key to making success criteria explicit for students. During the lesson, it is important for teachers to provide ongoing scaffolding that helps to remind children what the success criteria are for the activity. This support is especially important for young children who may not remember all the details provided at the start of an activity.

Evoking Evidence of Student Learning

Another important aspect of formative assessment is evoking evidence of student learning during the lesson. We documented the strategies of teachers in this study by using the observational protocol. Teachers can assess student learning during the lesson in a number of ways. For instance, teachers can ask children questions within the context of teacher-led whole-group discussions or they can facilitate opportunities for children to turn and talk with each other. They can also ask children to display their knowledge using a wide range of representational materials, like blocks, clay, string, or watercolor, for example. Importantly, evoking evidence of student learning helps teachers to determine what their next steps of instruction should be. Teachers can use information about student learning to capitalize on teachable moments, wherein they provide immediate, on-the-fly instruction to correct children's misconceptions or to introduce relevant information that expands children's current levels of understanding. Teachers should also use information about student learning to guide their future lesson planning, both in the short and long terms.

DESCRIBING FORMATIVE ASSESSMENT OF SCIENCE AND ACADEMIC LANGUAGE LEARNING

Our data and analyses allow us to paint a detailed picture of how kindergarten teachers used formative assessment during science instruction, both at the beginning and at the conclusion of our three-year teacher-researcher collaboration. In the section that follows, we briefly outline the study methods. An exhaustive description of methods used in the larger study can be found in other reports.[8]

Description of Participants and Instructional Context

Participants included teaching staff and children from kindergarten classrooms. The number of classrooms varied from four to three during the three-year study period due to fluctuations in school enrollment figures. Teaching staff also rotated to different grades over the three-year period such that just one teacher was involved during all three years and five others for varying lengths of time. As a result of these realities of working in schools, our intervention was aimed at shaping the overall curricular approach of the teaching staff rather than intervening at the level of individual teachers.

Each classroom had approximately twenty students. All children came from low-income Latino families, many with immigrant backgrounds, and all began preschool as Spanish-speaking ELL students. Overall, the charter K–5 elementary school enrolls 99 percent Latino students. All are in the free and reduced-price lunch program. The school's Academic Performance Index of 734 for 2008, while not reaching the state target of 800, exceeded the 2008 growth target set for the school. These demographics represent the experiences of many ELL students in the United States: ELL students are frequently from immigrant families with lower-than-average incomes and attend schools with lower overall academic performance.[9]

The six lead teachers and their teacher aides who participated in this study were bilingual in English and Spanish, and all had Spanish primary language backgrounds. Teaching experience spanned two to twenty-three years. All had received professional development that was heavily influenced by the Reggio Emilia constructivist approach to early childhood education and aimed at providing children with meaningful experiences designed to promote critical thinking and deep conceptual understanding.[10]

Study Procedures

The study procedures can be divided into three distinct phases.

Phase one: Establishing baselines in classroom practice. The first phase of the research project was devoted to establishing baseline characteristics of science and academic language teaching and learning in the kindergarten classrooms. A total of thirty-three science activities (five to thirty minutes each) were observed using a teacher- and researcher-created protocol. We calculated the percentage of all observed activities in which teachers made success criteria for science and language learning goals explicit to the children. We also documented instances when teachers evoked evidence of student learning and collected teacher lesson plans.

Phase two: Materials development. The second phase of the study involved a series of teacher-researcher strategy development meetings. During these meetings, researchers shared their impressions of what they had observed during the first phase of the project and teachers shared their perspectives on what the researchers had noticed. Together, teachers and researchers brainstormed about the curricular and pedagogical adjustments that might enhance student learning outcomes. As a group, we decided on several tools that could aid teachers in making adjustments to their teaching practices.

One of the curricular tools we devised was a lesson-planning and reflection guide designed to enhance existing lesson-planning templates that the teachers used. This guide was designed to help teachers become more strategic and varied in their formative assessment through the use of well-articulated learning goals and success criteria related to the California science and ELD standards. The guide also prompted teachers to later reflect on and document their use of formative assessment.

Phase three: Measuring changes in classroom practice. In order to document the efficacy of the collaboration, we collected data at two additional times: during the fall when the kindergarten teachers began to use the lesson-planning and reflection tools, and again in the spring, approximately four months after they had begun to use the new materials. A total of seventeen (five to thirty minutes each) science activities were observed and analyzed across the classrooms. We calculated the percentage of observed activities in which teachers made success criteria explicit to students, and we documented instances of teachers evoking evidence of student learning during the course of instruction. Lesson plans were collected from teachers, and one science lesson in each of the classrooms was videotaped.

Characteristics of Formative Assessment During the Baseline Year

Before any of the kindergarten teachers involved in the baseline year (phase one) had made conscious efforts to include formative assessment of science and language, 52 percent of observed science activities (aggregated across all four classrooms) contained teacher use of explicit success criteria for meeting science learning goals (see table 8.1). All teachers to greater or lesser degrees (ranging from 43 percent to 75 percent of observed activities in classrooms) included some success criteria for science. For example, all provided clear explanations of how students should conduct assigned tasks, and one teacher was observed to model exactly what she wanted her students to do. However, given the language learning needs of these young students, surprisingly just 10 percent of all the observed activities included teachers providing explicit success criteria for academic language learning goals. These ranged from not being observed in any of the activities in two of the classrooms to being observed at most in 25 percent of activities in another classroom. Teachers with a higher percentage of activities with success criteria for science also had the highest percentage of activities with success criteria for academic language learning goals. The percentage of success criteria

TABLE 8.1   Formative assessment in kindergarten: Usage and forms

	Phase 1	Phase 3 (early)	Phase 3 (late)
Explicit success criteria for science engagement (% of all observed activities)	52	67	100
Explicit success criteria for academic language use (% of all observed activities)	10	50	91
Ways teachers expressed science learning goals	Clear explanations of required tasks Modeling task completion	Clear explanations of required tasks	Clear explanations of required tasks Single out successful student as model Think aloud (model) during task demonstrations
Ways teachers expressed academic language learning goals	Word lists Labels	Word wall Sentence starters	Modeling pronunciation Sentence starters
Forms of formative assessment	Open-ended questions Students act out concepts Observing tasks	Diagrams for students to label Evaluating assigned work	Open-ended questions Prompting for vocabulary Evaluating assigned work Observing explanations to peers

used in one area appears to be related to the percentage used in another, which suggests a general pattern of success criteria usage rather than usage tied exclusively to a single content area.

Where success criteria were observed for language learning goals, teachers sometimes referred to word lists they wanted children to incorporate in their science tasks. One teacher modeled the labels to be used in the students' own science drawings. The four teachers used different forms of formative assessment to check for student understanding of science concepts and academic uses of language, including: (1) asking students open-ended questions, (2) asking students to act out their understanding using gestures and pantomime, and (3) observing students' work during assigned tasks.

Data from the baseline year of the project showed that while teachers engaged in a variety of formative assessment practices, they also missed opportunities for that assessment. Next, we describe patterns that we observed during the baseline year, with respect to setting learning goals, making success criteria explicit, and evoking evidence of student learning.

Setting learning goals. Lesson plans collected during the first year of the study revealed that teachers often had well-articulated science concept and language learning goals for children. For example, the teachers had clear ideas of what science concepts they wanted children to learn as well the accompanying academic vocabulary needed to support their learning. The teachers specified what they felt the important supporting concepts were, including "function of a root" and "parts of a root."

In the following interaction, drawn from a lesson observed during the baseline year, the teacher's goal was to review the concept of photosynthesis. Although photosynthesis is a highly complex and abstract process, and therefore a concept that is not typically taught in kindergarten, the teacher, Ms. Silva (a pseudonym), had modest learning goals, which made her lessons on photosynthesis more age-appropriate. With respect to science concept learning, the teacher's intent was to introduce the idea that leaves can produce their own food and in order to produce that food, leaves need sun, air, and water. With respect to academic language learning, the teacher's intent was to give children a chance to gain familiarity with specialized academic vocabulary (i.e., *glucose, energy, carbon dioxide,* etc.) that they will encounter again in later grades.

The children in Ms. Silva's class have been learning about photosynthesis. Silva begins today's lesson with a whole-group instructional period, during which she reviews what the children have learned about photosynthesis, using a diagram she has drawn on the white board.

> **Ms. Silva:** So everybody, you're a leaf. Ready?
> *[Ms. Silva adjusts her feet and stands up nice and tall with her hands by her side, pretending to be a leaf. The children, who are seated in front of her, sit up a little taller as well.]*
> **Ms. Silva:** You're getting the what?
> *[Ms. Silva points to the part of the diagram that represents energy from the sun.]*
> **A few children:** Energy.
> **Ms. Silva:** From the what?
> **Child:** The sun.

Ms. Silva: And then you get?

> [*Ms. Silva points to the part of the diagram that represents carbon dioxide.*]

Child: The carbon dioxide.

Ms. Silva: From?

Child: From the wind.

Ms. Silva: From the wind or the air. And then?

> [*Ms. Silva points to the part of the diagram that represents water.*]

A few children: The water.

Ms. Silva: The water. And then what does the leaf do?

> [*Ms. Silva wiggles her body, to represent the process of making glucose. The children follow her lead and wiggle their bodies as well.*]

Ms. Silva: It's making what? It starts making?

Child: Food.

Ms. Silva: Food. What is that food called?

Child: Glucose.

> [*Ms. Silva puts her hand to her ear and leans in towards the children to encourage them all to answer.*]

Ms. Silva: What is it?

Children: Glucose.

[Ms. Silva nods her head.]

Ms. Silva: It's almost like what?

A few children: Sugar water.

> [*Ms. Silva continues on in this fashion for a couple more minutes of review. Then she explains the small-group activities that the children will be engaging in.*]

Ms. Silva: So we're going to continue working on our representation of photosynthesis.

Ms. Silva: Some of you, I glued your leaves on another paper and you're going to show me on your leaf how photosynthesis works. You can use your resources to help you. OK, so you have to show me.

> [*Ms. Silva then holds up an example of one child's work for everyone to see.*]

Ms. Silva: Let's look at Roxanna's leaf. She's going to show me photosynthesis on her leaf. OK? . . . So here you're going to show me how photosynthesis works, OK?

> [*Ms. Silva holds up another example of a child's work.*]

Ms. Silva: And the same over here. Alexandra and Sherry, they used clay to show their representation of a leaf and they're going to go back and they're going to add how photosynthesis works with the clay.

Making success criteria explicit. We chose this excerpt because it exemplifies many of the lessons we observed during the first year of the project. Although as mentioned, the lesson plans we collected during the baseline phase suggested that teachers had clear goals and success criteria for children's learning, teachers often did not make their success criteria explicit to children. For example, in the excerpt, Silva explains to the children that they will be using a variety of media to represent photosynthesis, but her instructions are vague. She could have given children much more guidance about the level of detail she wanted children to include in their representations as well as her expectations for their academic language use. The success criteria would have been more explicit to children had she said something like, "I want you to represent photosynthesis. In your representations, I should be able to see glucose and I should be able to see all the different things your leaf needs to make glucose. I want you to really think hard about how you can represent the carbon dioxide in the air, the energy from the sun, and the water. Later, I will ask you about your representations, and I want you to try and use the new vocabulary we have learned to explain your representations to me." Importantly, teachers can continue to make the success criteria explicit and salient to children by providing guiding prompts as informal scaffolds during children's engagement in science activities. For example, in the excerpt, the teacher could have checked in with children as they were working and engaged children in conversations using increasingly close-ended prompts as necessary, such as, "Tell me about your representation. What does the leaf get from the sun? Do you remember the scientific word we use to describe the food that the leaf produces?"

Evoking evidence of student learning. During the first year of the project, we observed instances of teachers evoking evidence of student learning. As the preceding excerpt shows, teachers could ask children questions to assess whether they understood the concepts being taught. Questions, like those of Silva, allow teachers to check on how much specialized terminology has been retained during the lesson and clarify some early misconceptions.

IMPLEMENTING FORMATIVE ASSESSMENT OF SCIENCE AND ACADEMIC LANGUAGE LEARNING

The impact of implementing formative assessment of content and academic language during science instruction can be examined for its effects on teacher assessment practices and on growth in student science engagement and academic language use.

Impact on Teaching

Researchers made classroom observations in the fall of the third year of the project to determine practices with the kindergarten teachers who participated at phase three. These phase three (early) percentages are already higher than those reported for phase one of the project, most likely because this teaching staff had already been involved in discussion and some development of the new curricular tools, including formative assessment approaches during phase two. As table 8.1 also illustrates, the aggregate use of explicit success criteria for science learning goals changed to 67 percent of the activities (ranging from 33 percent to 100 percent across individual classrooms). The teacher who taught during all three years of the project used success criteria for science in 100 percent of observed activities, up from 75 percent in phase one. Teachers primarily used explicit success criteria by giving clear explanations of the science tasks they wanted students to carry out.

After these teachers had the chance to incorporate the new curricular tools into their everyday practices, researchers again made classroom observations (late in phase three). By this final phase of the project, the number of activities with overt science success criteria had increased to 100 percent, with all teachers now using clear explanations for carrying out tasks in all their activity settings we observed. Additional strategies included singling out and praising the performance of a student to serve as a model for others, and the use of reminders to include certain details while tasks were underway. One teacher used a think-aloud example of her own thought processes as she described plant parts and functions. This served as a model for the desired performance of her students (e.g., "I am looking for veins, the midrib that the food travels to . . .").

Use of success criteria for academic language learning goals was found in 50 percent of activities (ranging from 0 percent to 100 percent) in phase three (early) up from 10 percent at phase one, again with the teacher from phase one using success criteria for language at 100 percent, up from just 25 percent of her activities in phase one. Teachers directed students to use words on a *word wall*, an ongoing display of vocabulary cards that students have learned and can access at will as they continue their study, in order to accurately label their science sketches. They also gave students sentence "starters" that they expected to hear students use in their own talk about science phenomena (e.g., "I think that . . ." "I feel that . . ."). However, by phase three (late), 91 percent (ranging from 75 percent to 100 percent) of observed activities included explicit success criteria for academic language (the teacher from phase one sustained her use of success criteria for language across all observed activities). By the time the study was concluding, all teachers modeled correct pronunciation of new science terminology in English, which is not surprising given the students' Spanish primary-language backgrounds. They also continued to overtly model expected sentence starters for students (e.g., "I notice that . . .").

At phase three (early), there again appears to be a relationship between providing explicit success criteria for science and for academic language with the two teachers who used success criteria for science during all of their observed activities also using success criteria for language learning goals during all observed activities. The remaining teacher used success criteria for science in just 33 percent of observed activities and success criteria for language learning goals in no observed activities. At phase three (late), all teachers used success criteria in all observations for both types of learning, with the exception of one teacher who had a slightly lower percentage of activities (75 percent) with success criteria for language than for science (100 percent). Overall, this pattern of results supports the notion that using success criteria can be made a prevailing practice of formative assessment rather than remain tied a specific content area exclusively.

Teachers' chosen forms of formative assessment had also expanded by the close of the study to include: (1) asking students open-ended questions, (2) prompting for use of certain vocabulary, (3) evaluating students' assigned work, frequently representations of scientific processes or phenomena, and (4) asking students to explain their representations of scientific processes to a peer while the teacher listened. To summarize, our data show changes in formative assessment practices such that at baseline, teachers did not make their science and language success criteria explicit to children on many if not most occasions, but by the end of the project teachers consistently made their expectations for successful science and language learning overt.

Impact on Student Science Engagement and Academic Language Use

While the focus of this chapter has been on changes to teachers' formative assessment practices, we can bolster claims for the approach as a worthwhile endeavor with data collected on student science engagement and academic language use. Researchers rated student engagement in science content learning high during the majority of observed activities for all but one of the classrooms from the very start of the project. By the close of the project, they rated all observed activities in all the classrooms as exhibiting high student engagement in science. However, this uniformly high engagement could have been nonverbal (e.g., just getting on with tasks or responding to a request by pointing to diagrams, labels, etc.). Therefore, it is also important to know if language was supported to accompany high engagement in science content so students could both communicate their new science knowledge and demonstrate their academic language development.

We documented students' use of specialized academic vocabulary that is specific to a discipline (e.g., science terminology such as *embryo* and *seed coat*) and general academic vocabulary that cuts across disciplines (e.g., *explain, observe,* and *report*). We also documented students' engagement in scientific discourse that goes beyond the level of word usage to include the sentence and extended conversation levels. At the start of the project, students often used specialized science vocabulary, and this was a characteristic of every observed activity in each classroom by phase three (early) and sustained through to the end of the project. Much less ubiquitous and far more varied at the start of the project (and at the start of phase three) was student use of general academic vocabulary. However, by phase three (late), all classrooms on all occasions showed evidence of students also using general academic vocabulary.

Finally, there was great variation at the start of the project in the percentage of observed activities that included student science talk, but sentences and extended conversation were uniformly used by the start of phase three and then maintained through to the end of the project. At phase three (late), teachers prompted students to participate in science talk in a number of different ways by asking students to share their background knowledge (e.g., "My mom uses it [lettuce] in salad"), to report on their existing content knowledge (e.g., "The root is in the soil"), to recall their observations and their actions during tasks (e.g., "We saw veins in the leaves," "I cut the plant . . . I put the veins"), and to share their hypotheses (e.g., "The leaf is brown because it does not have water").

An Example of Impact on Teaching

During phase three, we observed many lessons in which teachers were skillfully integrating formative assessment into their science teaching. Figure 8.1 contains excerpts from a completed enhanced lesson plan. The questions prompted the teacher to explicitly detail the learning goals she set for language and science learning and make salient how she would know her students were meeting these goals.

We encourage readers, while reading the following interaction and examining the completed enhanced lesson plan excerpts in the text box, to reflect on the following three questions:

1. What were the science and language learning goals for this lesson?
2. What were the success criteria?
3. How did the teacher evoke evidence of student learning?

FIGURE 8.1   Lesson Planning and Reflection Guide

Pre-K–K Transitions Science Focus: Planning and Reflection

- *Setting learning goals:* Which student ideas will be built on from previous activities? What are the science concept learning goals? What are the language learning goals?

  - I started my lesson by asking my students this question: What do you think grows first after a seed is planted? I had pictures of the root system but I had *not* introduced them when I asked them this question. To my surprise some students were able to say, "The roots" (previous learning in action!). The science learning goals were for students to identify the different roots in the root system (primary root, secondary root, and root hairs) and to know their main function (to carry water, minerals, and nutrients to nourish the plant so that it can grow. The language learning goals were for students to use the new vocabulary while they were exploring the roots of Impatiens flowers.

- *Setting success criteria:* How will you know that learning goals were met?

  - I will know if the learning goals were met through their representations via block play, pipe cleaners, play dough, and sketches.

- *Evaluating learning goals:* Which science learning goals were met? What will you do differently next time? What student ideas emerged?

  - I feel the lesson went very well because the majority of the students were able to identify the three parts of the roots system and were able to tell me what their main function was. I will not use pipe cleaners as one of the representations because they were too flimsy and the student representations did not come out very clear for others to know what it was. The students asked the following questions: How does the water get up? Where does the water go? What happens when it doesn't get any more water?

- *Evaluating success criteria:* Were success criteria clear to students? Which success criteria were the right criteria for monitoring learning? Which were least helpful?

  - I feel that the success criterion was clear to the students because they had been exposed to the same expectations in the previous lesson of the seed parts. I did this on purpose because I wanted them to get comfortable with the scientific process and consistent practice is a good way to do it.

Source: Excerpts from a completed lesson plan.

All the children in the classroom are seated in a circle on the rug in front of the whiteboard. The teacher stands in front of them.

> *Teacher:* Good morning, boys and girls!
>
> *Children:* Good morning, teacher!
>
> *Teacher:* Good morning! Today we have a very exciting lesson about roots! Roots. Can you see the roots here?
>
> *[The teacher holds up a book with a picture of roots on the cover.]*
>
> *Teacher:* Can you show me, Isabel, where the roots are?
>
> *[The teacher holds the book in front of Isabel, and Isabel points to the roots.]*
>
> *Teacher: Very good. How about you, Carmen, can you show me where the roots are?*
>
> *[The teacher holds the book in front of Carmen, and Carmen points to the roots.]*
>
> *Teacher: That's right.*
>
> *[The teacher walks around the circle and asks three more children to identify the roots on the cover of the book.]*
>
> *[After several minutes of whole-group instruction and review have passed, the teacher explains the small-group activities she has prepared for the children.]*

Teacher: Today you're going to be looking at some plants—some flowers. They're called impatiens. And you're going to look like scientists.
[The teacher leans over and pretends to hold up a magnifying glass to her face as she scans the children in the room.]

Teacher: You're going to use your magnifying glasses and you're going to look for the primary root. And you're going to look for the secondary roots.
[As the teacher references the key vocabulary terms, she backs up to the diagram on the board and points to the corresponding parts of the root system as she reviews each word.]

Teacher: And then you're going to look for the tiny . . .
[The teacher pulls on her hair to give children a clue.]

Child: *Pellitos* (hairs)

Teacher: "Pellitos" in Spanish, and . . .

Child: Hairs.

Teacher: Hairs. Tiny root hairs.

Teacher: Now, that's not all we're going to do. Guess what? We are also going to try and make our own pictures of the roots growing out of the seed . . . I'll give you a black piece of paper, just like the one I got [the one she used to create the diagram on the board], except it's smaller. Right? It's not as big. And look—I made a drawing of a seed. You can make your seed any shape that you want because seeds come in different shapes, right? And then you are going to draw the primary root. And then what else?
[The teacher points at the secondary roots in the diagram on the board.]

Children: Secondary roots.
[Later, during small-group time, the teacher circles around the classroom, observing the children and asking them questions about their work. At some point, she goes to the block play area and asks the children questions about the block representations they have made.]

Teacher: Is this one yours, Julia? Let's see, sit down with it and show me. Show me what you've created. Tell me about your construction. Show me here. Where is the seed?
[Julia correctly identifies the part of her block construction that represents the seed.]

Teacher: OK. And where is the primary root?
[Julia mistakenly points to the root hairs in her block representation.]

Teacher: Are they primary? La primera que salio? (The first one to come out?)
[Julia correctly identifies the primary root in her block representation.]

Teacher: Yes. And where are the secondary roots?
[Julia correctly identifies the secondary roots in her block representation.]

Teacher: Yes. And where are the root hairs?

Teacher: Excellent. OK, let me take a picture of you and your construction.
[The teacher keeps these photographs of student representations as evidence of her formative assessment of their work and to later share student progress with parents.]

The preceding interaction and accompanying lesson plan excerpts exemplify several aspects of formative assessment. In her lesson plan, the teacher clearly communicates her science and language learning goals for the students in her class, as well as her success criteria, and her plans for formatively assessing her students' understanding through guided practice. The teacher in the excerpt is MaryLou Escobar, one of the chapter authors. By asking the students questions about their work, Ms. Escobar was able to determine whether they understood the root system (denoted by italics in the interaction). Specifically, the students were able to use their work pieces to walk her through their thought processes.

Lessons Learned

The implementation of the new resources for formative assessment of science and academic language learning coincided with changes in kindergarten teachers' formative assessment practices and in student outcomes. These changes included the increased use of explicit success criteria for science and language learning goals by teachers and an expanded repertoire of formative assessment strategies by the final observation point compared with baseline and early phase three characterizations of these practices for the school's kindergarten staff. Further study is needed in order to replicate these findings, and a larger set of classrooms will be needed before being able to definitively attribute improvements to the new resources developed here. But the project findings speak to the potential of formative assessment in changing teacher instructional practices and student learning outcomes. As Ms. Escobar explains, the power of formative assessment lies with "using formative assessments to help me to consistently gather evidence about my students' learning or lack of learning. By knowing where my students are in their learning, I can adapt my lessons and plan for differentiated instructional experiences that will fill in their individual gaps."

The results of this study suggest that there is a tendency to use success criteria across both science and language, if teachers were using success criteria at all. Even so, there was a bias toward a greater proportion of success criteria for science than for language learning goals until the project intervened with teacher lesson-planning and reflection guides that prompted the setting of overt success criteria in both areas of learning. Like the teachers in this project, other teachers may already be using explicit success criteria in the content areas, but to help young English language learners succeed in school, teachers must become aware of the need for salient success criteria for the academic language that is related to those content learning goals.

Also to help young English language learners succeed in kindergarten, we suggest teachers consider expanding the ways in which they express learning goals to students for both science and academic language, as well as consider expanding their repertoire of formative assessment types to include an array of methods for evaluating students' scientific understanding and language development. Teachers who document student performances when assessing formatively can use the resulting artifacts, observational notes, or photographic evidence to communicate student learning outcomes to parents in ways that tangibly tie outcomes to curricular goals and activities.

On occasion in this project, teachers' misconceptions of science were revealed as a result of the need to overtly set learning goals as part of the formative assessment process. This aspect of the approach may prove threatening to teachers. However, if learning goals can be set by teachers working together in collegial team settings, this aspect could be turned into a strength of the formative assessment approach. Teams are more likely than individuals to catch and address any content misconceptions during the setting of learning goals. Relatedly, such team planning can also address concerns with the appropriateness of chosen learning goals. This project suggested some science content (e.g., photosynthesis) that may have been challenging for young learners. Planning teams might be better equipped collectively to determine whether and how best to teach complex scientific concepts and what language might best be integrated to support these goals.

To conclude, the characteristics of the teacher-researcher collaboration that was adopted in order to bring about the reported changes are noteworthy for any future attempts at replication. This approach to formative assessment, while used with young children in this study, is also applicable within any classroom that is working to improve the quality of moment-to-moment oral formative feedback. The collaboration was built on the complementary expertise of teachers and researchers: teachers articulated knowledge of students, content, and instructional strategies, whereas study design, data collection techniques, and analysis were the purview of researchers. The principal also gave strong leadership, and the funding source awarded support jointly to the charter school agency and the researchers. The project outcomes may also have benefited from the focus on just science and related language to concentrate efforts most efficiently. And finally, the teachers showed a willingness to grow in areas of science-concept learning and instruction, academic language use and support, and new ways of conducting formative assessment with both. This willingness was irrespective of the amount of teaching experience they had and encouragingly suggests that schools will not need personnel with years of teaching experience in order to attempt a replication of this approach. Rather, what is important is that teachers demonstrate a strong desire to further their own and their young students' learning.

The final word goes to Ms. Escobar to whet appetites for assessing formatively and to engender just that desire in teachers everywhere:

> *Formative assessments are created collaboratively between the teacher and her/his students. The students actively participate in their learning and the teacher becomes the keen observer of their learning and then helps facilitate the learning by adapting the lessons to their current level. This might sound complicated and overwhelming but I assure you it is not. Just think of it as a puzzle. When you know the piece that is missing, you can find it more easily. Formative assessments provide you and your students with the missing pieces and now you can complete the puzzle together.*

We would first like to thank the students and teachers of the respective Early Childhood Center and Charter School classrooms. It goes without saying that their collaboration along with the support of administrative staff was paramount and full of the joy of sharing their teaching and learning experiences. We also extend a special thank you to graduate student researchers Anna Osipova and Stacey Beauregard who joined the project in its final year. This work was made possible by the support of a grant awarded jointly to the Para Los Niños agency, Alison Bailey, and Margret Heritage by the Center for Community Partnerships at UCLA. Finally, we would like to thank Penny E. Noyce and Daniel T. Hickey for the insightful feedback they provided to us and for their editorial acumen throughout.

CHAPTER 9

Two for One

Assessing Science and Literacy Using Writing Prompts

JENNIFER L. TILSON, ALISON K. BILLMAN,
SETH CORRIGAN, AND JACQUELINE BARBER

Recent efforts to improve educational opportunities for all students have resulted in a new consensus of what students are capable of learning as well as what students need to learn in order to be college-ready.[1] This new consensus is embodied in the Common Core State Standards documents for English language arts, as well as the emerging Next Generation Science Standards. The common core movement signals a course of change for our nation. This course of change is about clear and high expectations for all students. It also heralds an emphasis on teaching students to employ strategies to engage with the literacy demands of the disciplines, essentially calling for an integrated approach to instruction.

For instance, science teachers are expected to help students learn how to read informational science text, write science texts, and communicate effectively in the ways that scientists do.[2] The current draft of the Framework for New Standards for Science Education states, "learning [science] requires significant opportunities to talk the language of science and engineering, to write in its standard genres . . . every science or engineering lesson is a language lesson" (p. 5–20).[3] Additionally, for the first time, the importance of being able to read and understand science and technical text has been highlighted in English language arts standards, with a notable increase in emphasis on teaching even very young students to engage with information.[4] This represents an increase in the understanding that we live in a world that is full of constantly emerging information and that students need to be well versed in science ideas, processes, and ways of thinking in order to interpret and make sense of the information that they will encounter in school, work, and life. Not only do students need to understand scientific ideas and be able to interpret evidence, they also need to be able to formulate, organize, and communicate these ideas both orally and in writing.

To the extent that the new standards represent a shift from current approaches, there is much to do at the state, district, and classroom levels as educators transition from *adopting* the common core standards to *implementing* them. A central challenge for educators is learning how to align their instructional approaches, resources, and assessments to the new common core standards. Doing so is crucial in order to fully realize the promise of these focused and challenging standards and improve students' college and career readiness.

In order to implement the common core standards in ways that realize their potential, it will be imperative that teachers have curricula and assessments that align with ways of thinking about disciplinary learning and literacy in a more integrated way. In this chapter, we describe formative assessment tasks—with a particular focus on writing in the context of science—and highlight the features of these assessments that we believe are important to successfully support integrated teaching and learning. We begin by describing the curricular context of the formative assessments, the Seeds of Science/Roots of Reading integrated curriculum, and follow with examples and descriptions of writing prompts and scoring guides developed to complement the curriculum. We argue that in an integrated instructional approach, it is essential to also employ integrated assessments as a source of valuable information about student development of scientific understanding as well as skill in using the language of science to present these understandings in written form.

SEEDS OF SCIENCE/ROOTS OF READING INTEGRATED SCIENCE LITERACY CURRICULUM

Seeds of Science/Roots of Reading is an ongoing collaboration between the Lawrence Hall of Science and University of California, Berkeley, Graduate School of Education. The project explores the power of integrating science with literacy in meaningful and authentic ways while also emphasizing a balanced approach to learning in both domains. Three principles are central to this curriculum: (1) engage students in first- and second-hand investigations to make sense of the world; (2) strategically employ multiple learning modalities; and (3) capitalize on synergies between science and literacy. The synergies can be thought of as the sweet spots where science and literacy overlap.[5] For example, posing questions is pivotal in both domains. Posing questions before, during, and after reading is a comprehension strategy that can help readers make sense of text and inquire into ideas as they read. Similarly, scientists—like readers—pose questions to make sense of the natural world as they design and carry out investigations. While some questions may be answered during the investigation, new questions emerge as the scientist collects and analyzes data. This continual questioning drives science forward.

It has been our stance that the overlap between science and literacy—the places where the two domains share highly complementary learning goals or cognitive processes—provides instructional opportunities to support learning and development in both domains. Literacy skills and strategies—such as navigating informational text, using reading comprehension strategies, and learning science vocabulary—are those that students genuinely need in order to engage with and understand scientific ideas and make sense of their investigations. In addition to the alignment of an integrated approach with the Common Core State Standards, we are finding increasing evidence that teaching in an integrated way helps students learn both science and literacy better.

Integrated Formative Assessment

During the development of the Seeds of Science/Roots of Reading integrated science-literacy curriculum, it became clear that rather than assessing each domain separately, some formative assessments could—and should—capitalize on the integration of science and literacy. In practice, this meant developing assessments in which students were asked to demonstrate knowledge and skills across both domains. One piece of student work would then be scored with different focuses on student performance. For example, a single piece of student writing could be analyzed to gather information about students' science knowledge, writing organization, use of evidence, and vocabulary use.

To be meaningful and useful in meeting instructional and learning needs, we have found that integrated formative assessments must have four key characteristics. They come at the *right time* during a unit of study, they require the *right performance* from the students, and they are both *useful* and *time wise* for the teacher. Each characteristic is described next.

Right time. Integrated writing prompts work best if they fall at points in a unit of study when students have learned enough about a topic to have something to say in response to a question, but when there is still adequate instructional time to revisit and engage further with the ideas. We call these points *critical junctures*. A writing prompt might, for example, be given near the end of a two-week sequence of instruction that includes firsthand science investigations, reading informational science texts, and a focus on using evidence to support ideas in writing.

The following scenario is drawn from an integrated science and literacy unit on light in which the learning goals include: (1) developing understanding of the concept that all visible materials reflect light, and (2) developing facility with the science practice of supporting scientific ideas and claims with evidence. In this lesson sequence, students first investigate how light behaves by using a flashlight and materials such as foil, felt, plastic, and wood. Students record their observations and subsequently use the observations as evidence in a discussion to argue whether or not they think all materials reflect light. Next, students informally write their initial ideas about which of the materials reflected light, citing the evidence they previously discussed. Students then read a book that explains how humans see—light is reflected off objects and travels to the eye. The class then discusses how the ideas in the text change their understanding of reflection. In the subsequent investigation they make diagrams to explain their new understandings of how light travels to the eye. This is a critical juncture—the *right time* to administer a formative writing assessment. At this point, students have had experiences conducting investigations exploring reflection and practice constructing and defending oral arguments *before* they are asked to respond to a writing prompt. Students are now asked to write a response to the question, *do nonshiny materials reflect light?* In writing about this topic, students bring to bear evidence from their firsthand experiences—investigating with flashlights and materials—and evidence from their secondhand experiences—reading about how people see.

The teacher then uses science and writing scoring guides to examine students' writing to understand progress toward the learning goals—To what depth do students understand that all visible materials reflect light? Do they provide multiple examples of this phenomenon at work? Can they bring evidence from both their reading and their firsthand investigations to bear when explaining reflection? Answers to evaluative questions like these help teachers use student responses to determine the progress of the class toward the learning goals and plan instruction accordingly.

Teachers can identify critical junctures in their own science curriculum by determining at what point students have had chances to explore big ideas, and by identifying literacy opportunities that are inherent in the process of scientific investigation. As
illustrated in our example, the critical juncture came when students had science and
literacy experiences that allowed them to use evidence from various sources to support
claims. Those experiences were necessary background to engage with the assessment.
Critical junctures can also be thought of as points beyond which it might not make
sense to proceed if students do not have particular understandings. For example, in a
unit on weather, students need to first understand that there is invisible water vapor in
the air before they can effectively learn about why it rains. In such a unit, an assessment might occur after students have had experience detecting water vapor as humid-
ity in the air, but before students investigate clouds and precipitation.

Right performance. Integrated formative assessments need to be included at the *right time*
during the course of study in order to assess the *right performance*. *Right performances* are
those that are aligned with and measure progress toward understanding curricular and
standards-based expectations. Formative assessments in Seeds of Science/Roots of Reading are designed for students to demonstrate science knowledge and literacy skills. In
terms of science content, the assessments that yield the greatest and richest information
are those in which students are expected to communicate what they have learned about
the big ideas and core science concepts in the unit of study. While specific examples are
often used to build conceptual understanding, it is important to remember that the
more important goal is for students to understand big ideas in science. For instance, in a
soil habitats unit, students might study isopods—a common decomposer that lives in
the soil. Students observe them firsthand in terrariums as well as read about their behaviors and body structures. Although there are many important reasons to learn about
isopods, the bigger conceptual idea drawn out in this unit is the concept of *adaptations*—a central idea in biology. To elicit the *right performance*, an integrated assessment
question or prompt should be tied to the key concept—that all organisms have adaptations that help them survive in their habitats. In demonstrating an unfolding understanding of the concept of adaptation, a student might draw from the examples used to
build an understanding of adaptation, in this case, the isopod.

In terms of literacy, the assessment needs to require students to employ writing
skills they have had opportunities to practice. Eliciting the right literacy performance
requires assessment prompts that define the boundaries of the student response and
that reference the writing skills that respondents are expected to employ. For example,
in the soil habitat unit, students create a piece of informational writing that is based on
their observations of isopods. Students are prompted to include a description of the
organism's adaptations and explain how these adaptations help the organisms survive
in their soil habitat, as well as a detailed sketch of an isopod that depicts the adaptations described in writing. Through this piece, students demonstrate not only their
understanding of science ideas, but also their ability to organize these ideas in writing
and display their understanding visually through drawing.

Usefulness. It stands to reason that assessments that elicit the *right performance* from
students are more likely to be useful to teachers because teachers are able to under-

stand to what degree students understand key ideas. However, in the case of formative assessment, usefulness also extends to how well the assessment provides information that can guide adjustments to instruction. In the example of the unit on light, if a teacher evaluates students' writing and discovers that many include just one source of evidence in their response, she can plan to provide additional instruction to support students' use of evidence in their writing. This may include an instructional emphasis on the importance of including evidence from multiple sources, more practice gathering different pieces of evidence, and supports to help students include and organize evidence in writing.

To be useful, an assessment and scoring system also needs to provide discrete information that teachers can easily interpret and then translate into instructional plans that will support or extend learning opportunities for a wide range of student achievement levels. Integrated formative assessments can provide opportunities to look for evidence of student progress on more than one skill or idea at a time. Teachers can think of this as evaluating student work on different *dimensions*. In the unit on soil habitats, a teacher might look for student understanding of science ideas about *adaptations* in their writing. She might also look to see to what degree students are able to use key science vocabulary such as *adaptation*, *survive*, *habitat*, and *isopod* in their writing, or the extent to which students use evidence to support claims. In this example, one piece of student writing is assessed with three or more dimensions—science content understanding, science vocabulary use, and the use of evidence. These dimensions can shift based on the assessment needs of the teacher and the class at a particular point in time. Assessing student work on multiple dimensions can provide information that may be used to identify the learning needs of a whole class of students, as well as to identify subgroups of students within the class who have similar strengths or needs in order to plan for targeted enrichment or reteaching opportunities.

Time wise. A good assessment serves no purpose if it is not practical to administer. Teachers are under enormous time pressure in the classroom—there never seems to be enough time to accomplish all of the myriad teaching and learning tasks. We believe that integrated formative assessments should *save* teachers time, not add to an already crowded school day. Therefore, it is important that assessments be integrated with the curriculum in ways that capitalize on authentic tasks students are already completing in the course of their learning. In addition, selecting dimensions on which to focus (as described earlier) is an efficient way to approach assessment for the teacher without overassessing the students. The same piece of student writing can be examined for multiple student outcomes, but these outcomes might be different at the beginning of the school year than at the end, depending on the instructional needs of the class. Finally, the tools that teachers use to evaluate student learning should be clear and concise, and should tie very closely with learning goals, standards, and expectations. Examples of these tools—scoring rubrics and writing checklists, along with examples of their use—are discussed in the remainder of this chapter.

The Tools

Formative assessment tools include the assessment items themselves as well as scoring guides and checklists designed to evaluate responses on a range of dimensions. All of these elements work together to help teachers get as clear a picture as possible of what students know.

To demonstrate the use of a set of formative assessment tools, we have included two samples of student writing from the Seeds of Science/Roots of Reading curriculum. The first sample (see figure 9.1) is a third-grader's piece from a unit on soil habitats that answers the question, *Why is soil important for plants?* The second sample, shown in figure 9.2, is a fourth-grader's explanation written in response to the question, *Do non-shiny materials reflect light?* Through analysis of these student examples, we hope to provide a picture of how the formative assessment tools provided in this chapter work in practice, and how one piece of student writing can be evaluated on multiple dimensions. The first of these dimensions is science content.

FIGURE 9.1   Third-grader's writing sample

Directions. Write the question that you will write about in the space labeled "My Question." Then write about your question. Illustrate about your writing in the space provided.

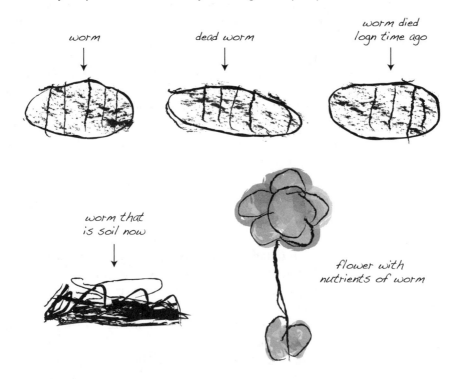

My Question: *Why is soil important for plants?*

Soil gives nutrients to plants. When nutrients get to roots the plant grows stronger. Funguses can help give nutrients too it breaks things down and things break down turn into soil.

Source: Seeds of Science/Roots of Reading, *Terrarium Investigations.* Copyright © 2004 by The Regents of the University of California.

FIGURE 9.2   Fourth-grader's writing sample

Do Non-Shiny Things Reflect Light?

Write an explanation that answers the question "Do non-shiny things reflect light?" Include a claim and support it with evidence. Make an illustration that supports your thinking.

Non-shiny things reflect light. For instance, when we did our investigation we saw that wood reflected light. In addition, the reflected light shone on the table. Similary, the moon reflects the light from the sun. Therefore, we can see it from Earth. Ive can conclude that non shiny things reflect.

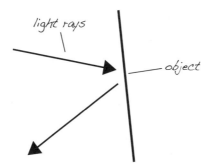

Science scoring guides. Scoring guides, also called rubrics, can be an essential tool for identifying student understanding and areas for future instruction. Rubric-based scoring takes many forms. A curriculum program may include very specific scoring guides, one for each assessment item or task. These specific scoring guides have the advantage of being highly targeted and detailed; the disadvantage is that it can be difficult for teachers to engage with a new scoring guide each time an assessment is called for. Specific scoring guides are also more difficult to share with students, as they are less generalizable and must be introduced anew with each task. The other extreme is providing a general scoring guide that can be used with any prompt regardless of the topic students are studying. While these general scoring guides can be easier to learn initially, they do little to convey sufficient information about the degree of scientific understanding that should be expected from students. We have found in our work with students and teachers that the most effective science-content scoring guides are tied to key science ideas (rather than individual assessments), and that the levels of scoring reveal the typical stages of understanding (partial understanding and misunderstandings) of scientific phenomena.

Therefore, we designed the science scoring guides in Seeds of Science/Roots of Reading to take a middle-of-the-road approach—they are neither very general nor specific to just one prompt. Rather, the scoring guides can be used for a range of prompts related to a concept. An example of this can be seen in table 9.1, which shows a scoring guide for the topic *decomposition*. This scoring guide is organized into levels of understanding from 1–4, as follows: (1) represents *inaccurate understanding*, (2) represents *partial understanding*, (3) represents *appropriate understanding*, and a score of (4) represents *beyond expectations*. The key concepts associated with the topic of the scoring guide are

TABLE 9.1   Science Content Scoring Guide for the topic, *decomposition*

Scoring Level	Key concept: process of decomposition	Key concept: role of decomposers
4 Beyond expectations	Student describes how dead things are broken down (decay) and links decomposition to detailed and varied evidence of decomposition.	Student provides examples to support the claim that decomposers help enrich the soil by making nutrients available to plants and refers to their role in the nutrient cycle.
3 Appropriate understanding	Student describes how dead things are broken down (decay) or links decomposition to detailed and varied evidence of decomposition.	Student describes how decomposers help enrich the soil by providing nutrients for plants.
2 Partial understanding	Student defines decomposition and/ or provides irrelevant evidence.	Student describes a decomposer but does not link the organism to providing nutrients.
1 Inaccurate understanding	Student describes observations he has made but does not like observations to decomposition or decomposers. Student may describe decomposition or decomposers inaccurately.	Student repeats the prompt or provides an inaccurate description.

shown across the top—process of decomposition and role of decomposers. Note that a scoring guide might have more than one key concept if there are multiple parts to a scientific concept, as in table 9.1.

Science scoring guides can help teachers anticipate and identify levels of student understanding and make instructional plans for further teaching, as in the following examples. In figure 9.1, the student has identified—in writing and in the accompanying illustration—the process by which the plant gets nutrients from the soil. The student work demonstrates an understanding of the way in which organisms break down, become part of the soil, and subsequently provide nutrients to plants. While the writing shows understanding of different aspects of decomposition and parts of the nutrient cycle, it is more focused on describing soil and its importance for plants. Even so, it demonstrates appropriate understanding of both the process of decomposition and the role of decomposers (a score of 3 on the rubric scale).

The writing prompt shown in figure 9.2 is focused on the physical science concept that all materials reflect light. A scoring guide for this concept, and the related idea that all materials absorb light, can be found in table 9.2. This student has demonstrated his understanding both in writing and through his illustration, a ray diagram that shows a beam of light from a flashlight reflecting off an object. The writing provides specific examples of reflection and indicates that the student understands that nonshiny objects such as wood and the moon reflect light. The illustration indicates that this student is beginning to generalize the concept of reflection to all objects. Thus, this piece can be said to demonstrate appropriate understanding (a score of 3 on the rubric scale).

Teachers can use science scoring guides or rubrics from a variety of sources as part of a formative assessment system—for example, scoring guides may be included with

TABLE 9.2   Science content scoring guide on the topic, *reflection and absorption of light*

Scoring level	Key concept: When light is blocked by a material light is both reflected and absorbed.
4 Beyond expectations	Student includes details to support understanding of interactions with materials when the path of light is blocked.
3 Appropriate understanding	Student cites evidence of reflection and/or absorption of light. Student accurately describes and records the path of light when it is reflected and/or absorbed.
2 Partial understanding	Student cites evidence of reflection and absorption of light. OR Student describes how path of light is blocked when light is reflected or absorbed by a material.
1 Inaccurate understanding	Student describes alternate conceptions about what happens when light is blocked by certain materials (only shiny things reflect light, transparent materials do not absorb light).

published curriculum materials or they may be part of school or district developed assessments. Scoring guides should be *useful* in providing clear information about the development of student understanding as related to key science ideas. And, scoring guides are more likely to be *time wise* if they can be used with a variety of prompts and tasks, but are not overly general.

Science writing checklist. The science writing checklist (see figure 9.3), developed by the Seeds of Science/Roots of Reading curriculum development team, provides opportunities to examine a piece of writing for key characteristics of science informational text. The checklist guides teachers in their examination of students' (1) writing organization, (2) use of evidence to develop ideas, and (3) vocabulary and use of language. Taken together, these elements provide a window into students' use of scientific language to express their science understanding.

Writing organization. Many students (and adults!) struggle with writing organization. This complex skill involves providing readers with a logical progression in which one idea follows from the next. In figure 9.1, the student has organized ideas about plants getting nutrients from soil into a single paragraph. The first sentence states this main idea of the piece. The ideas in the piece are closely related to each other and no irrelevant information is included; however, the relationship of the sentences one to another may not be entirely clear to the reader. The piece lacks a conclusion. A next instructional step for this student (and likely others who need to master this element of writing) could be to model conclusions and ask students to practice writing them.

In figure 9.2, we can see that the student's writing is organized into a single paragraph. The answer to the question, also called the claim, is clearly supplied in the first sentence. The body of the piece presents ideas (first about the observations of light as it strikes wood, then the information about how we see reflected light from the moon) that are related. The conclusion "Ive [sic] can conclude that non shiny things reflect" wraps up the piece and brings the writing to a close.[6]

FIGURE 9.3   Science writing checklist

Key	Description
+	Effectively addressed this component.
✔	Only partially addressed this component.
–	Did not address this component.
N/A	The directions/format does not lend itself to incorporating this component.

Writing organization

	Indicate +, ✔, –, N/A
Ideas are organized into paragraphs.	
Beginning clearly states what the piece will be about.	
Body of the piece presents a group of related ideas.	
Ending summarizes key ideas and/or brings the writing to a close.	

Use of evidence to develop ideas

	Indicate +, ✔, –, N/A
Multiple pieces of evidence are used to support ideas.	
Evidence included is relevant to information requested in the prompt.	
Ideas fit together logically.	
Visual features (such as diagrams or drawings with captions) support or extend the evidence provided.	

Vocabulary and use of language

	Indicate +, ✔, –, N/A
Topic-specific vocabulary is incorporated.	
Word choice shows an awareness of purpose (e.g., to explain, to describe, to compare, etc.).	

Use of evidence to develop ideas. Making evidence-based claims is the heart of science; supporting ideas with evidence is at the heart of good informational writing. When evaluating students' writing in science, teachers should pay close attention to how students are using evidence to support their ideas. Often, students will focus on only one source or piece of evidence and fail to take all of the available evidence into account. Conversely, some students may list evidence and many ideas in their writing, but not attend to how these pieces fit together to make a coherent explanation. Using evidence in a way that shows awareness of audience and clarity is a skill that takes time to develop. Examining students' science writing throughout the course of a school year can help teachers identify specific needs in this area.

In figure 9.1, the student explains that plants get nutrients from the soil and that the breaking down of material contributes to getting nutrients to the plant. Multiple and relevant ideas are included; the piece could be improved if the student linked the ideas together more logically. The piece lacks a strong tie between the question—*Why is soil important for plants?*—and the response provided.

In figure 9.2, the student is drawing upon evidence from two different sources, thus meeting the expectation that multiple pieces of evidence be used to support ideas. He has experienced light reflecting off wood and has observed this light shining on a table. The phrase "when we did our investigation we saw . . ." lets the reader know that this evidence has come from the writer's firsthand experience. This student also knows that the moon, which is made of dull rock, appears bright to us because it reflects light from the sun. The source of this information is not made clear. The piece could be improved if the student explicitly stated that he, for instance, read this information in book. A teacher might also suggest to this student that he include more evidence, citing one more example to back up his claim.

Students should not only use evidence in their writing, but ensure that the evidence make sense to the reader by ensuring that the connections between evidence claims are clear. Both ideas—wood is not shiny and yet it reflects light, and the moon is not shiny yet it reflects light—are clearly relevant to the prompt. The student's use of transition words helps make the piece clear and readable (note that using transition words was part of the lesson during which students wrote this piece). Words such as *for instance* and *similarly* help the evidence fit together logically so one idea flows into the next. And, in this case, the illustration supports the student's ideas by providing a general illustration of the scientific principle he describes in the piece.

Vocabulary and use of language. In an integrated curricular approach, it can be useful to think of words as concepts. Words, after all, are simply labels for concepts and ideas. As students investigate the natural world through their firsthand experiences and through reading, they develop understandings about scientific concepts such as adaptations, the reflection of light, erosion, ecosystems, and weather patterns, and so on. Regardless of what topic students are investigating, their conceptual development includes development of understandings about words. Writing prompts provide rich opportunities for students to use the science vocabulary they have been learning for an authentic purpose—to share and explain their thinking. Therefore, one element of student writing that can yield fruitful information for teachers is individual students' use of vocabulary.

The science writing checklist allows teachers to take a quick look at students' use of vocabulary in their writing. In figure 9.1, we can be fairly confident that this student understands the word *nutrients*, since she has written that "the plant grows stronger," but we may want to look at how the student uses this word in other unit activities, such as oral discourse, to be sure. As evidenced in her illustration as well as in her writing, this student has a command of the word *soil*. However, while the student clearly exhibits understanding of the process of decomposition and the role of decomposers, she uses neither word in her writing, instead using the term *break down* instead of *decompose*. This suggests that she may have an understanding of the process of decomposition but has not yet associated the scientific term with this process. We can say that this piece begins to incorporate some topic-specific vocabulary, but the student could use support in expanding her use of words related to decomposition.

Conversely, the student in figure 9.2 demonstrates active control over the word *reflect*, which he has used throughout, instead of choosing the everyday term *bounce off*. Occasionally, some students may even include a hefty dose of scientific terms in their writing, without an apparent understanding of what they mean. This can happen at the beginning of a unit of instruction, as students are just beginning to learn new terms; we have found that a continued focus on using scientific vocabulary to accurately explain ideas in oral and written discourse counteracts this phenomenon.

In addition to the inclusion of topic-specific vocabulary in writing, it is helpful to know which words students are using and how often. Teachers can get a good sense of which words students understand conceptually by keeping a list of core science vocabulary from a unit alongside as they score student writing (for example, words taught in the soil habitats unit by the time the assessment is given and that we might expect to be in this piece of writing are *soil, organism, nutrient, habitat, decompose, decomposition*, and *decomposer*). A tally of the vocabulary words students have used in their writing can be a quick way to identify the words students understand well and the words that may require more instruction or practice.

As we have demonstrated, student writing can be evaluated on multiple dimensions at once. Looking at student work in different dimensions can be thought of as different lenses—ways to look at a piece that change slightly depending on the focus. Students may be strong in one dimension and weaker in another—for example, they may have well-organized writing that shows little grasp of scientific concepts, or writing that is scientifically accurate and complete yet uses everyday language instead of scientific terms or is poorly structured. Even a quick read through student writing, when a specific lens is applied, can yield information about instructional next steps. Teachers need not attend to all possible dimensions for each piece of writing; rather, choosing a few on which to focus can provide information for providing targeted feedback to individual students as well as inform instructional plans for the class or small group.

Impact on Students

Through formative assessments of students' writing, researchers have been able to examine the characteristics of students' written pieces, see how they changed over time, and learn the extent to which integrated science and literacy instruction results in greater student gains in science writing. In a recently conducted efficacy study of the Seeds of Science/Roots of Reading curriculum for grades three through four, students in two groups of classrooms were compared. Teachers in the treatment group taught a Seeds of Science/Roots of Reading unit, and teachers in the control group taught the same science content, but used a different curriculum. In the study, all students responded to a writing prompt before and after instruction. Using a carefully developed rubric, the student responses were scored along several dimensions, including science content, use of evidence, strength of introduction, strength of conclusion, clarity, and vocabulary (figure 9.3).[7] On each of the dimensions, students using the Seeds of Science/Roots of Reading integrated curriculum outperformed students in the control classrooms.[8] Similar positive results have also been found for grades four through five English language learner students in a smaller study of 115 students.[9]

Potential Barriers to Implementation

While there is a growing body of evidence supporting use of formative writing assessments, there also exist several barriers to their widespread implementation in the classroom. A long-standing barrier to teachers' implementation of formative assessments is the time required to score and interpret the assessments. Supporting teachers' *time-wise* use of formative assessment should include helping them to become strategic in choosing assessments—it is unnecessary or inefficient to use every assessment in a curriculum program or to assess students at every available opportunity. It is important to understand when to focus in on elements of student work that will yield the most relevant information for a particular class at a particular point during a unit of study, as well as when it is expedient to focus in on elements that align with district or school initiatives.

One example of focusing on a select number of learning goals comes from a large, urban school district that has begun implementing the Seeds of Science/Roots of Reading curriculum in its summer school program. The district's goal was to increase the academic achievement of students who are typically assigned to summer school. A large number of these students are English language learners with a need to develop oral language and vocabulary. To respond to this need, the district chose to focus one of its assessment efforts on vocabulary growth as measured in student writing (as well as by a summative vocabulary assessment). The district also chose to focus on science content understanding in order to gauge the extent to which the summer school program resulted in acquiring content knowledge beyond that learned during the school year. This example demonstrates decision making at a district level. But this type of thinking and decision making holds true for selecting the aims of assessment at the school or classroom level as well. We want to underscore that it is important that assessments be targeted to meet particular priorities related to student needs and learning goals. Selecting assessments based on priorities and needs will minimize the amount of time spent administering assessments and ensure that time spent is well spent because it provides useful results.

Whether a curriculum program provides a formative assessment system with items and scoring guides or not, teachers can capitalize on integrated formative assessment methods like those we describe here.

First, capture the *right time*. Identify one or more critical junctures in the curriculum, situated after students have had some rich foundational learning experiences that they need to understand key concepts, but before moving on to subsequent concepts that build on those ideas. Teachers can ask: Is this the right time to assess students' progress? Have the students had multiple opportunities to learn about the big idea? Have they had multiple opportunities to communicate evidence-based claims?

Second, develop the *right performance*. Select a writing prompt that provides students with the opportunity to make a claim and support it with evidence. Teachers can ask: Does the prompt outline expectations in a way that helps students understand what content should be represented in the response and what key elements or characteristics the response should have?

Third, ensure that the prompt will provide *useful* information to the teacher as part of her instructional plan. Teachers can ask: Will evaluating student responses to this prompt provide information about students' progress toward the learning goal I am concerned with? Will it help inform my instructional decisions?

Fourth, be *time wise*. Remember that fewer assessments can be a better time investment. Teachers can ask: What lens(es) do I want to use to assess this work? Can I use this one piece of writing to assess multiple goals?

The writing checklist supplied in this chapter can be used for any science writing prompt. Teachers can use initial experiences evaluating student work to develop scoring guides for particular science concepts. Reading student work will give a sense of students' partial understandings. After implementing an assessment, teachers can revisit these questions to reevaluate and refine the prompt and any scoring guides in preparation for use the next time the topic is taught.

We acknowledge that time is at a premium in today's classrooms and that the pressures related to time may be a barrier to implementing this type of assessment. While we support using assessment-guided instruction, we do not endorse overassessing students. Teachers should carefully select opportunities for assessment and also choose which of those opportunities to deeply evaluate. In some situations, it is possible that an informal reading of student responses will provide enough information to get a sense of the class's progress as a whole. In another scenario, a teacher may have more concerns regarding the progress of a subset of students and may save time by evaluating that subset of responses deeply while evaluating the rest of the groups' responses more informally.

CONCLUSION

The Common Core State Standards movement has increased the importance of integrating disciplinary learning with literacy. As instruction shifts to meet this new vision, so too must assessment. Effective, assessment-guided instruction involves integrated formative assessments that provide *right time* and *right performance* tasks that are also *useful* and *time wise* for teachers. Using open-ended, yet clearly directed writing prompts yields rich information to inform instructional decisions related to disciplinary knowledge, language, and literacy. These open-ended writing prompts should be tied to students' conceptual learning, access big ideas in science, and allow enough flexibility for students to respond using the language of science they have been learning. Students should have enough experience through firsthand investigations and reading to allow them to leverage evidence to support their ideas. And, as we have demonstrated, student writing is a valuable means for assessing both science-content knowledge and scientific language use, when these different dimensions are examined simultaneously.

Scoring student writing on several dimensions is *useful* in helping teachers get a clear picture of areas of strength and weakness and support subsequent planning for instruction. Assessment of science writing is *time wise* for teachers and for students, when this writing is an authentic task that allows students the opportunity to demonstrate what they have learned both about key science ideas and about the practice of communicating ideas clearly in writing. Integrated curriculum and assessments provide students with real reasons to write to share their evidence, findings, and ideas.

CHAPTER 10

Shared Data

Technology-Enabled Formative Assessment in the Science Classroom

DANIEL DAMELIN AND KIMBERLE KOILE

Science teachers engage students in examining and explaining ideas on a daily basis, encouraging students to experiment; to collect, analyze, and present data; and to build understanding through classroom conversation and scientific debate. Technology has transformed these activities. Now when students investigate scientific concepts, they can collect data via digital sensors, analyze data using sophisticated computer tools, and interact with computational models of physical phenomena. In addition, technology can help teachers collect and assess a wide range of student work with greater frequency than was previously possible. Technology can support formative assessment by allowing teachers to use data about student work to make informed decisions regarding instructional practice and content. Such data can be used during class, between classes, or between uses of curriculum units. Regardless of which time scale is chosen, however, the amount of information that technology-enabled assessment makes available to teachers and students can be enormous. The challenge is not in collecting such information, but rather in managing and constructing meaning from the information, and using that meaning to guide teaching and learning.

The two projects described in this chapter, Concord Consortium's Rhode Island Information Technology Experiences for Students and Teachers (RI-ITEST) and Logging Opportunities in Online Programs for Science (LOOPS) projects, take on that challenge. Both projects provide examples of using technology to support formative assessment through which meaning is constructed from the wide variety of student work in science classrooms. These projects go beyond the current generation of technology-enabled formative assessment systems commonly known as "clicker" systems. Such systems have been extremely successful in providing teachers with formative feedback, but data collected with such systems are limited to multiple-choice or matching questions. RI-ITEST and LOOPS technologies enable the collection and use of a wide variety of artifacts that are created in real time as students interact with computational models, diagrams, graphs, and open-response questions. The LOOPS technology also logs information about student actions as the artifacts are created, providing insight into the method or depth of student exploration. We discuss the goals, implementation details, results, and lessons learned from each project in the following sections.

A FOUNDATION FOR RI-ITEST: THE MOLECULAR WORKBENCH

The RI-ITEST project was the culmination of ten years of National Science Foundation (NSF)–funded work on model development, pedagogical design, and teacher professional development, all beginning with the creation of the core software tool—the Molecular Workbench. The goal of the Molecular Workbench team was to develop a way for students to use an inquiry approach in learning about and making sense of the unseen atomic world. When the project started, the only tools available to chemistry teachers for helping students understand the dynamic nature of the atomic world were videos, static images, handmade drawings, and the proverbial waving of hands. The team's experience in chemistry classes and with chemistry students made it clear that students' understanding was limited. What students really needed was a way to do "experiments" at the atomic level—to manipulate molecules in the way they could touch beakers and balances, to "see" atoms and molecules in motion. At this time, there were no interactive simulations geared toward middle and high school students, so it was fortuitous that work on the Molecular Workbench had now begun. The software that we envisioned would allow students to perform virtual experiments with atoms and molecules, and to see the results of their experiments in real time.[1]

The initial implementation of the Molecular Workbench was very crude compared to the full activity development and assessment system into which it has evolved today. It was first piloted in an eighth-grade science class. We handcrafted each simulation as its own software application that depicted a model driven by a molecular dynamics engine and that included a set of controls for students to adjust model parameters. In this first eighth-grade classroom, the topic was the kinetic theory of matter—the idea that atoms and molecules are in continual motion and that this motion is related to temperature. One of our simplest interactive models involved a simulation populated with atoms, a slider to allow students to adjust the temperature of the system, and the ability to trace the path of selected atoms. Students observed how atoms move (in a straight line until colliding with another atom), that this resulted in seemingly "random" movement for any particular atom, and that the speed of the atoms correlated with the temperature of the system.

For three weeks, these kinds of models were interspersed with the teacher's traditional pedagogical tools, such as videos, handouts, demos, and labs. Students enthusiastically engaged with the Molecular Workbench models and reported that they felt models helped them learn. The teacher also commented on how much students seemed engaged while using the models. While it was evident that some students incorporated their experiences with the Molecular Workbench into class discussions and other types of assessment, it was not clear exactly what each individual learned from the models or where the models themselves might have been sources of misunderstanding. Because the models were not embedded in a context that included ways to probe student knowledge, and because there were no mechanisms for feeding such information back to the teacher, the teacher was unable to efficiently use the Molecular Workbench for adjusting classroom lessons or for addressing any lingering student confusion. This situation inspired the developers of the project to create a formative assessment system that would inform both teachers and curriculum writers, fostering improvements in the classroom efficacy of the model-based activities, while simultaneously promoting positive changes in the underlying materials.

Despite the positive initial responses from both teachers and students, the Molecular Workbench team felt that it needed a better way to gather data about student learning, both for research purposes and to give teachers deeper insight about the level of understanding being achieved by the class as a whole and by each individual student. Over the next series of projects, we added several features to the Molecular Workbench environment, including the following enhancements in the area of assessment and feedback:

- A much more flexible authoring system that allowed teachers and students to construct their own model-based activities with embedded assessments.
- A selection of various assessment types used to gauge student understanding.
- A system for electronically collating student work and making this feedback available to teachers and researchers.

Our initial data-collection efforts used only classroom observations to determine how the model-based materials were working. While this method is still a crucial tool, the amount of data that could be collected was limited. Developing a system to electronically monitor student interactions and answers to embedded assessments would greatly expand our ability to collect data from large numbers of diverse students, teachers, and classrooms. So the Molecular Workbench team first developed typical assessment items such as multiple choice, multiple selection (which are like multiple choice but with more than one correct answer possible), and open response questions. The initial purpose of these assessments was to provide information to researchers and teachers about how the models and activities were affecting student learning. Researchers enjoyed greater access and ease of data collection to quickly inform materials development, while teachers felt the added assessments would provide a way to hold students accountable for their work and to better guide pedagogical decisions regarding what to do next, once students had completed a particular activity.

Although the original purpose of the assessments was to provide information to researchers and teachers, the Molecular Workbench team quickly received feedback from both teachers and students that students wanted a way to self-check their understanding as they progressed through an activity. This feedback led to the inclusion of a "check answer" button on many of the multiple-choice questions. At first, just a "correct" or "incorrect" indication was given, but this feature soon evolved to include custom feedback to students based on their particular choices. Each choice could be scripted to provide feedback that included text, images, or even changes in the state of the model to help illustrate a point or reveal a hidden component. Typically, incorrect responses would call up suggestions for other experiments to try with the model, further engaging students in using the model to deepen their understanding. Hints such as these helped students to see subtleties in the models that they might not have otherwise noticed, while helping others to better interpret models, improving their responses to formative and summative assessments.

Although the check-answer feature provided formative feedback to students, it reduced the number of items researchers and teachers could use to gauge student understanding, since students could now work with the models and activities until they got the right answer. To counteract this reduction, we included open response questions, concluded activities with a summary page of questions that had no check-answer buttons, and developed a new question type we dubbed the "image question."

Image questions were an outgrowth of using visual tools. Prior to the use of image questions, we would ask students to describe in open response items what they saw in the model and to explain how the model demonstrated a particular concept. Much student writing would be devoted to describing what they saw, rather than to interpreting a particular model state. To better focus on conceptual understanding, we added the ability to take a snapshot of a model, and we provided tools for students to annotate the snapshot with text, arrows, and shapes. In figure 10.1, for example, the student has annotated a ball in the left screen to show that it has little movement and low kinetic energy at the peak of its bounce, while in the right screen, a student has correctly identified hydrogen bonds depicted in a model.

Once students create an annotated snapshot, it is added to a collection of all snapshots taken by them during that session. They are then able to use annotated snapshots as responses to image questions by opening their collection and selecting an image to represent their answer. Annotated model snapshots were a key innovation in the development of a comprehensive formative assessment system.

Not only did image questions eliminate the need for students to describe models, they also allowed teachers to quickly see a selected model state, rather than trying to interpret a student's verbal description. In addition, image questions gave activity developers a simple way to include performance assessments as part of the formative feedback to teachers and researchers. In an activity about diffusion, for example, we could ask students to provide an annotated snapshot of a model once it reaches equilibrium, or we could ask students to create a model that is out of equilibrium and use an annotated snapshot to show that they have completed and understood the performance task. The concept of an image question has since been extended by other projects at the Concord Consortium to include snapshots of graphs, illustrations, and

FIGURE 10.1   Student annotation tool (left), and image question populated with student answer (right)

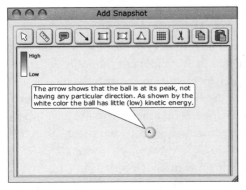
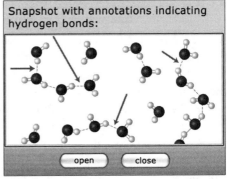

other model types that we embed in our activities, including models we've made using NetLogo and Phet models developed at the University of Colorado in Boulder.[2]

The technological innovations described provided a framework for developing interactive model-based activities with embedded assessments that could be easily collated and reported to the teacher. Still missing, however, was a professional development program to help teachers get the most out of these activities and formative assessment systems. This professional development became a key element in the development of the RI-ITEST program.

THE RI-ITEST PROJECT

RI-ITEST was a comprehensive professional development (PD) program to support teachers in the classroom use of a set of Molecular Workbench activities that were previously developed by the NSF-funded Science of Atoms and Molecules (SAM) program. SAM developed twenty-four two-day activities to engage students in topics across the science spectrum with concentrations in physics, chemistry, and biology. Primarily a materials development grant, SAM had limited professional development as part of its program. Participating teachers attended a two-day workshop in the summer before they were to incorporate the models into their classes. Given the unique nature of the materials and the short duration of the PD program, it was not surprising, in hindsight, to observe that teachers had not made changes in practice that would optimize the use of the student materials and the formative feedback data found in student reports. These findings inspired the development of the RI-ITEST PD program to meet this need. A central goal of the RI-ITEST project was to provide teachers with the necessary professional development and technology tools to incorporate computer-based materials in science curricula. A crucial component of the technology tools was a system for providing formative feedback to teachers and students.

Training in technology and pedagogical techniques involved 120 hours of PD activities spread over two years, including summer institutes, online courses, face-to-face meetings during the school year, and frequent e-mail contact between participants and project staff. The framework developed for the PD experiences was guided by the concepts of pedagogical content knowledge and its logical extension in this case—technological pedagogical content knowledge. Research in these areas points to the idea that teachers develop a specialized kind of knowledge that goes beyond the content itself, primarily focusing on how to teach a specific concept and, when technology is a significant component, how the affordances of the technology have an impact on teaching practice.[3]

For RI-ITEST teachers, the PD program needed to address two levels of pedagogy. First, the program needed to address how to teach using interactive computer-based models. Teachers worked with each other and with project staff to develop strategies and patterns of classroom use that would maximize student engagement and learning while using models. Together as a community, we—the project staff and teachers—supported each other in building this kind of pedagogical content knowledge, sharing ideas within and across schools. Second, RI-ITEST worked with teachers to understand how the formative feedback system built into the activities and Web portal could be used to guide pedagogical choices. The SAM activities were designed to be used over a two-day period with opportunities for teachers to examine formative feedback data after each day. Before participating in RI-ITEST, few teachers had ever used a system that could give them the level of detail they received about student work with interactive computer-based materials. Over the course of the project, teachers in the program helped us to greatly improve the formative feedback system. Initially, the only report available to teachers was a full report on each student that contained his or her answers to assessment questions each time an activity was launched and some work was completed. Improvements made over the course of the grant included the following, each of which will be describe in detail:

- Cumulative reports that collate multiple student sessions with the same activity
- Dynamic group assignment
- Full-class summary reports
- Summary views of individual questions
- Teacher customizable reports

Cumulative Reports

Teachers wanted to collect all student work from an activity into a single report. Initially, they got a report from each student or group of students, which carried information from only a single activity session. If students revisited an activity, multiple reports from the same activity would be generated. Teachers found it cumbersome to have more than one report per student for the same activity, in some cases with overlapping assessment items because students revisited pages to update their responses. By changing the system to collate all student work on an activity, a more coherent report was generated, showing the student's most recent understanding of the concepts.

Dynamic Group Assignment

Teachers wanted the flexibility to assign activities to individuals or small groups. Computer access varied significantly by teacher, so some kind of grouping mechanism was needed. (In fact, based on our prior work in classrooms, we consider pairs of students working together to be best practice.) To make grouping easier for the teacher and to address issues of absenteeism as well as limited access to computers, we developed a system through which students could select who, if anyone, was working with them each time they launched an activity. This approach allowed the greatest flexibility for the teacher to dynamically change groups as necessary. It also allowed students to start an activity together in school but complete it individually outside of school, if necessary. This functionality, combined with the collated reports described previously, gave the teachers the most flexibility in assigning work, while maintaining a coordinated set of formative assessments for each student.

Summary Reports

While having individual student reports gave teachers a complete set of data, they wanted easier ways to compare student work across the class. Creating summary reports helped teachers keep track of student progress through an activity and provided teachers with a snapshot of where the entire class was in terms of understanding various sections of an activity, as well as their progress in completing it. The report shows which students worked together and which multiple choice answers they selected (color-coded for correct or incorrect); it also includes the text of student responses to open-ended questions and links to student-generated images.

Summary Views of Individual Questions

As part of the overall summary report, teachers could request a report on a specific item. This report would collate student responses for just that item and provide a specialized view. For multiple-choice questions, teachers were given a histogram showing how many students chose each answer, helping them quickly identify which distractors were most successful in drawing students from the correct answer. Additionally, each individual's response (color-coded to indicate correct answers) was shown. This feature helped teachers make decisions about whether to address the entire class regarding a particular misconception or to direct attention only to certain individuals.

Customized Reports

Probably the biggest hurdle in using formative assessment data was the sheer volume of data available. Each of the SAM activities had approximately thirty assessments spread over twelve pages. Some teachers just ignored the data, even though it was available. One teacher noted, "At first I graded the entire report, which I found overwhelming and not motivating." If a teacher wanted to provide feedback to students by printing out individual reports, it would take almost a ream of paper per class. A solution to this problem was to allow teachers to generate a customized report for individual students that would only include assessment items the teacher chose. This approach was helpful for three reasons: teachers could focus on the assessment items they felt were most informative, a more manageable data set was generated, and teachers could give individualized feedback to students. The teacher quoted earlier commented later, "Using the selection features of the reporting allows me to focus on the questions that I feel most crucial to understanding a concept and assisting my students."

As part of our teacher surveys, thirty-two respondents provided information regarding their usage of student reports. The most common usage was to "look over the student results to consider next steps in my teaching of the concepts or to decide which models to revisit with the class (64 percent)," which was our intention in creating the reporting system. Teachers also indicated that "I make customized reports so I can grade a subset of questions (56 percent)," "I grade the entire report (40 percent)," and "I use the reports to find examples of student work to discuss with the whole class (40 percent)."

RI-ITEST Impact on Students and Teachers

Efficacy of the RI-ITEST program was gauged qualitatively through surveys, focus groups, and classroom observations, as well as quantitatively through a molecular concept inventory (MCI) pre-post test measure specifically designed to get at conceptual understanding of the atomic nature of various science topics. Both teachers and students took versions of the pre-post MCI. Students took a version of the MCI most appropriate for the course they were taking (physics, chemistry, or biology), and teachers took a combined MCI that included items from all three fields of science.

There were two cohorts of students and teachers who participated in RI-ITEST. In both cohorts, there were significant gains in conceptual understanding as measured by the MCI test. Both students *and* teachers showed gains. If students were further divided into subgroups by the number of activities completed, there was a correlation between completing more SAM activities and greater gains on the MCI post-test. The largest overall gains were actually achieved by the second cohort of teachers, whose average pre-post scores went from 72 percent to 80 percent correct. The fact that there were any significant content-knowledge gains by teachers came as a surprise, because, as we had suspected, their initial scores on the pre-test MCI were already quite high. Our first cohort of teachers had statistically significant, but small-effect size changes, while the second cohort of teachers showed a more dramatic improvement.

One possible explanation for the difference in performance between the first and second cohort of teachers might be changes in the PD program, as well as improvements in the reporting mechanisms of the RI-ITEST platform. The first cohort of teachers helped to pilot the PD program and was the primary group to field-test the formative feedback systems. By the time we began the second cohort, we had the fully developed formative feedback mechanism in place, and there was a greater emphasis on its use in the PD sessions. While there is no direct evidence that this was a causal factor in the increased pre-post gains, it does seem plausible that a greater focus on assessment items may have helped to fill gaps in a teacher's own content knowledge.

Formative assessment can provide an avenue for a positive feedback loop that continually increases teacher content knowledge, quality of feedback to students, and student learning. As noted by D. Royce Sadler, the numerous experiences teachers have with student work in a formative assessment context "exposes teachers to a wide variety of ways in which the students approach problem solving, and how they argue, evaluate, create, analyze, and synthesize. Many of these ways will be beyond the ability of the teacher to imagine, so that the teacher learns from the students."[4] As teachers gain greater exposure to the variety of ways students approach and think about problems, their own understanding grows and the quality of their feedback increases. This cycle of evaluation and feedback is accelerated and enhanced in classrooms employing formative assessment.

RI-ITEST Lessons Learned

Teachers' engagement with student work and students' exploration of inquiry-oriented models greatly increases if these types of activities are embedded in a context that supports data collection and reporting.

Computer-based materials can generate large amounts of data, more than teachers who are already pressed for time can digest or utilize. So systems for collecting data must be well organized, and they must include mechanisms that allow teachers to synthesize results and create customized views of that data.

We found, however, that even when good systems for synthesizing and customizing data are available, one key barrier to successfully using technology tools for assessment in classrooms is ready access to computers. Not only must computers be available to students so that data can be collected about their understanding, but computers must also be available to teachers so that they can work with the student data in a timely manner. The data collected from students are only formative if they can be processed in proximity to when students are still studying the same concepts.

In addition, even when computers are readily available to both students and teachers, professional development must be provided so that teachers can develop skills in using data collection tools and in creating meaning from the large amounts of data that can be collected. Without such PD opportunities, even the best tools rarely achieve their true potential.

LOOPS: LOGGING OPPORTUNITIES IN ONLINE PROGRAMS FOR SCIENCE

The goal of the NSF-funded LOOPS project is to provide teachers with timely formative feedback that provides insights into student learning and gives teachers instructional options that are informed by data. We are exploring this idea in the context of guided explorations that use computer-based models and sensors. Our research questions focus on how providing feedback—during class, between classes, or between uses of curriculum units—has an impact on both teaching and learning. The project is a collaboration of physical scientists, computer scientists, and learning scientists at Concord Consortium; University of California, Berkeley; and University of Toronto. Project members are working closely with teacher-developers to create materials for the middle school topics of force and motion and chemical reactions.

LOOPS is both a technology and a pedagogical approach. To "LOOP" (verb) is to use student-related information, for example, a summary of student progress or artifacts created in a lesson, to inform instructional practice. A "LOOP" (noun) is a feedback loop, which is used as in the following scenario:

Imagine that you're teaching an eighth-grade science class on motion. Your students are working in pairs using motion sensors attached to laptop computers. One student in each pair is walking back and forth in front of a sensor, which causes a position versus time graph of her motion to be displayed on the laptop's screen. The other student sits at the laptop manipulating the software that displays the graph. The students are very engaged in the activity, and as you walk around the room, you hear conversations that you think indicate that the students understand the idea of position versus time graphs. But how do you really know? Could the students just be playing with the sensors and not understanding the underlying concepts?

Now imagine that while the students are using the motion sensors, the students wirelessly submit their work, and your computer gives you a summary of that work—on which step in the activity each pair is working, how many times they've created a particular graph, whether their graph "makes sense," whether they're getting correct answers to the questions in the activity. You can use this information to gauge student understanding and to know, for example, which groups to help with misconceptions or when to bring the class together for a discussion of underlying concepts. You can choose several examples of student work and display them anonymously on a public display and on students' machines, focusing on similarities and differences in answers and different problem-solving strategies.

This scenario illustrates the technology-enabled formative assessment loop central to the LOOPS project: Students submit their work. The teacher uses that work, along with summary information about student progress and understanding, to guide instruction. If the teacher chooses, student work can be selected and shared with the class, thus completing the loop from student to teacher and back again. These formative assessment loops make students' classroom work transparent to the teacher and students and provide for flexible lessons tailored to the students.

LOOPS Classroom Example

LOOPS technology and curriculum have been used in six California and Massachusetts middle schools with ten teachers and their students. Critical to supporting science teaching and learning in these classrooms has been embedding LOOPS in an environment in which the technology is, as articulated by John Bransford et al., "mediated by learning conversations with peers and teachers."[5] LOOPS supports these conversations by logging student interaction with computational models, sensors, graphs, and drawing tools as students explore and refine scientific ideas, and by making that information available to teachers and students.

Next is an example of these classroom conversations, illustrated by means of student work for a motion curriculum unit and a teacher display related to that work. In the described activity, each pair of students has just experimented with a motion sensor and practiced interpreting the position versus time graphs produced by the device. Each pair is then presented with the story of a Pony Express rider traveling on a particular route. The students are asked to draw a position versus time graph that matches the story and to submit their graph to the teacher for anonymous sharing and discussion with the class.

In the Massachusetts classroom from which this example was taken, each pair of students used a wirelessly connected tablet computer. The teacher used an identical tablet computer, with the keyboard folded out of the way beneath the computer screen. A projector was connected to another computer in order to create a public display machine, which communicated wirelessly with the teacher's computer. This setup enabled the teacher to carry her computer and interact with students, choose their work, display work on the projector, and lead class discussion in her usual style of circulating in the classroom. She was able to guide discussion while walking among her students or while standing next to the projected image of student work.

Shown in figure 10.2 is the teacher's view of two student graphs created to match the Pony Express story. There are five kinds of information presented in this kind of display: the fraction of student pairs who have completed this activity step, the most recent graphs drawn by each pair, the percentage correct of the most recent graph, what is correct or incorrect about the most recent graph, and the number of graphs each pair drew and submitted to the teacher. With each kind of information, the teacher needs a visual display that is easy to navigate and one that employs easily scanned imagery. The display shown in figure 10.2, which enables a teacher to pick any number of student answers for viewing, illustrates both of these principles. A pie chart near the top of the display indicates what portion of student pairs has completed this step (all have in this example). The most recent graph submitted for each pair is visible in the display, along with easily identifiable icons for interacting with the graphs. Two such graphs are shown in figure 10.2; the teacher can scroll or resize the display to see more student work (scrolling and resizing are not shown in the figure) and tap on a "+" associated with a graph to zoom in and see more detail. Next to the names of the students who created each graph is a percentage that represents the portion of the graph that is correct compared with a teacher-supplied rubric written in terms of segment start and end points and slope. The correctness or incorrectness of the graph is represented by different kinds of highlighting and labels on the segments. Correct segments are highlighted in green, and incorrect segments are highlighted in red. For an incorrect segment, start or end points that are incorrect are labeled with "X," while an incorrect slope is labeled with "D." In figure 10.2, for example, the graph on the left is 100 percent correct. The graph on the right is 84 percent correct, with an incorrect slope and ending point for the fourth segment, and an incorrect slope for the fifth segment. (Note: Students are not penalized twice for an incorrect ending point that results in an incorrect starting point or slope for the subsequent segment.) Next to the percentage correct is a count of the number of graphs a student pair submitted. The history of each student pair's work is currently available in an after-class report similar to the RI-ITEST report described in the previous section and can be used to gauge the extent of students' exploration and progression of understanding. In the next version of the software, teachers will have access to this history during class by tapping on the count of submissions.

To share students' work with the class, the teacher selects their answers by tapping on the squares to the left of their names in the work display and then creates a public display by tapping on "Public Display" in the lower right corner. This action creates on

FIGURE 10.2   Teacher view of an activity step

The teacher can glance at the display and see what portion of student pairs have completed the step, what percentage of each pair's graph is correct and what is correct or incorrect, and how many times each pair submitted a graph

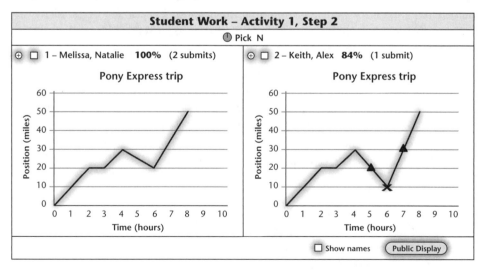

the teacher's machine a window of the selected work and also displays that window on the projector (by communicating wirelessly with the computer connected to the projector). If the "Show Names" option is not selected, the student work will be displayed anonymously. The wireless communication between the teacher's machine and the projector's machine enables the teacher to have a private view of the work before selecting it for public viewing via the projector. The selected work also appears on the students' machines in a public display window that stores a history of all publicly displayed work. The history enables the teacher to refer back to previously selected work, for example, asking students to reflect on particular items.

LOOPS Impact on Students and Teachers

The LOOPS project is in its fourth of five years, so our research is ongoing. To date, we have investigated the effect of the LOOPS curriculum and technology in Massachusetts and California middle school classrooms, looking at student performance on pre-tests and post-tests, and at teacher practice.

Student learning. We have collected data from pre- and post-tests in both Massachusetts (163 students) and California (654 students) classrooms for five-day curriculum units aimed at helping middle school students learn how to create and interpret position versus time graphs. The Massachusetts classrooms used the version of LOOPS technology described earlier (see www.loops.concord.org); the California classrooms used a similar version developed for the WISE4 platform by the project's Berkeley and Toronto team members.[6] We saw statistically significant gains in performance with both cohorts of students. Graph test items were scored using graph rubrics similar to the one described for graphs in figure 10.2. Open response test items were scored using rubrics based on a knowledge integration framework developed at the University of California, Berkeley.[7]

Teacher practice. In interviews conducted after teachers ran LOOPS curriculum units in their classrooms, teachers reported substantial benefits from reviewing, selecting, and displaying student work during class. They thought that students were engaged and motivated to reflect on and revise their ideas. Teacher-led discussion of selected work helped to highlight for students common misconceptions. It also focused students' attention on the science content and prompted their own self-monitoring of understanding. One teacher, for example, remarked:

> [Projecting student graphs in whole-class discussion] gave students an opportunity to actually see the misconceptions. [Students] finally realized that just because a graph has a positive slope, it doesn't mean that the person is going uphill and a negative slope doesn't mean they are going downhill. I can tell them that [idea] once or twice or even three times and it still won't stick, but allowing them to see lots of student work really cemented in their minds that these are misconceptions.

Another teacher commented:

> I could see [many students] weren't getting [a particular idea] by my walking around and looking over their shoulders, listening to their conversations, or looking at their work on my screen. Then I could choose a couple of examples and stop everybody so we could talk about it in real time. You saw their "aha" moment."

Teachers found the student review of peers' work particularly beneficial to their learning. Teachers reported that it not only motivated students to assess and revise their thinking, but also made them feel more successful about their work in the project, compared to when they received only teacher feedback. One teacher, for example, commented:

If [students] didn't understand the question or how to do it, they could look at these examples. Then they'd go back to their own and go, "Oh, that is what the question was asking me."... I think if I asked [my students] about this activity, they would say they loved it; they usually have a question but they don't want to ask because they feel stupid. With this [strategy] they have another way to ask—by looking at the other students' work—and they didn't only have to ask me for help. It empowers them.

Another teacher commented:

A lot of kids wouldn't think intuitively to look at others' work and say, "What did they do to arrive at that solution?" They don't do that. This process [sharing student work] helps them understand the learning steps in arriving at answers. This isn't only about getting the answer right, it's about the students understanding how others think about the same problem, and maybe thinking about their own processes.

In classroom observations, we noted that teachers with different teaching styles or backgrounds often chose to use the formative assessment information differently: teachers who were accustomed to using student work as the focus of a lesson used the information to lead classwide discussions about different student ideas and were able to do so almost immediately after introduction to the technology; other teachers used the information instead to target students who seemed to be struggling with the material. In either case, students benefited, as the pre-post test data for the different classes showed gains on the same questions. Teachers were able to use formative assessment information to either slow down or speed up a class, depending on how well their students understood the material. One teacher, for example, noticed that many of her students were only submitting one or two motion sensor graphs, and she had the class go back and repeat their experimentation so that they explored a wider variety of motion conditions. A lively class discussion followed after the additional experimentation. Another teacher noticed that many students were not correctly drawing position versus time graphs to match a story, and he stopped the class to have the students do a drawing exercise on paper that he made up on the fly. The exercise helped students understand the material and served as a good example of trying out new curriculum ideas that, if successful, can be incorporated into later versions of the unit. (It also reminded developers that curriculum need not always be technology-based to be successful.)

Teachers in both California and Massachusetts thought they and their students benefited from the ready availability of student work afforded by the technology. Both groups of teachers, however, found it difficult to know how to select work for discussion or reflection. This issue was borne out in both classroom observation and teacher interviews. As one teacher commented, "There's no problem with the technology, the computers . . . it's easy to learn, we spent only about fifteen minutes getting to know it.

I like the ability to see how each kid has finished and submitted the assignment. It's just really hard to choose which ones to sample for the class."

LOOPS Lessons Learned

Teachers were unanimous in liking the technology and in the ability to see their students' thinking. They thought the formative assessment data, especially when available during class, gave them a valuable window into what students were doing. With information about student learning easily and quickly accessible, they were able to identify struggling students more readily than without the technology. They also were able to more easily and quickly tailor their lessons to their students, for example, not dwelling on a topic that students already understood. As pre-post test results showed, their students benefited.

It is critical, however, that teachers know how to teach using formative assessment data, especially when they have access to that data in real time. Without professional development, the cultural context of a teacher's background was evident: teachers who had practice with a curriculum that emphasizes focus on student work and formative feedback made effective use of formative assessment information more easily than those who had not. As expected, however, teachers' use of formative assessment data improved with practice.

In addition to helping teachers learn to choose student work examples for use in a lesson, professional development can help teachers identify which assessments are appropriate for particular time scales. Lengthy reflection questions that enable students to articulate their understanding of particular concepts are extremely valuable but difficult for a teacher to scan in real time in a classroom. Answers to these sorts of questions take time to analyze and are best used on days following their implementation in the classroom. Graphing questions, however, are easier to use shortly after they are answered, since graphs are fairly easy for teachers to scan. With professional development to help teachers identify visual characteristics that make for good class examples, graphing questions can be very effectively used in real time.

In addition to professional development, building into the technology the automatic analysis of certain types of student work will relieve the teacher of some of the burden of scanning large quantities of work in order to identify different kinds of answers. As illustrated in figure 10.2, we are working, for example, on encoding graph analysis routines so that teachers can see quickly how their students' work compares to a teacher-supplied rubric.

Finally, teacher mobility in the classroom in an important issue: technology can support a classroom interaction model that enables teachers to continue to circulate among their students. We saw evidence of better classroom management and teacher engagement, and resulting student engagement, when teachers were using a mobile computer instead of a stationary one.

CONCLUSION

As illustrated by the RI-ITEST and LOOPS projects, technology-enabled formative assessment holds great promise. It can successfully link teaching, learning, and assessment by making students' thinking more visible to teachers, students, and researchers. With technology, students can use computational tools to explore, create, and experiment. Teachers can use this work as formative assessment data: to identify individual students who may need specialized attention, to get a bird's-eye view of learning both during class and between classes, and to inform class discussion and curricular choices. When designing and implementing technology with these capabilities, there are several key issues to consider:

- The types of data collected
- How data are presented to the teacher
- The design of a comprehensive and inclusive PD program
- Who uses the formative assessment data

The types of data collected. In gauging student understanding, both projects made use of typical multiple choice and open response assessment items, as well as visual data. Image questions in RI-ITEST helped capture students' work with models, while graphs in LOOPS captured both student-drawn data and actual data collected with probes. The process of generating annotated model snapshots and graphs helps support student inquiry and provides rich artifacts for analysis by both teachers and researchers. Visual data, while containing a great deal of information, are also processed more quickly and easily than other types of open-ended student work, so they lend themselves well to the fast turnaround necessary if student work is to guide teacher practice from class to class or moment to moment.

How data are presented to the teacher. Both projects placed special emphasis on organizing data for the teacher. Large volumes of data can be collected easily when students use computer-based tools in science. If the point of collecting these data is to help inform next steps in the classroom, it is crucial to organize and present data in a meaningful way for teachers. RI-ITEST found much greater use of student data when it gave teachers options to customize reports. LOOPS has spent considerable time in refining presentations of the data so that teachers could process whole-class aggregate feedback, allowing them to quickly choose one or more examples for in-class discussion. Volumes of data are not useful unless they are easily accessible.

The design of a comprehensive and inclusive PD program. Developers of an innovation have a particular vision for how that innovation should be implemented, and it is the rare occurrence when implementation closely resembles the initial vision, especially in technology-based projects that frequently push teachers' pedagogical content knowledge limits. A greater desire for fidelity was one of the key factors that inspired the development of RI-ITEST, a PD program that extended the work of the SAM project, which found that teachers needed more PD to see the greatest benefit from innovative activities. Having data available in real time, as in the LOOPS program, was entirely new for the LOOPS teachers. PD helped the LOOPS teachers to understand how and when to access these data, and how to include student work as an active teaching component. Using formative feedback often requires a change in teaching practice, something that is rare without a PD program to help teachers look at their own practices in detail and reflect on best practices for using formative assessment data.

Who uses the formative assessment data. Usually, formative assessment data are thought of as something used by the teacher. In the RI-ITEST and LOOPS projects, however, two additional groups used and benefited from formative assessment data—students and program developers. In RI-ITEST, some questions provided customized feedback to students, suggesting alternative ways to explore the models and allowing them to check their understanding. Teachers were also encouraged to use student work in class discussions. The main focus of LOOPS was the immediate in-class feedback from student to teacher and back to students for whole-class discussion. Ultimately, the student data were fed back to program developers in both projects and were used, along with teacher feedback about data representations, to improve the quality of both the student activities and the formative feedback mechanisms.

Through implementation of the RI-ITEST and LOOPS projects, we have learned valuable lessons about effective use of formative assessment data in a wide variety of classrooms. These types of data can guide curricular choices and lead to measurable improvements in student and teacher content knowledge, as was shown in both the RI-ITEST and LOOPS projects. The current trend toward technology-based curricular components bodes well for greater integration of systems such as those developed in RI-ITEST and LOOPS, making formative assessment practices more commonplace and thus providing a better education for all.

The authors of this chapter are listed in alphabetical order.

PART IV

Perspectives and Reflections

CHAPTER 11

Interactive Technology for Formative Assessment

How We Got Here and What Comes Next

PAUL HORWITZ

In April 1983, the National Commission on Excellence in Education delivered to the president a report entitled "A Nation at Risk: The Imperative for Educational Reform." In contrast to most government reports, this one had a significant effect on national policy, perhaps because of the forcefulness and eloquence of its language. I know it had a major effect on me. All these years later, I still remember fondly one particularly over-the-top quote: "If an unfriendly foreign power had attempted to impose on America the mediocre educational performance that exists today, we might well have viewed it as an act of war." Wow!

At the time, I was working at the Cambridge, Massachusetts, research firm Bolt, Beranek and Newman. My job was to try to find ways to use computers, which were relatively new back then, to "make things better." This open-ended mandate authorized me to dabble in all sorts of ventures I knew nothing about—from automating the analysis of data retrieved from a torpedo to using artificial intelligence to generate advice to nuclear reactor operators—a hot topic in those post–Three Mile Island days. It also gave me license to dream about how those newfangled machines might help to achieve the goals the president's commission had described so passionately.

My starting point was the realization that *science is a game*. (I should point out that as a scientist myself—my PhD thesis was titled "A Quark Model of Mesons"—I felt I had the right to an opinion on the matter.) Not that I consider science trivial—on the contrary, some of mankind's most significant endeavors can fairly be classified as "games"—but that it is gamelike in having definite rules and goals, the latter largely internalized, in that their value is defined primarily within the game itself. (Would humanity really be better off with a working quark model of mesons? Wouldn't that be something like finding Waldo, or winning at Scrabble?) So if science is a game, why don't we teach it that way?

Video games were just becoming popular (for those with long memories, we had progressed beyond Pong and were smack in the middle of the Pac-Man Age), and it seemed a reasonable assumption that if students learned to play a game that had Newton's laws for rules, they would become acquainted with those laws and thereby learn some physics. It seemed so reasonable, in fact, that I was moved to send a proposal to the National Science Foundation (NSF) to check it out. And so was born ThinkerTools.

Lest there be any doubt, let me hasten to admit that my ideas about human cognition and learning were extremely naive, even for those primitive times. It should have been, and has since become, abundantly clear to me that it is perfectly possible for someone to become proficient at playing a science game without learning very much science. That unhappy observation, in fact, will recur throughout this chapter, so let me repeat it here: *getting good at the game does not imply learning the science behind the game*. But I didn't know that back then. I just knew that I really wanted to build a physics game.

Fortunately, I had a partner in this enterprise. Barbara White had recently earned a doctorate at MIT in cognitive science and actually knew something about how people learn. So together we made a great team: I had lots of ideas for games and knew, or could figure out, how to program them.[1] Barbara knew how to get them to teach the physics.

THINKERTOOLS: PHYSICS GAMES

ThinkerTools was supported by NSF from October 1984 through September 1986. The target audience was sixth graders, and the goal was to teach them enough Newtonian mechanics to enable them to reason about the effect of forces on point masses (solid objects that didn't rotate or vibrate) moving in two dimensions. In addition to the software that implemented the games, Barbara produced an eight-week module with detailed lesson plans covering the effect of impulses (forces acting over very short times) in one and two dimensions, the transition from sequences of impulses to continuous forces, and the effects of friction and gravity.

The software consisted of a set of computer-based gamelike learning activities that led students through the sequence of topics. These games were built from three simple components: dots, walls, and data crosses. Dots were colored disks representing point masses. They had positions and could move, but had no rotational or other internal degrees of freedom. Walls were just stationary lines on the screen, oriented vertically, horizontally, or at forty-five degrees to those directions. Dots could detect collisions with walls and react either by exploding or by bouncing off them. Each data cross represented the velocity of a particular dot. Data crosses resembled four rectangular "thermometers"—two horizontal and two vertical—that could be partially filled with color to represent the horizontal and vertical velocity components of the dot. (The actual direction of the velocity vector could be estimated from the data cross but was not directly represented by it.) Velocity could also be represented in another way: dots could be made to leave "wakes" by dropping small markers at regular time intervals. The trail of these markers then represented the dot's trajectory and the distance between them its past velocity. Figure 11.1 illustrates these ThinkerTools features.

The ThinkerTools games followed a carefully worked-out sequence. At the first level, they introduced students to motion in one dimension under the influence of impulses that imparted a fixed, finite increment of velocity to the right or to the left. The basic rule, as the students discovered, was that these velocity increments added and subtracted just like signed numbers, with impulses to the right corresponding to positive numbers and impulses to the left, negative ones.

FIGURE 11.1   An example of a ThinkerTools screen

The data cross on the left indicates the velocity of the large dot, which is moving up and to the right. The smaller dots constitute the "wake" of the big one. Since they are dropped at constant time intervals, their even spacing indicates that the dot has been moving at a constant velocity.

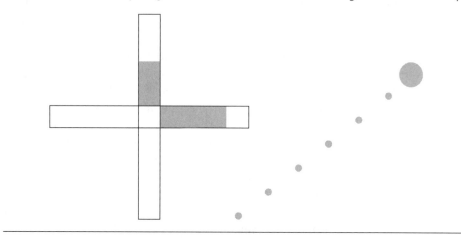

The second level of game broadened the domain to motion in two dimensions. At first, we had two students control the same dot, one of them restricted to imparting right or left impulses, the other up and down. Their joint challenge was to steer the dot over a specified path, taking care to avoid bumping into a wall (which was of the type that would explode the unfortunate dot). This required close coordination between the two students, but limited the cognitive load on each and reinforced the notion that arbitrary velocities (in two dimensions) can be composed from just two components. Once they were proficient at such tasks, the students were presented with more difficult challenges that required them to control both components of the dot's motion.

The third level of the ThinkerTools games introduced continuous forces through a limiting process whereby the students could reduce the magnitude of the impulses in successive steps while simultaneously increasing the frequency of their application. In the limit, the impulses came so close together that they approximated a continuous force, but the students could reason about their effect by mentally decomposing them into the finite impulses they had already become familiar with.

Finally, at the fourth level, we introduced two common examples of continuous forces, gravity and friction, and created games where students could experiment with each, first in one dimension, then in two. The final game in this sequence involved investigating projectile motion in a uniform gravitational field, both with and without air resistance.

RESULTS FROM THINKERTOOLS PROJECT

In the spring of 1986, we ran the ThinkerTools materials in two sixth-grade classes comprising a total of forty-two students. The same teacher who taught those classes also taught two others, which were used as a control. The control classes, a total of thirty-seven students, followed a traditional curriculum, which in this instance was a unit on invention.[2] This within-grade comparison would have satisfied the requirements of the grant proposal, but in a fit of chutzpah inspired perhaps by one of the reviewers who opined that ThinkerTools required "thinking . . . available only to formal operational students," we added two more control groups composed of high school physics students in the same suburban school district.[3] Two of these classes, forty-one students in all, had just completed a unit on Newtonian mechanics similar to, and in fact slightly longer than, the ThinkerTools unit—but without the software, of course. Another forty-five students were just beginning their physics classes and had not yet encountered Newtonian mechanics.

We administered a written test designed to measure understanding of forces and motion as they apply to real-world situations. The test was composed of items drawn from the cognitive science literature that had been used to study misconceptions among physics students. All required reasoning from basic principles, rather than algebraic problem solving. We broke the items down into three categories: those that involved problems and concepts that had been covered explicitly in the ThinkerTools curriculum, a second group that required students to apply concepts they had been exposed to in ThinkerTools to an unfamiliar context, and a third group of items that were entirely new to the students, both in concept and in application (e.g., problems involving circular motion, which was not covered in the ThinkerTools unit). To summarize our findings briefly, the ThinkerTools students outperformed all three control groups—including the high school physics students who had just taken the unit on Newtonian mechanics—on all items except those in the third (unfamiliar concept and application) category.[4] On those items, in fact, there were no significant differences among any of the four groups—in particular, the high school students who had completed the mechanics unit did not score significantly higher on those items than those who were just starting the physics course.

The assessment of the ThinkerTools project made no use of the computer; it was in the form of a summative, multiple-choice choice test administered on paper. The software itself, though it reacted to students' actions in real time, did not log those actions and offered no formative assessment, either to the teacher or to the students themselves. Yet, barring a few technical details described later, it would have been possible to provide such assessments. We could have reported, for instance, how many times Susan tried, and how often she accidentally hit a wall, before she managed to stop her dot on the target. We could have figured out whether Tom got closer and closer to the goal of launching his dot through the virtual basket or whether he just picked random starting velocities until he got lucky. Information of this kind might have been extremely valuable to the teacher and could also have been used to formulate insightful hints to help students improve their performance by teaching them the underlying physical principles. We might, for instance, have used such information to guide students toward special "tutorial sessions" based on an analysis of their actions. Why, then, did we not do these things?

For one thing, we didn't need to. Barbara and I were able to observe and actively participate in each ThinkerTools class. We would wander about the room, often interacting with the students, who worked in pairs or larger groups due to the scarcity of computers. Based on our observations, we were able to offer help and explain things—providing the kind of feedback we might otherwise have tried to generate from an automated formative assessment function, had there been one built into the software.

Moreover, implementing an automated formative assessment system would have been quite challenging, given the primitive nature of the technology available. The ThinkerTools computers were not networked, so the reports from each session would have had to be recorded on each computer and later collated. Moreover, the Commodores we used did not have a hard disk, so each assessment report would have had to be collected on a floppy disk from each machine, printed out, and analyzed separately or aggregated by hand with reports from other computers. Today, it can be assumed that every computer in a school is "on the net," which makes it possible to keep track of every student's progress on a central server. We can create a portal in a central location and use it to deploy and maintain software in many schools at once. Such a portal can also support the registration of new schools, teachers, classes, and students, maintaining and updating a database of such information. It can store student-generated data and use it to generate reports of differing granularity, aimed at many different stakeholders, from the students themselves to teachers, administrators, parents, researchers, or policy makers. Such portals did not exist in 1986 but they do today, and their application to education, and to formative assessment in particular, is an indispensable context for the discussion in this chapter.

GENSCOPE AND BIOLOGICA: TOOLS FOR GENETICS

GenScope was supported by two successive NSF awards, running from 1992 through 1997.[5] It was designed as a general-purpose tool, written in C++ and running only on the Apple Macintosh platform, intended to assist in the teaching of genetics. It consisted of six separate but integrated models representing genetic phenomena and processes at six different levels: DNA, chromosomes, cells, organisms, pedigrees, and populations. The levels were linked so that manipulations at any one level could have ripple effects, as appropriate, at any of the others. For example, a modification of an organism's DNA would show up at the chromosome level as a change in a gene—a mutation.[6] The mutation, in turn, might affect the organism's observable traits and might be transferred to an offspring through the processes of meiosis and fertilization. This would then show up at the pedigree level in the form of a statistical distribution of the traits of offspring of the original organism. At the population level, students could run virtual experiments to determine how the change in reproductive fitness associated with the mutation affected its diffusion through a population of randomly mating organisms, and observe the spread of the new trait on an evolutionary timescale.

In contrast to ThinkerTools, GenScope did not integrate curriculum activities with the software. The program did not offer challenges to students, nor did it provide them with feedback of any kind. Instead, we provided learning activities either in the form of oral instructions to students or via handouts and worksheets. This gave teachers a great deal of control over the use of GenScope and encouraged its adoption as an open-ended tool for inquiry in genetics. GenScope proved to be very engaging for a lot of students and was popular as well with many teachers who reported that they particularly liked the fact that it did not constrain them to adopt a particular curriculum.

But the use of an unstructured tool like GenScope comes with a certain risk. In the absence of a curriculum explicitly designed to link the behavior of the computer model with its associated real-world analogs, it is possible for students to become proficient at using the model to solve problems without learning the science behind the model. We observed this in several trials in which students who had used GenScope performed no better than control groups taught the same material by conventional means. When we eventually achieved success, it was by incorporating a set of offline activities in the form of paper-and-pencil worksheets, collectively called "Dragon Investigations," designed to bridge the gap between the computer model and the underlying scientific concepts. When we did this, students taught in classrooms that used both the Dragon Investigations and GenScope significantly outperformed a control group taught the same material using more traditional means.[7]

Our experience with GenScope led us to rethink the educational utility of stand-alone tools. It was clear to us that something more was needed to connect, in the students' minds, the representations and affordances of the model with their counterparts in the real world. In our zeal to replace the static, boring textbook with "active learning," we had swung the pendulum too far, providing opportunities for inquiry but skimping on explanation. We needed a hybrid technology that would link static materials designed to explain complicated concepts to open-ended exploratory environments. And once we had it, we could use it to provide insightful formative assessments by observing and analyzing students' actions in both regimes: tabulating their answers to questions while also evaluating their inquiry skills and problem-solving strategies.

Enter BioLogica

In 1998, we started work on BioLogica, a Java version of GenScope that ran on both Macintosh and Windows computers. BioLogica had all the features of GenScope but was designed to run as a set of structured learning activities. In software terms, BioLogica is a collection of interoperable components that cannot stand alone but are invoked and run by an external *script* that implements an interactive learning activity. This architecture separates the functionality of the biology model—the software embodiment of the science content—from the pedagogy and assessment functions, which are embodied in the scripts. Rather than a general-purpose tool, BioLogica presents itself to students as an *interactive curriculum*—a set of learning activities, each focused on a separate topic. The shift in focus has implications for both pedagogy and assessment.

Using BioLogica, we could embed the GenScope multilevel model of genetics in a variety of different contexts. The generic term for this sort of thing is "scaffolding," and it can be put to many uses.[8] It can guide students to make connections between model and data by linking real-world phenomena and processes to the corresponding behaviors of the model. It can encourage students to reflect on what they are learning by posing questions before, during, or after their interaction with the model. And by moving students back and forth between answering questions and manipulating a model, it can help them bridge the gap between knowing how to do something and knowing how to answer questions about it. Question-and-answer tests force students to translate conceptual understanding, as demonstrated by their ability to solve problems in a domain, into a linguistic performance. Students who experience difficulty with such translation can benefit from practice in the context of an active, exploratory environment.

Scaffolding also frees us from having to rely solely on question-and-answer data for assessment purposes. By analyzing students' actions in the context of specific problem-solving challenges, we can create *performance assessments* as well. We can first set up a context in which students are trying to achieve a particular goal (e.g., "breed a blue fire-breathing dragon with wings, in no more than three generations"), and then monitor the students' use of the model to see whether they succeed at the task. And we are not constrained to look only at success or failure; often the process a student uses to solve a problem can be interpreted and used to distinguish, for example, a systematic exploration of alternative strategies from a scattershot approach that leads to a lucky guess. In such situations, the feedback can go beyond the simplistic "Well done!" or "Try again" and give meaningful hints on how to improve performance. If a student repeats a particular error, the computer can generate a sequence of hints, starting with general advice (e.g., "Think about the dragon's genes"), then becoming more and more leading ("What does it take for a dragon to have wings?"), and eventually, perhaps, linking the student to an animated demo or a tutorial specifically tailored to particular obstacles or misconceptions.

Formative Assessment for Teachers

If we can provide performance-based feedback to students, why not provide it to teachers as well? If we can analyze what students are doing in order to give them appropriate feedback, we ought to be able to use the same analysis, perhaps at a slightly higher level, to generate formative assessments for teachers.

We traveled partway down that road with BioLogica, but we didn't get very far. In the long run, the only reports we were able to generate for teachers provided information about the answers that students gave to embedded questions but did not track their manipulations of the model. Much later, after all the implementations were over, we were able to analyze all of the performance data that had been generated—approximately 1.5 gigabytes of data—and try to draw inferences from it. The work was difficult and time consuming, and we ran out of time on the project before we could complete the job.[9] Still, we saw enough promise in this approach to give us hope that eventually we would be able to work out the details and provide automated reports to teachers that would draw valid inferences from observing the students' actions as they attempted to solve problems. This should include evaluations of their conceptual understanding of the domain as well as of their inquiry skills, as manifested by their ability to perform, and learn from, virtual experiments.

One of the lessons we learned from our work with BioLogica was that for an activity to produce meaningful formative assessments, it must be designed from the start to do just that. It must not be so constrained, for instance, that students can perform only one action at any given time; one can't learn much from their behavior if they are given no choice about what to do! On the other hand, if an activity is too open-ended and unstructured, then there's a good chance that many students will either flounder around aimlessly or, even worse, make up their own challenges without telling us about it, so that their actions make sense to them but are mysterious to us and likely to be misinterpreted.

Here is an example of the sort of thing that can go wrong. A recent project of ours, called Evolution Readiness, also supported by NSF, is using BioLogica-based activities to teach about adaptation and natural selection to fourth graders.[10] Early in the project, during a pilot test of the software, we observed a child working with an activity that involved planting virtual seeds at different points in a field to find out where they would grow best. We watched as this student figured out that some of the seeds grew best at the top of the field where there was the most sunlight, others grew best in the middle where the light level was intermediate, and the third variety grew best at the bottom of the field, in the shade. We were encouraged because this was exactly what the activity had been designed to teach. On the next page, the student was challenged to use as few seeds as possible to grow as many plants as possible within five generations. This required that she plant just a few seeds but be careful to place them where they would grow best. The student, however, invented for herself a very different challenge: she tried to draw a smiley face![11] For the eyes, she used the plants that grew best of the top of the screen; for the mouth, she used the plants that grew at the bottom of the screen; and for the nose, she used the intermediate plants. This was very clever of her, but of course it was not what we had intended and it required her to use many more seeds than the optimal minimum. Had we not been observing her actions directly, we would have had a lot of trouble figuring out what she was attempting to do. An automated analysis algorithm would most likely have failed to recognize this student's creativity and would have reported erroneously that she had missed the central point of the lesson.

So, for these interactive activities to work and provide useful evidence of student knowledge, they have to strike a happy medium. They must be open-ended enough to let the student demonstrate understanding through actions, but they must have enough structure to enable teachers to interpret those actions with reasonable confidence. In designing such an activity, the question one should always ask is: if an expert and a naive student were both to attempt this challenge, would I be able to distinguish one from the other just by looking at their respective log files? If the answer to that question is no, then you probably don't have the right design.

Designing good formative assessment activities is more of an art than a science, however. Some examples are in order.

Playing with Dots

When the ThinkerTools project was in its infancy, Barbara White and I had the pleasure of trying out an early version of the software on a world-renowned physicist: Richard Feynman (who shared the Nobel Prize in 1965 for fundamental research in quantum electrodynamics). At the time, we were both at Bolt, Beranek and Newman, and Feynman was giving a guest lecture there. Someone got the bright idea that he might be interested in a project that was attempting to teach the principles of Newtonian mechanics to sixth graders, so our little office became a stop on his pre-speech visiting tour.

On the screen of our brand-new computer, we showed Feynman eight stationary dots of different colors, enclosed in a rectangular box. One of the dots—the blue one—could be controlled by a joystick. When the joystick was pushed in any direction, the blue dot would accelerate in that direction. In this way, the dot could be "pushed around" by the user. The other dots were not controllable externally, but they reacted to collisions between themselves and with the walls. All such collisions, as we explained to our distinguished guest, were "elastic," meaning that they conserved energy.

I demonstrated to Feynman how I could manipulate the blue dot by giving it small accelerations in different directions, being careful to avoid letting it collide with any of the other dots. Then I gave it a big push, causing it to crash into a nearby dot, which bumped into another, and so on. Immediately, all eight dots were moving quite rapidly, bouncing many times per second off each other and the walls of the containing box. The situation was chaotic and seemingly quite uncontrollable. I handed the joystick to Feynman and told him to "slow them all down." He stared at the wildly colliding dots and said, "It can't be done!" Then, half a second later, he said, "Oh, yes it can!" and proceeded to do it.

What he had figured out was that all he had to do was take energy away from the system, so he focused his attention on the blue dot and used the joystick continually to slow it down. If the blue dot was moving downward, for instance, Feynman would push the joystick up. A second later, it might be moving mainly to the right, say, and he would push the joystick to the left to slow it down. Of course, the dot changed direction and picked up speed every time it was hit, but it was not terribly difficult to keep track of the general direction in which it was moving and manipulate the joystick in the opposite direction. The net effect is to take energy away from the blue dot and thus from the system of dots, which causes them all to slow down. The effect is almost magical; in fact, it takes remarkably few collisions before all the dots are practically stationary again. Even Feynman was impressed, I think, at how quickly that happened, though the principle had obviously been clear to him from the start.

It is possible, even likely, that a beginning physics student might have discovered Feynman's strategy for slowing down the dots, but it would surely have taken much longer and would likely have entailed any number of false starts and blind alleys along the way. Had ThinkerTools been able to monitor and record their actions, it would have been easy, just by looking at the two log files, to determine who was the expert and who was not.

Tracking What They Look At?

In designing learning activities that make good formative assessments, it pays to keep in mind that one can learn a great deal not only from what students do but also from what they choose to look at and pay attention to. While it seems that it might be difficult to do this (do we have to hook them up to an eye tracker?), appropriate design of the computer interface can yield reliable information of this kind. Here is an example.

In BioLogica, a student can observe an organism's genes by clicking on it with a special "chromosome tool." In designing a performance assessment, therefore, after first making sure that the student knows how to use this tool, we can challenge her to do something that requires her to know what genes an organism carries. When we make this challenge, we don't explicitly tell the student to use the chromosome tool but we do make sure she knows that it's available. Then if the student doesn't use the tool, we will know that she is not observing the genes, attending instead solely to the organism's macroscopic, observable traits. This is a very useful observation, since we know from experience that beginning genetics students have a natural tendency to attend to the outward appearance of an organism without considering what that appearance may imply about the genes that the organism carries.

Sometimes we radically tinker with what students can see and what they can't see. Hiding information can add to the fun of the challenge (think how uninteresting poker would be if you could see everyone's hand), and by manipulating what students can see, we also affect what they think about. If we want students to reason about the center of mass of a collection of ThinkerTools dots, for instance, why not hide one of the dots and show the center of mass instead? Then the task can be to figure out where the invisible dot is and click on it. Performance on such a task clearly correlates with an understanding of how the position of the center of mass depends on the positions and masses of the individual dots.

Invisible Dragons

One of the more successful BioLogica learning activities that we developed was called "Invisible Dragons." The students were presented with two dragons: one male and one female, both invisible (they were represented on the monitor by question marks). The challenge was for students to find out everything they could about the dragons. They could mate (the technical term is "cross") the two dragons and see their offspring, and they could cross the offspring, either to each other or to one of the parents—a so-called "back cross"—and look at *their* offspring. They could also look at the genes of any dragon except one of the parents, using the chromosome tool described earlier.

The catch was that each of these actions cost virtual money; a single cross (which produced a litter of exactly forty offspring—enough for statistical trends to be observable) cost $1,000 and an examination of genes cost $5,000. The students were given a research budget of $50,000 and allowed to perform any action they wanted until the money ran out. Whenever they felt they were ready, they could answer questions about the invisible dragons: whether they had wings, how many legs they had, what color they were, and so forth. For each correct answer, the students received $2,000, but each incorrect one cost $1,000, which discouraged guessing. The goal, of course, was to amass as much money as possible—and not to go broke!

The game was quite challenging, inasmuch as it required students to reason backwards (from visible appearance to invisible genes) as well as between generations, and to recognize and interpret statistical data. Although such reasoning is thought to be beyond most secondary students, the game turned out to be very popular, and by examining the particular crosses a player decided to make (it was a bad idea to use the chromosome tool—too expensive, and it tended to provide redundant information), we had the groundwork of a system that could help us quickly separate the "Feynmans" from the beginners.[12]

WHAT'S UP NEXT?

We have come a long way in our exploration of the use of interactive models for formative assessment—from simple environments like ThinkerTools that did not keep track of students' actions to more complicated ones like BioLogica and finally to full-fledged scaffolded activities that not only track students actions but generate reports for students and teachers that make inferences about the students' knowledge and understanding of the underlying concepts. We have only just begun to work with the last category, and there are still many areas that remain to be explored. In this section, we list a few of these.

We have not discussed activities that support group interactions, yet the extensive literature on social cognition makes it clear that having students work in pairs or small groups can be very beneficial.[13] The social dimension of learning opens a wide range of interesting questions for the design of interactive curriculum. How can one best scaffold interactions between students? When should a learning activity run on a single computer, and when, and for what purposes, should it be run on separate, networked computers (or tablets or smart phones) for each student? What is the best use for interactive whiteboards or projectors—shared artifacts around which to foster group interactions? What are the implications of social learning activities, either collaborative or competitive, for formative assessment? Note that such activities need not be high-tech. In fact, the paper-and-pencil Dragon Investigations referred to earlier were designed to foster "feedback conversations" as students worked together to discuss their initial answers to challenging problems.[14]

This raises important questions that we continue to explore in our research at the Concord Consortium: How can we best design social activities to support assessment? If the activity is to run on a single computer, can we distinguish the input of each student in the group? If we can't, are there strategies for scoring or otherwise placing value on the activity that will maximize the engagement of each member of the group? Can we design challenges that can only be solved if all the students work together? If the activity ran on multiple computers and the students were physically separated, we could monitor not only their actions but the messages between them. What information could we glean from an analysis of such communications, particularly now that the technology for analyzing open-ended text is reaching maturity?[15] How could we boil down such a rich source of information to make it useful for the teacher? Clearly, the field of automated formative assessment of collaborative effort and social cognition is wide open for future research.

Another issue to be explored involves the role of the teacher in any classroom where students spend a significant fraction of their time on computers. When we started developing computer-based learning activities, we conceived of the teacher's role as simply to observe and be available to individual students when they seemed to need help (often helping them to get the software to work at all). We have now moved to a situation where software glitches, though not unheard of, are no longer a major problem, but classroom management issues have arisen in their place. Students progress at different rates and are therefore often working on different activities, or at least on different steps of the same activity, at any given time. The teacher can only observe and interact with a small number of students at a time, so trying to get a sense of whether anyone is learning anything can be quite challenging.

There are technological fixes for this kind of thing, of course, such as building stopping points into an activity—places where students are instructed to raise their hand and talk to the teacher before they go on. One can even arrange things so that the teacher can inhibit the students from proceeding beyond such checkpoints until they have been debriefed. Is that a good idea, or does it needlessly kill free-ranging inquiry in the pursuit of control?

Beyond looking to technology for an answer, what kind of professional development would help teachers to run a classroom full of computers effectively? And getting back to the theme of this book, what do we know about the appropriate design of assessment reports for teachers? We need to figure out how to produce reports that enable teachers to get a bird's eye view of the learning of an entire class in just a few minutes, but also let them drill down to examine the work of any particular student in finer detail. There is also a question of the timescale of such reports. Should they be produced during the class period, every day, at the end of a unit, or all three? And how should they be structured at each level of granularity? A current, NSF-funded project called LOOPS, reported in chapter 10 of this book, is currently exploring questions such as these.

With the advent of scaffolded learning activities comes the possibility of customizing such activities for different purposes. Different students have different learning styles: some prefer a lot of structure, while others are more comfortable if they are left alone to experiment. Students come to the classroom with differing background knowledge, including idiosyncratic misconceptions, as well as different strengths and weaknesses. Some students are verbal, others are more visual, some learn by doing, others by memorizing. We should try to design our interactive curricular activities so that they can adapt to accommodate a broad range of students. This will not be easy, but if we succeed in building an activity that can adjust itself to the needs of individual students, then that very adjustment will be a useful input to the teacher and may well constitute a formative assessment in itself. We have touched on this issue elsewhere in this chapter, when we discussed the fact that the feedback we give in response to repeated error conditions need not be repetitive. We described a strategy of starting with general hints and then continuously making them more and more specific until they culminate in a tutorial designed to help the students overcome a particular difficulty. An activity that incorporates such an adaptive teaching strategy can be used for formative assessment simply by reporting to the teacher how many hints and tutorials particular students have received.

No discussion of the use of performance data for formative assessment would be complete without recognition of the fact that such use poses a challenge to the psychometric community. As we have seen, performance data can be a rich source of information, fundamentally different in kind from the information one gets from the traditional question-and-answer assessment instruments. But we don't yet have a solid mathematical foundation upon which to evaluate and interpret performance data. The measurement theories used to create traditional tests assume that all data points (typically, individual questions) are independent of one another. In other words, the theories posit that whether a student gets a particular item right or wrong has no direct bearing on how that student will perform on a subsequent item. This assumption is clearly not justified for performance data on complex tasks consisting of multiple, interdependent subtasks. The challenge is to come up with ways of evaluating such complex performances that map reliably onto the underlying cognitive processes, conceptual understanding, and procedural skills that are the subject of the assessment.

CONCLUSION

For better or worse, in the United States at least, we live in the Age of Accountability. Owing primarily to the No Child Left Behind Act of 2001, the fortunes of teachers, schools, and school districts are significantly affected by the scores students achieve on standardized tests administered by their respective states. Test scores have become so critical to the success or failure (not to mention the budgets) of schools that most systems devote substantial instructional time to preparing their students to take them—often with mixed result.[16]

This begs the question, "How good are the assessments?" to which the answer seems to be, "Not good enough." After all, if we believed that test scores were a reliable indicator of the educational outcomes that we truly care about, we would have no problem with the current emphasis on "teaching to the test." The opinion—held by many educators and policy makers, as well as the general public—that we are placing too much emphasis on test results arises from a shared concern that the tests we are using do not adequately measure the full range of students' knowledge, understanding, and skill.[17]

It is an often overlooked truism that an assessment, no matter how cleverly constructed and exhaustively validated, can only measure the subject's ability to take the test. The entire enterprise, therefore, is founded on an inferential leap: that performance on the assessment is a valid *marker* for the educational outcomes of interest. Traditional testing methods rely almost exclusively on soliciting answers to written questions; as such, they make specialized demands, for instance, on language skills, that may have little to do with the characteristics of the student that the assessment is designed to measure. The mismatch can create paradoxically dysfunctional incentives, as when schools explicitly teach test-taking strategies that fly in the face of more fundamental educational goals. For instance, students are routinely advised, when faced with a body of text followed by questions, to read the questions first, looking for "marker" words or phrases, and then search for those in the document and try to guess the answer from the surrounding text. Similarly perverse strategies abound in other domains.

From the assessment point of view, the pot of gold at the end of the research rainbow may well be the invention and ultimate adoption of radically new ways to evaluate what students know and how broadly and effectively they can apply what they know. This will not result in the elimination of question-and-answer instruments, but it will liberate us from our current near-total reliance on that methodology, and give us the ability to triangulate question-and-answer test scores against performance data obtained by other means. I have argued here that with the advent of modern information technologies, the ability to accomplish that has fallen in our lap. The requisite technology is becoming widely available. Ninety-seven percent of schools in the United States have Internet connectivity, and, driven largely by commercial interests, specialized software exists for registering, tracking, and monitoring the actions of large numbers of users.[18] Personal computers, increasingly complemented "above and below" by interactive whiteboards and tablets, get cheaper every year. Institutional barriers remain, but those too will eventually disappear—even inertia doesn't last forever.[19]

Information technology is changing the way we teach; our challenge now is to follow that path to its logical conclusion and change the way we assess. If we succeed, we will erode an artificial barrier between instruction and evaluation, blending the two to create interactive and engaging learning environments that report on students' progress. As an added benefit, we will loosen the stranglehold of the high-stakes tests whose use as a tool for sorting human beings has so greatly exceeded their relevance to the world outside of school.

CHAPTER 12

Commentary

A Gentle Critique of Formative Assessment and a Participatory Alternative

DANIEL T. HICKEY

This volume is one of the several that will be published this year about formative potential of classroom assessment, in the United States and around the world. At the same time, hundreds of studies will be conducted and dozens of academic papers will be published. Meanwhile, two massive assessment consortia are underway within the 2010 Race to the Top assessment program at the U.S. Department of Education. The central role of classroom assessment in these current reforms illustrates the evolution of formative assessment since the publication of Paul Black and Dylan Wiliam's landmark 1998 article.[1] Rather than focusing primarily (and sometimes exclusively) on classroom assessment, researchers are increasingly using classroom assessment to *coordinate* instruction with high-stakes achievement tests.

This shift to the coordinating role of formative assessment illustrates how the sharp distinction between "formative" classroom assessments and "summative" external tests has given way to a more nuanced appreciation of the crucial role that classroom assessment can play in the larger enterprise of education.[2] For many leading researchers, the dichotomy between formative and summative assessments has been replaced by a consideration of different assessment *purposes* and a continuum of *formality* that ranges from very informal observation to highly formal achievement tests.[3] In this way, many now see the major purpose of formative assessment as coordinating the very informal assessment that is a natural part of classroom instruction with the highly formal external tests that have become a permanent feature of most educational institutions.

While none of the other chapters in this volume directly focus on this coordination, some of them touch on it in important ways. In particular, chapter 1 by David Foster and Audrey Poppers shows how the coordination across informal assessments embedded in the mathematics curriculum led to substantial improvements on more formal performance assessments; these improvements in turn were echoed in gains on the state's high-stakes multiple-choice test. The chapter provides some compelling evidence that coordinating instruction, assessment, and testing can lead to broad systemic improvements that in turn lead to improvements in multiple learning outcomes.

In this chapter, I aim to articulate both my excitement and my concerns about this expanded and more nuanced consideration of formative assessment. Many of my concerns are the result of using a single model of learning to establish "coherence" across formative and summative assessment practices. In that context, I propose a somewhat different way of thinking about formative assessment that addresses these concerns. This alternative emerged from two multiyear studies of the GenScope computer-based modeling curriculum described by Paul Horwitz in chapter 11. Building on contemporary "situative" theories of learning and assessment, this alternative aligns learning across three or more assessment levels. Across levels, students practice using their knowledge in increasingly formal and abstract ways, starting with informal curriculum activities and ending with highly formal achievement tests.

REASONS TO BE EXCITED ABOUT EXPANDED FORMATIVE ASSESSMENT

For those of us who have long appreciated the potential of formative assessment, there are many reasons to be excited about this increased and nuanced interest. Consider, for example, that the No Child Left Behind Act paid little attention to formative assessment. The current large-scale assessment reforms assume that this is one of the reasons that NCLB failed to deliver promised achievement gains on targeted tests, while undermining teaching and learning of content that was not included on those tests. Thus, the most obvious reason to be excited by the new interest in formative assessment is that using it to coordinate instruction, assessment, and testing promises to deliver improvements in all three that are consistent with current expectations for each.

Increased Appreciation of the Complexities of Reform

The increased and nuanced interest in assessment is also causing more stakeholders in education to appreciate how truly complex the educational enterprise really is and how difficult it is to reform education on a large scale. In particular, this interest has helped highlight how the unintended negative consequences of reforms can often outweigh their positive outcomes. More broadly, this increased focus on multiple learning outcomes is resulting in more knowledgeable discourse about those outcomes. Wider appreciation that educational *outcomes* differ from the learning *process*, and that both differ from teaching *practices*, is helpful for coherent discussions of educational reform.

This expansion of interest from (1) tests that measure academic achievement to include (2) assessments of learning and then (3) assessments *for* school learning has helped illuminate the crucial role of *context* when considering learning. A consideration of the context in which knowledge is used helps distinguish educational assessment from achievement testing. This is not to say that conventional achievement testing is not a form of educational assessment. But externally developed multiple-choice achievement tests are just one of many contexts in which knowledge can be assessed. Consider this: what we ask students to do with a multiple-choice test item is choose which of four or five loosely related associations is the least incorrect. A typical achievement test will have students perform this task on dozens of unrelated items. This is an inherently peculiar way to *know* something.

Cognitive scientists have proven that the human mind can memorize thousands of specific associations well enough to distinguish between correct and incorrect associations. But the same knowledge that can be used to *recognize* something may not have been learned deeply enough to *recall* it when solving open-ended problems or to *apply* it in real-world situations. This is why test-preparation programs "work." In order to maximize scores on targeted multiple-choice tests, test-prep programs train students to recognize hundreds of these relatively weak recognition-level associations. Those associations are useful for ruling out some incorrect responses and sometimes recognizing correct ones. Because of the way tests are created and scored, such associations can help students get a few otherwise difficult items correct, resulting in significantly higher scores.

This effect leads to two of the most worrisome consequences of No Child Left Behind. One is the dramatic expansion of such test-preparation practices. The computer-based test-preparation industry exploded within mandated tutoring at schools that failed to meet NCLB achievement growth targets. The second consequence is the expanded use of interim achievement tests. Dylan Wiliam is credited with coining the label *early warning summative assessments* to describe such tests. This label highlights that, in practice, it is very difficult to use a student's score from an achievement test in ways that are directly useful for that student. While interim tests have become quite popular with schools, there is remarkably little evidence of positive impact. Leading assessment scholars have expressed outrage that both products are increasingly being marketed as "formative assessment."[4]

New Appreciation of Different Views of Knowing and Assessing

Another positive consequence of the expanded interest in assessment is a new appreciation that there are very different definitions of *knowing* and (therefore) *learning*. Each definition has distinct implications for teaching, motivating, and assessing learning.[5] In the context of assessment, this relationship was explained in the 2001 report by a National Research Council (NRC) committee led by James Pellegrino. While the report was called *Knowing What Students Know*, it went to some length to remind readers that we never *really* know what students know. Rather, we first create some sort of a situation or task where we can observe student performance. Then, we interpret what students do in that situation. In order to do this, we must articulate our assumptions about knowing and the model of learning that those assumptions support. Assumptions about knowing and learning make up one of the three vertices of an assessment triangle, along with observation and interpretation. The NRC report highlighted the fact that these assumptions often remain unexamined and taken for granted. The report cited evidence that classroom assessments are typically based on teachers' intuitive or qualitative models of learning, while large-scale assessments are almost always based on statistical models of learning.

The NRC assessment report embraced modern cognitive science perspectives on knowing and learning that focus on broad conceptual representations of knowledge and higher-order skills such as problem solving and inquiry. The report critiqued the limitations of conventional multiple-choice achievement tests that have come to dominate high-stakes testing: "The central problem addressed by this report is that the most widely used assessments of academic achievement are based on highly restrictive beliefs about learning and competence not fully in keeping with current knowledge about human cognition and learning."[6]

In response, *Knowing What Students Know* argued that both classroom assessment and external tests should be based on the "best available understanding of how students represent knowledge and develop competence in the domain." As subsequently elaborated by Drew Gitomer and Richard Duschl, and Mark Wilson, the report argued for increased coherence between classroom assessments and external tests by having both strongly embrace the same modern cognitive representational theory of knowing and learning.[7] The report also took issue with the common practice of using a single assessment for multiple purposes. It argued that "the more purposes a single assessment aims to serve, the more each purpose will be compromised."[8] As I will elaborate later, there are reasons to qualify both of these arguments.

REASONS TO BE CONCERNED ABOUT EXPANDED
FORMATIVE ASSESSMENT

But there are also reasons to be concerned about a rapid expansion of formative assessment. Perhaps the most obvious reason is that formative assessment does not always work. On some occasions, the hours and effort devoted to formative assessment might have been better devoted to additional instruction. This is typically because the feedback from the assessment is not useful or not used in ways that are actually formative for students and/or teachers. It may also be used in ways that actually undermine learning. There are several reasons why this is so.

Tensions among Instruction, Assessment, and Testing

Many of the challenges for formative assessment are the result of the aforementioned complexities. While the increased focus on assessment has helped many appreciate these tensions, it has not resolved them. Instruction, assessment, and testing can each embrace very different assumptions about the nature of learning. These assumptions are often taken for granted and often conflict with one another. Conflict is compounded when different assumptions are present in the same practices. Different assumptions make tensions across practices inevitable. These tensions result in problems like those that Horst Rittel and Melvin Webber called "wicked problems."[9]

These wicked tensions pervade the enterprise of education. They are most obvious when policy makers try to use high-stakes tests to reform teaching and learning, a practice currently most apparent with NCLB. But some of the reasons to be concerned about the current large-scale assessment reforms are rooted in a prior wave of reforms in the 1990s. Reflecting a relatively modern perspective on knowing and learning, these reforms led to the expanded use of portfolios and open-ended performance assessments in many U.S. states and of some of the national tests in other Western countries. These reforms were pushed back by concerns such as increased cost and decreased reliability compared to conventional tests and perceived lack of promised improvements in instruction.[10] Rejection of these reforms helped pave the way in the United States for NCLB at the turn of the century.

Many of the fundamental challenges in coordinating instruction, assessment, and testing have to do with *validity*. Validity refers to the trustworthiness of specific interpretations made from evidence. (Validity should not be confused with reliability, which refers to the precision of a score on a particular assessment.) The late Samuel Messick (the father of modern test-validity theory) published an influential paper in 1994, in the midst of the earlier wave of reforms, that helped many appreciate the validity issues associated with open-ended performance assessments and related problem-solving measures.[11] The paper highlighted some of the fundamental challenges inherent in the notion of "tests worth teaching to." Messick explained how providing learners with formative feedback on performance assessments can compromise the validity of similar assessments. This threat to validity hints at a fundamental concern that this chapter aims to address: the way that this happens is hard to understand in theory and almost impossible to address in practice.

The issues that Messick raised prompted guidelines for appropriate preparation for open-ended performance assessments. These guidelines continue to be both relevant and widely ignored. William Mehrens, W. James Popham, and Joseph Ryan pointed out that most educational assessments are used to make claims about student ability beyond the actual assessment tasks.[12] They argue that when this is the case, one has to be careful not to prepare students for summative assessments with formative feedback on similar problems: "The drawback of providing students with direct practice on tasks that are clones of the task embodied in an end of instruction performance test is that students may learn to master a specific type of task, yet be unable to generalize the skills and knowledge that have been learned to other somewhat dissimilar types of tasks."[13]

This helps explain why formative assessments may actually result in *less* learning in some classrooms. As I suggested above, the ultimate explanation of this result is rooted in newer situative theories of knowing and learning. But it can be partly explained within the modern cognitive view of learning advanced by *Knowing What Students Know* and embraced by most assessment researchers. As attested to by numerous chapters, articles, and conference papers, increased interest in formative assessment has resulted in an increased number of empirical studies that compare learning with and without formative assessment. Arguably, many of these studies test whether students who are provided with formative feedback when solving problems learn to solve those problems better than students who do not get feedback. This ultimately is nothing more than a test of educational malpractice: withholding feedback from students simply short-circuits the entire teaching and learning process.

What is both surprising and illustrative about many of the experimental studies of formative assessment is the trivial size of the advantage sometimes found for the formative feedback group; some even find no advantage or even greater advantage in the comparison group. This is quite surprising, because feedback is so important and it is difficult to learn without it. The frequency of negative results is informative because it suggests that many of these studies ignore the fundamental premise of formative assessment (and this chapter): in order to be educationally valid, feedback must be *useful* and *it must be used* in ways that advance learning. This is one of the core points made by Black and Wiliam, and while it is appreciated by assessment experts, it appears to be widely ignored in studies of formative assessment. While it is beyond the scope of this chapter to review this literature, one of the markers of the problem is the scant attention that many studies pay to the usefulness and use of feedback. Most studies describe the feedback provided, but few provide convincing evidence that the feedback was actually used by the learners or teachers in specific and useful ways. Part of the problem is that demonstrating use can actually be quite challenging with many kinds of formative feedback in typical classroom-based educational research. This problem is confounded by the validity issue raised earlier, but it may also be that it is a lot harder than we think to provide formative feedback in typical formative assessment contexts in ways that are truly effective. If the resources devoted to poorly enacted formative assessment take time and attention away from other curricular activities that would have been well enacted, then the introduction of formative assessment practices is likely to result in reduced learning.

Issues Facing Formative Assessment Research

Some of the concerns with expanded formative assessment stem from continued efforts to prove that formative feedback works. We already know that feedback works. Embracing the experimental gold standard that is touted by many assessment and measurement specialists, some studies go to great lengths to establish well-controlled designs, sometimes randomly assigning students and even teachers to conditions. These sorts of experimental controls can be quite challenging in classroom research. The specific concern is that the effort to achieve such controls may come at the expense of efforts to ensure that feedback is useful and used. Rather than experimental studies of formative feedback, what are needed are more studies of assessment using what has come to be called "design-based research." As illustrated by this chapter and others in this volume, and elaborated later, such studies should use more interpretive methods to ensure that feedback is indeed useful and used. Once the usefulness and use of learners' feedback has been established with such interpretive methods, research should include additional outcome measures for which students have not been provided formative feedback and that are appropriate for use in controlled experimental studies.

The concerns I raise here are primarily directed at more structured activities that are the primary focus of formative assessment research. As illustrated by many of the chapters in this volume, such semiformal formative assessments are resource-intensive. They take up a lot of student and teacher time to administer, complete, score, and then deliver and use feedback. The worry is that while most classrooms can manage assigning and completing formative assessments, many classrooms may fall short on the more complicated process of interpreting student performance and then providing and using feedback in ways that advance learning. Consider, for example, a mathematics teacher who elects to include an open-ended formative assessment during a week-long unit. Even though most students complete the assessment within fifteen minutes, one-half of a class period is set aside to ensure that all students can complete it. The teacher then spends an hour of grading time reviewing the completed assessments and identifying persistent misconceptions. She then devotes fifteen minutes to a whole-class discussion about students' misconceptions and fifteen more minutes with a subset of students who still seem to be struggling.

There are the obvious concerns with the amount of downtime, the issue of whether or not students were engaged in the whole-class discussion, and the concern that the feedback may or may not have connected with their current understanding of the concept. Likewise, the teacher may or may not use the insights gained from the assessment to adjust the rest of the unit or teach the unit differently. The specific point here is that depending on how well-designed the unit was and how well it was being enacted in the classroom, the resources devoted to the formative assessment might have been more productively applied to carefully and systematically completing the unit as it was originally designed. The larger point is that we should be careful in assuming that time taken away from lessons for more formal, formative assessment practices will always lead to increased learning. There are many other factors at play. Some of these factors are most apparent from the perspective of contemporary situative views of cognition, which support a much broader definition of learning.

HOW SITUATIVE THEORIES TREAT ASSESSMENT AS LEARNING

As articulated by cognitive scientists like James Greeno and linguists like James Gee, situative theories characterize learning primarily in terms of broader social, cultural, and technological change.[14] Contrary to popular misperception, situative views do not dismiss or ignore learning by individuals. Rather, they treat change that happens to individuals as a special case of these broader forms of interactive learning. Following the groundbreaking work of Jean Lave and Etienne Wenger, these views characterize learning in terms of *trajectories* of interactive participation.[15] This makes it possible to treat seemingly isolated learning by an individual as a specific type of trajectory of interaction with socially defined artifacts. The most obvious implication for assessment is that *all* of the changes that result (or might result) from the process of assessment, testing, and accountability systems are forms of learning. This leads to the argument that assessment in all of its different functions (formative versus summative) and types (individual understanding versus group achievement) has the potential to support learning.

A less obvious implication of situative theory for assessment is that all learning involves assessment, because all learning involves interaction: "In every moment of interaction, participants produce information that reflects their current understanding of each other's statements and intended meanings, and this information plays a major role in the way the interaction progresses. In this sense, assessment is inherent in all interactions, although the function of assessment is, for the most part, tacit."[16]

Just as the narrow summative notion of assessment *of* learning was expanded with the more formative notion of assessment *for* learning, situative perspectives lead to an even broader notion of assessment *as* learning. From this perspective, to-be-learned knowledge consists of social and technological tools that learners must first pick up before they can practice using them. This initial practice provides the context that is necessary to understand how to use those tools appropriately in particular contexts. The fundamental concern is that prevailing formative assessment practices lock in an overly narrow characterization of important knowledge as abstract understanding that people carry around in their minds. In doing so, they discourage initial participation in domain-specific discourse and interaction that is crucial, especially for struggling learners. Of course, this perspective is counterintuitive for many assessment specialists and seems heretical for many measurement specialists. As such, it calls for elaboration.

THE FIRST GENSCOPE ASSESSMENT PROJECT

This proposed alternative approach to formative assessment is rooted in two multiyear collaborations with Paul Horwitz involving the GenScope computer-based modeling software described in chapter 11. Designed for one of the first color graphic computers (Apple IIe), GenScope presented very sophisticated graphic models of complex multilevel processes that students could manipulate. With GenScope, students could literally insert a mutation into an organism's DNA, watch the "dance of the chromosomes" to see if and how the mutation was transmitted to offspring, examine a pedigree chart for multiple generations of offspring, and even run a model of evolution to see if the mutation was carried forward. The software featured fanciful dragons, the various interfaces were simple and intuitive, and the GenScope team had developed guided-inquiry lessons that most students found fun and deeply engaging.

The National Science Foundation requested that an outside team create a comprehensive assessment of GenScope and help use it to evaluate learning. This work was carried out at the Center for Performance Assessment at the Educational Testing Service. The assessment development was led by Ann Kindfield and was based on her prior research on learning progressions in introductory inheritance.[17] This work distinguished between simple cause-to-effect reasoning (e.g., how particular traits are expressed) and effect-to-cause reasoning (like using a pedigree chart to figure out how a particular trait was inherited, a common task for geneticists). The latter implies that the individual has a robust cognitive model of the relationships between the various elements. GenScope was designed to support the sort of inquiry-oriented learning that would let students construct such a model. A comprehensive performance assessment using a new organism (the "NewWorm") and traditional representations of genetic information was created.[18]

Unfortunately, even after dozens of hours of guided inquiry, many students were unable to solve the simpler cause-to-effect problems, and none of them could solve the more sophisticated effect-to-cause problems on the NewWorm performance assessment. This raised the question of whether the new organism and representations were confusing students or whether they were really not learning the underlying principles of inheritance. To answer this question, a second performance assessment was created using screen shots from the GenScope software. But the same students did only a little better on our new assessment. This convinced everyone that students were really *not* discovering fundamental rules of inheritance in their inquiry-oriented activities in GenScope. The obvious solution was to use the new assessment as a formative assessment.

Feedback Conversations for Social Learning

The new assessments were transformed in the Dragon Investigations described in chapter 11. For each investigation, a dense and detailed *answer explanation* was created to help teachers explain the solutions to the students. After students completed several of the guided inquiry activities in GenScope, they would complete a Dragon Investigation and discuss their answers with their classmates. This part of our work was inspired by the paper on "assessment conversations" that science educator Rick Duschl and assessment scholar Drew Gitomer published in 1997.[19] The answer explanations were originally designed for the teachers so that they could help lead the conversations, provide feedback, and correct misconceptions.

What was exciting was the way that the GenScope activities left behind a rich, *shared* understanding of the GenScope dragons and their various features. This helped students participate in remarkably sophisticated conversations about the way they solved the problems. Students seemed to quite naturally recognize that the new technical terms they were encountering in the answer explanations (e.g., homozygote) were new to everyone; they also readily used the features of the GenScope software to make sense of these terms (e.g., "the thingy in the meiosis window"). And they adjusted their choice of words and their interactions accordingly, completing each other's sentences. In the conversations, many students would struggle to initially pronounce the new technical terms that were introduced in the Dragon Investigations, but there was something about the informal nature of the conversations that encouraged students to help each other out. One student might say "the hetero . . . ummm . . ." and a classmate would say "heterozygote," and the first student would use the term correctly and continue on.

Scores on the summative performance assessment started going up with these conversations. This led to an intensive multiyear effort to search for ways to refine the conversations. This search started with the aforementioned situative theories of learning. These theories (and related sociocultural studies of classroom discourse) suggested looking past the knowledge that presumably was developing in the minds of individuals. Rather, these theories suggested focusing on the knowledge that was stretched across the different participants, technologies, and representations that made up this new formative assessment context. Right away, these theories helped explain something very interesting about the conversations. During the GenScope activities, the high school students sounded a lot like, well, high school students. They made up everyday words to label the representations and processes they observed. They gave the dragons names of friends and family members. But their conversations around the Dragon Investigations began to take on a rather different tone. Students would help each other try out the technical language of the domain. Students and teachers finished each other's sentences; more experienced students helped less experienced students use more of the technical language of inheritance. Situative theories of identity helped us appreciate the conversations as a context in which students could collectively try on the identities associated with being a geneticist. Sociocultural theories of classroom discourse helped explain why seemingly productive conversations among students could abruptly cease when a teacher (or even a more authoritative student) gave the correct answer to a problem.

In the search to improve the conversations, various configurations were tried. In some classes, the conversations consisted of teachers explaining the solutions to the problem using the technical language and diagrams in the answer explanation. In retrospect, the conversations were relatively boring, and there was a sense that those students did not do particularly well on the NewWorm. But in other classes, students were given copies of the answer explanations and allowed to struggle through them on their own. And this was when the power of the prior GenScope activities really became apparent. The answer explanations were written for high school biology teachers. They used small type, big words, and complex diagrams; reading-grade level analysis showed them to be well into the college level. The shared experience with the GenScope activities allowed even struggling students to work together with their classmates to make sense of the answer explanations.

Across several cycles of refinement, the original idea of a teacher-led assessment conversation gave way to small-group, student-led feedback conversations. This label was used to communicate the idea that the conversation itself was feedback. In other words, individuals were not expected to provide feedback on each other's problems in the traditional sense. Rather the feedback was intended to be much more informal. Much of the feedback consisted of students indicating whether they understood what other students were saying. This is different from indicating whether they think what the other student said was scientifically *correct*. While students also provided "correctness" feedback, situative theories of learning were suggesting that the former very informal feedback was necessary before students could provide the latter more formal feedback.

As the conversations were further refined, students did better on the NewWorm assessment. A *lot* better. In sixteen of seventeen high school biology classrooms, we documented gains unlikely to have occurred by chance. These gains averaged about one standard deviation. In measurement terms, this is the difference between the fiftieth percentile and the eighty-fourth percentile. A follow-up study with two matched comparison classrooms obtained gains of three standard deviations in the GenScope classroom, which was twice as large as the gains in the comparison classroom where the teacher used a conventional textbook curriculum.[20]

Design-Based Alignment of Different Assessment Levels

While the first GenScope project eventually included comparison groups, it was not really an experimental study. Rather, we used a growing appreciation of participation in domain-specific discourse in this context to directly improve the feedback conversation, while examining the indirect consequences of these improvements on individual understanding. This work was occurring at the same time that the notion of *design-based research* (DBR) was emerging. Particularly as Paul Cobb and colleagues described it in 2003, DBR starts out by considering the *practices* that students need to engage in. Practices in this sense refer to using the conceptual, representational, and linguistic tools of the particular domain (e.g., sex-linked inheritance, Punnett squares, and "homozygote") respectively.[21] Rather than helping students understand these things in the abstract, the goal becomes one of preparing students to use these tools appropriately in specific social and technological contexts. The next step is developing an informal theory for moving communities of learners from their current practices to these desired practices. In our case, this first meant transforming the informal everyday conversations around the GenScope activities into more formal conversations that looked and sounded more like ones that geneticists would have. But these conversations needed to leave each student able to use his or her new tools of inheritance appropriately in the very different context of the NewWorm performance assessment.

What began to take shape was the notion of design-based alignment of very different knowledge practices across different assessment levels. This is different from the more typical approach of having students practice solving increasingly difficult problems in the same way. Rather, there were increasingly difficult problems *within* the

GenScope activities, the Dragon Investigations, and the NewWorm assessment. What was changing was how formally students were engaging with the domain knowledge at each level. The GenScope activities were very informal: the assessment at this level consisted of the collaborative groups figuring out whether they were doing what they were supposed to be doing and then assessing what was happening in the program. The Dragon Investigations and the feedback conversations were semiformal. Though various schemes for grading (and not grading) were tried out, the focus was always on maximizing engagement in the feedback conversation. In contrast, the summative performance assessment was formal. Students completed it individually, and the research team carefully scored their answers with a conventional rubric.

The idea emerged that the formative potential of the GenScope activities was summatively assessed with the Dragon Investigations and feedback conversations, while the formative potential of the Dragon Investigations and feedback conversations was summatively assessed with the original performance assessment. What became apparent was how learning at each level could focus on the unique formative potential of that level because of the accountability provided by the unique summative potential of the next level. These insights helped the GenScope design team resist the tendency to include more domain-specific language and representation in the GenScope activities. When beginning a particular activity, students lack the situated experience to comprehend these abstract terms and ideas. Including too many of them too early makes the activities dense and confusing.

In the same way, the summative function of the NewWorm helped discourage using Dragon Investigations only to summatively assess individual understanding. The NewWorm provided accountability that could discourage teachers' tendencies to ask conversation-killing known-answer questions or transform the feedback conversations into lectures using abstract textbook language and examples. This is *really* important when teaching inheritance in typical ninth-grade life science classes. It is the first time that many students will be asked to solve problems that involve proportional reasoning about things that cannot be directly observed and that occur at unimaginable speed. A premature focus on the abstract processes leaves many students overwhelmed and confused. Rather than picking up the new tools to practice using them, students try to memorize the definitions and the specific steps used to solve the particular problems. Or they just give up.[22]

The Problem of "Construct-Irrelevant Variance"

The earlier discussion about appropriate performance-assessment preparation practices raises the issue of whether the improved scores on the NewWorm were the result of simply more "teaching to the test." The informal Dragon Investigations used problems that were similar to the ones on the more formal NewWorm assessment. For the easier problems, it was certainly possible that students were merely memorizing procedures for solving problems without appreciating the underlying principles and concepts. But the answer explanations and feedback conversations focused more on the underlying concepts and less on the step-by-step procedures. And for the more complex problems, it was impossible to memorize the solutions for all the possible combinations of the problems.

But, in an important way, Samuel Messick *was* right. Using the same types of problems in both the Dragon Investigation and the NewWorm presumably meant that at least some of the gain was due to students getting practice solving those problems. This threat to trustworthiness of scores is what Messick labeled *construct-irrelevant variance*: differences in scores that are the result of acquired knowledge (e.g., memorized step-by-step procedures) that is irrelevant to the knowledge one intended to assess (i.e., the student's understanding of underlying processes). Messick emphasized the difficulty of distinguishing between the deeper conceptual understanding (that presumably could transfer to different types of problems and contexts) and knowledge of specific proce-dures for solving particular types of problems. In order to address this concern, we might have deliberately used entirely different problems across the Dragon Investiga-tion and the NewWorm. But this would have been much harder to do and would have made the NewWorm a lot less useful for guiding refinements along the way.

The more fundamental issue we were confronting was this: it is difficult in theory and impossible in practice to determine how much construct-irrelevant variance is introduced when providing formative feedback on one set of problems in order to prepare students to solve a similar set of problems. On one hand, the way we created the Dragon Investigation and answer explanation fixed the degree of transformation across the Dragon Investigation and the NewWorm. On the other hand, some feed-back conversations focused more on the underlying processes, while others focused more on the specific procedures used to solve the problems. Furthermore, there was less concern with learning the procedures without understanding the processes on the more difficult items. A central point of this chapter is that this is a *huge* theoretical and practice problem when coordinating formative and summative assessment prac-tices. A related point is that this problem is worsened when using a single model of learning for both practices.

There was another factor at play at this time. Our work was occurring in the con-text of a massive shift toward test-driven accountability that brought with it a strong focus on traditional experimental designs with rigorous, externally developed achieve-ment measures. Regardless of efforts to the contrary, skeptics were likely to dismiss the NewWorm as a hopelessly biased researcher-developed assessment. We also felt a moral obligation to the high school students we were working with. In some of their schools, a third of the students were failing the science subtests on the high school graduation tests. Typically, biology is one of three subtests, and as many as a third of the biology items might concern inheritance. Unfortunately, it is nearly impossible to obtain scores on high-stakes tests for specific topics. Even if it were possible, most students would not take the test for at least another year; and without any pretest, it would im-possible to figure out how much the curriculum was actually contributing to scores or whether this contribution was larger than with traditional instruction.

The Unique Formative Potential of Standards-Oriented Achievement Tests

We sought to address this issue of external achievement in the second GenScope as-sessment project. For these studies, we created a genetics achievement test using re-leased items from the SAT II Biology Subject Test. Rather than the research-based learn-ing progressions model underlying the NewWorm assessment, the items were selected based on their difficulty relative to each other. The validity of scores on such tests rests on the assumption that learning means building and strengthening numerous tiny links between elements of knowledge. This is precisely the sort of test that *Knowing What Students Know* had criticized.

By using a sample of items that were not embedded in any particular context, the test was independent of any particular curriculum. Because the items came from the SAT, they were well aligned with the state biology standards. This made for a standards-oriented test, as opposed to the curriculum-oriented NewWorm. While a standards-oriented test is necessarily less sensitive to the impact of any particular curriculum, it is very unlikely that a given curriculum provided practice and feedback on the items that ended up on the test. This separateness gives such tests several unique functions. It makes it possible to efficiently obtain valid evidence for comparing learning across multiple curricula targeting the same standards. It also gave us a valid measure for judging the improvement of our curriculum from one year to the next. This was important because we had no way of knowing how much construct-irrelevant variance was being introduced with each refinement. And to reiterate, the broad view of learning in situative theories of assessment treats all of these insights as learning. Thus, this seemingly summative achievement test actually presented the project with unique and critically important formative potential.

After we created the test, we did something that was very important: we put it away. We did not consider the items as we refined the curriculum. Rather, we took the test out only to administer it before and after students completed the curriculum and the NewWorm pretest and posttest. In other words, we did not consider the items in any way when we were developing the curriculum, and we never allowed the GenScope teachers to see the items. We did this because multiple-choice tests are so easily compromised.

In the first year of the second GenScope assessment project, students in four classrooms taught by the focal GenScope teacher showed modest gains on the NewWorm (over a half of a standard deviation), but almost no gains on the achievement test. We then improved the curriculum, the Dragon Investigations, and (particularly) the feedback conversations. The next year, that same teacher's classes showed much larger gains on the NewWorm, with a corresponding gain on the achievement test. The next year, after a few more refinements, his students gained almost two standard deviations on the NewWorm and over one standard deviation on the achievement test. We also administered both measures to a comparison class at the same school. These students were taught by an experienced teacher who devoted the same number of class periods to genetics using the standard textbook. These students gained very little on the NewWorm (just a quarter of a standard deviation). This was not surprising, because that test was not oriented to the textbook in the same way. But the achievement gains in the comparison classroom, one-half standard deviation, were half the size of the gains that were ultimately obtained in the GenScope classroom.[23]

MULTILEVEL DESIGN-BASED FORMATIVE ASSESSMENT

By this time, the core multilevel assessment model had emerged: (1) use informal assessments and feedback materials like our Dragon Investigations to (2) directly refine students' and teachers' shared participation in domain discourse around resources like our answer explanation, in order to (3) indirectly affect performance on a more formal curriculum-oriented assessment like our NewWorm. The results of the curriculum-oriented assessment are then used to (4) directly refine the entire curriculum, in order to (5) indirectly affect achievement on an external standards-oriented achievement test. The important point here is that we never used the curriculum-oriented assessment to provide feedback or even guide the teacher. Rather, we used more informal, activity-oriented Dragon Investigation assessments and ultimately discouraged teachers from even *looking* at individual students' responses.

This underlying model was implemented in two separate studies funded by the National Science Foundation and NASA. Including GenScope, we completed design-based formative assessment studies of five different inquiry-oriented multimedia and video-game science curricula. In four of the five studies, we obtained a similar pattern of improvement, whereby the increasing gains in the curriculum-oriented assessment were echoed in the smaller gains on the achievement measure. After one or two rounds of refinement, the achievement gains became statistically significant. These gains were as large or larger than the gains we found when we were able to identify valid comparison classrooms and measure gains on achievement.[24]

But this model is not appropriate for all curricula. One of the NASA multimedia curricula turned out to be a relatively straightforward spreadsheet activity about regenerative life support. As such, the curriculum focused on very specific procedures that were either right or wrong. The specificity of the procedures left students with nothing meaningful to discuss. A similar conclusion emerged when the model was applied to an entire fifth-grade mathematics curriculum (Everyday Mathematics). Even after three annual refinement cycles, the feedback conversations never progressed beyond students comparing the specific procedures they used to solve the problems in the chapters. We tried to focus on the concepts behind the procedures and had some success, but the feedback conversations were never as engaging or meaningful as in the other studies. Not surprisingly, the gains on performance assessments or achievement were never significantly larger than well-matched comparison teachers who used more of the curricular activities instead of our informal assessments and feedback conversations.

Participatory Assessment for Discourse, Understanding, and Achievement

It is now clear that what was missing from the curriculum in the two unsuccessful assessment design studies was ample opportunity for meaningful shared discourse. As illustrated by the efficiency of test-preparation programs and individualized drill and practice, conversation is an inefficient way to learn specific facts and procedures. The curricula in the successful studies focused on more open-ended problems. While they certainly gave students practice using specific procedures and facts, that practice was embedded within student-directed inquiry and was not the focus of the activities.

Put differently, the types of curricula where this model works are those that are capable of fostering shared participation. Learning in situative theories is primarily characterized as increasingly successful participation in the practices associated with a particular domain of knowledge. What these participatory theories have in common is a resolute concern with the social and technological contexts in which groups or communities of individuals engage in these practices. Hence, it makes sense to label the new approach to assessment and accountability as *participatory assessment.*

CONCLUSION: DESIGNING FOR PARTICIPATION IN TWENTY-FIRST CENTURY LEARNING

Increased interest in assessment has helped many educational stakeholders appreciate that there are different and competing ways to characterize knowing and learning. At the same time, an explosion of digital social networking has helped some of these stakeholders appreciate situative views of learning and participatory approaches to teaching. The neologism *blogosphere* points to the growing importance of knowledge that is being socially constructed outside of traditional media and research contexts. Wikipedia has helped us appreciate that seemingly objective knowledge is socially constructed via negotiation. The most important knowledge in many industries and scientific domains is increasing the "crowd-sourced" user-generated knowledge that is stretched across digital social networks. The amount of knowledge is growing exponentially, and the way it is accessed and represented is changing rapidly. It is becoming impossible to know even a fraction of that vast store of knowledge. Increasingly, success is defined as participating in the construction and definition of that knowledge.

For these reasons, school knowledge should increasingly be learned in ways that makes it useful in relevant, networked digital contexts. To this end, the current implementations of this multilevel assessment model use digital social networks for the feedback conversations. These include secondary language arts curriculum using the ning.com digital social network social network and university e-learning courses using "wikifolios" with with an online course management system.[25] Both examples extend the reframing of standards-oriented tests described earlier by treating them as a bizarre form of digital social network contexts that serve a specific formative function.

The participatory assessment model that has emerged across these studies lends itself well to emerging "connectivist" instructional approaches that focus more directly on networked knowledge and to the emerging open education resources (OER) movement.[26] This connectivist model begins to address the very real pressures of accountability and supports the development of specific factual and procedural knowledge. But its ultimate promise may arise from its ability to alter students' thinking about the nature of knowledge, the creation of new knowledge, and their role in that process. In addition to promoting the conceptual understanding that is the target of most formative assessment practices, participatory assessment leaves behind what Melissa Gresalfi calls a *disposition* that helps learners use that knowledge appropriately in particular contexts.[27] In this way, it helps students see that the context in which concepts are learned fundamentally shapes the meaning of those concepts. This contextual knowledge is a crucial ingredient in twenty-first century education. Many of the current efforts to standardize, teach, and test such knowledge as so-called "twenty-first century skills" are missing the point: characterizing this knowledge as a skill to be carried from one context to another strips away the contextual relevance that makes it meaningful.

For More Information

Some of these new strategies for participatory assessment and learning are now organized around five general design principles within a model called Designing for Participation. Space limitations preclude elaboration in this chapter. Interested readers may
wish to examine the networked working examples that show how the five general principles have been turned into more specific principles. Some of these examples feature
educational video games, secondary language arts, and university e-learning contexts.[28]

*I am indebted to numerous scholars and colleagues beyond those explicitly referenced in this chapter. Kate
Anderson, Michelle Honeyford, James Gee, Jenna McWilliams, Pamela Moss, Nancy Schafer, Gita Taasoobshirazi, Stephen Zuiker, and many others participated in the studies described here or contributed directly to the ideas as they were unfolding. Paul Horwitz and Ann Kindfield provided feedback on prior
versions of this chapter, while Rebecca Itow and Susie Gronseth contributed to its preparation. The writing
of this chapter was supported by grants from the MacArthur Foundation and Indiana University; the studies described were supported by the U.S. National Science Foundation, the NASA-sponsored Classroom of
the Future Program, and the U.S. Department of Education. The opinions expressed here are entirely my
own and do not represent the positions of Indiana University or any of the sponsoring agencies.*

Conclusion

*Lessons Learned, Controversies,
and New Frontiers*

PENDRED E. NOYCE

AND DANIEL T. HICKEY

This book has described efforts to use and improve formative assessment in educational settings from kindergarten through twelfth grade, in three subject areas, and in ways that address the needs of English language learners, students with disabilities, and students along a broad spectrum of achievement levels. The chapters have presented tools that range from handwritten planning guides to sophisticated technology for sharing students' manipulation of computer-generated graphics. Throughout the chapters, a number of common findings have emerged. These findings can be thought of as principles that underlie both the promise of formative assessment and the challenges faced by those who mean to use it. They can also be thought of as hard-learned lessons constructed over years of effort to build durable systems of formative assessment from the ground up. As such, the findings are worthy of consideration by anyone—from the curriculum developer to administrator to professional developer to classroom teacher—who wants to incorporate formative assessment and effective feedback into the teaching and learning cycle.

FINDINGS AND LESSONS LEARNED

Leaders of the formative assessment projects presented in this book had to figure out the key skills and concepts they wanted students to learn and what tools would help them communicate these expectations to students and teachers. They sought efficient ways to help teachers use the tools, and they devised systems to share assessment information with teachers in manageable chunks.

The First Step: Deciding What's Most Important to Learn

Developers and users of formative assessment need a clear, nuanced sense of what they most value and most want to assess in student learning. While defining what we want students to gain seems like an obvious first step in designing any instruction, in practice teachers often find themselves following the curriculum in a textbook or district pacing guide simply because it is there. Thinking analytically about how to assess student progress creates a new level of critical awareness among teachers about where they are headed. It also helps them distinguish between the more explicit practices of teaching and the more implicit processes of learning.

Because not everything can be assessed, designing or choosing an assessment instrument necessarily means creating a hierarchy of values. Figuring out what matters most often reveals remarkably different perspectives on learning and on evidence in educational systems. Defining good writing, for example, was a challenge for the teachers in Audrey Poppers's chapter on Every Child a Reader and Writer. Mathematics teachers working with David Foster's Silicon Valley Mathematics Initiative had to select the core mathematical concepts to be assessed between grades two and ten; they then had to assign points in a rubric for every mathematical performance task administered. This process led inevitably to discussions about the relative importance of getting the right answer versus being able to articulate an approach to the problem or being able to generalize the solution to similar problems. Similarly, in their study of young children's mathematical understanding, Herbert Ginsburg and colleagues delved beneath the level of correct answers to examine the kinds of strategies and principles students rely on to solve even simple problems, such as whether they use an understanding of base ten in addition and subtraction. In a particularly good example of this phenomenon, teachers using the templates for assessing students' science writing in the Seeds of Science/Roots of Reading project in chapter 9 had to agree on the core scientific concepts they wanted students to master as well as their goals for improving students' use of evidence in writing.

The process of defining assessment learning goals often highlights the friction between the goals of teachers and the goals of external accountability. Under the pressures of external accountability, some communities and administrators may define the success of an educational program as primarily a matter of students doing well on standardized tests. But the process of creating a reliable and efficient measure of achievement that is independent of any particular curriculum results in tests that are simplistic characterizations of the targeted standards. The resulting scores provide only a shallow, easy-to-measure slice of what we want our children to understand about a subject. Such scores say a lot more about students' educational and socioeconomic history than about any specific curriculum or particular teacher. This disconnect presents a real threat to formative assessment systems in the United States, because the level of teachers' time and administrative support required to sustain a strong program of formative assessment understandably leads to demands that formative assessment prove its worth. Such proof, if it is to take the form of demonstrated progress on standardized tests external to the program, is often hard to come by, as many chapters in this book reveal. Nevertheless, these chapters provide some useful examples and evidence of how formative assessment can help affect achievement scores without undermining worthwhile instruction.

The issue of alignment between formative and high-stakes summative assessment is directly addressed in Lisa Lineweaver's discussion of the FAST-R assessment of reading comprehension. The FAST-R team analyzed the Massachusetts state test, MCAS, in order to understand the components of reading comprehension addressed by the English language arts exam. The team decided that in this case, the standardized test was probing aspects of reading that were important and relevant. Building off past released tests, the team constructed its own hierarchy of finding evidence and making inferences, and then developed assessment items that identified these skills for teachers and students in a way that made direct instruction possible. Such close coupling of formative assessment and external tests may be most effective when the curriculum targets relatively specific procedural knowledge, such as early literacy and arithmetic, and provides remedial instruction on those topics.

David Foster's Silicon Valley Mathematics Initiative provided perhaps the most compelling illustration of how a concerted, large-scale formative assessment effort might have an impact on external achievement. What is most impressive is that the patterns of improvement found on the performance-based MARS summative assessments were directly echoed in a pattern of equally impressive upward shifts on the corresponding high-stakes state tests. We believe that this pattern of results provides convincing evidence that the external achievement gains were indeed the result of concerted efforts to learn from the MARS formative assessments.

Formative Assessment as Professional Development

Formative assessment often exposes areas where teachers' knowledge is itself thin or shallow. Gaps occur both in teachers' knowledge of the domain itself—content knowledge—and their understanding of how this knowledge unfolds and can best be presented to learners—pedagogical content knowledge. This phenomenon is particularly troublesome in the domain of mathematics. Chapters 1 through 4 illustrate how formative assessments that help teachers analyze student work and thinking can also reveal teachers' own misconceptions. Even when a teacher knows how to teach one or two effective procedures for solving a class of problems, underlying misconceptions can undermine and interfere. Limited understanding of a concept and corresponding solution strategies may lead a teacher to prematurely and inappropriately shut down a fruitful line of student reasoning. In particularly promising developments using computer technology, the mCLASS program in chapter 3 and the Agile Mind program in chapter 4 were designed to bolster teachers' understanding with built-in guidance or commentary.

The impact of formative assessment on teacher knowledge is evident in other domains as well. The Every Child a Reader and Writer initiative in chapter 5 increased teachers' familiarity with "craft moves" in writing—the teachers' own writing as well as that of their students. Likewise, Boston's FAST-R assessments of students' reading comprehension in chapter 6 worked best when situated within an inquiry cycle of collaborative professional development. A particularly impressive example of teacher learning is provided in chapter 10, where Dan Damelin and Kimberle Koile show teachers' learning gains in understanding chemistry from implementing the Molecular Workbench and its embedded formative assessments in their classrooms. Damelin and Koile's experience shows that externally developed formative assessments can themselves serve as both formative and summative assessments for learning brought about by teachers' professional development. These findings are tremendously important in light of recent pressure to increase teachers' content-specific course work, knowledge, and achievement. Because of this pressure, many future teachers have less time than in the past for courses focusing on pedagogical content knowledge and educational methods more broadly, such as course work on formative and summative assessment. The chapters in this book show how innovative formative assessment practices can yield a convergent solution to the dilemma of seemingly divergent goals—content versus pedagogy—for professional development.

These collected chapters offer the good news that a sustained, collaborative focus on formative assessment can become an effective vehicle for enhancing teacher knowledge. When teacher confusion or uncertainty appears in the midst of collaborative work or in the presence of a supportive coach, there is a real opportunity for efficient, relevant, just-in-time teacher learning. Wrestling with questions and explanations can help both the questioner and the explainer bring their understanding to the next level. Thus, collaboration around designing and implementing formative assessment becomes a durable, continuous process for building teacher understanding, curiosity, and even identification with their students.

The Importance of Tools

In most instances, effective formative assessment depends on teachers' continuous refinement of their diagnostic acumen. No paper instrument, checklist, or built-in automatic tutor can replace teachers' intuition and knowledge of students, but tools can help teachers develop this acumen by giving them an organized approach for understanding student thinking. This book presents a wealth of such instruments, ranging from the simple to the computationally complex. These include low-tech tools such as templates for lesson planning and for anticipating how students will perform on a mathematical task; sample rubrics, scoring schemes, and meeting agendas; and annotated examples of student work. Such instruments also include high-tech tools that offer increasingly sophisticated ways of gathering and displaying student responses to prompts. The kinds of student work that can be gathered range from selected answers to multiple-choice questions to spoken responses to puzzlelike items to student-created graphs and diagrams. These responses can be automatically analyzed and collated in many ways—by item, by student, by class, by school, by performance level, by gender. The possibilities are virtually unlimited.

The sheer volume of information that such automated formative assessments make available to teachers creates additional challenges. While Jennifer Tilson and colleagues stress in chapter 9 that all assessment needs to be time wise and efficient, this warning is especially germane to high-tech approaches. Given how much data computers can generate and given the risk of losing sight of the most useful information, innovators need to be realistic about how much information teachers can use. There is a limit to how much feedback and information about student performance teachers can absorb. Teachers could theoretically spend so much time delving into a pile of student data that they never manage to surface long enough to teach the next lesson. In practice, the designers of curriculum projects like Agile Mind in mathematics, FAST-R in reading, and RI-ITEST in science suggest approaches for judiciously selecting, organizing, and highlighting the most useful information. Presentation matters. Color-coding, placing questions right beside summed student responses, coding or commenting on where students might have gone wrong, and allowing teachers to slice the data along different dimensions are strategies that can help teachers focus on what is most important in the wealth of data that technology makes available. This problem of

data overload is perhaps one of the most important challenges facing the next generation of formative assessment, and we hope to see others building from these examples
and helping refine these strategies in new contexts.

Digital Technologies Can Change the Relationship of Assessment to Curriculum

The use of digital technology in assessment began with computerized drill and practice with built-in progress monitoring. This use of computers could be considered a
series of mini-summative assessments allowing students to claw their way up steps of
atomized knowledge. The essentially reductionist task of assessment developers was
to slice the material into the smallest steps possible so that feedback about what was
correct or incorrect could be specific. In technological terms, that conception of technology-enabled assessment is generations out of date. While such approaches are still
widely used, we contend that they are only appropriate when the knowledge targeted
by the curriculum can be meaningfully represented in terms of such elements of
knowledge. Examples include the specific procedures or skills associated with initial
fluency in reading or mathematics, and the more arbitrary associations such as vocabulary when learning foreign languages. As exemplified by several chapters in this
book and in current work on artificially intelligent tutors, the most worthwhile formative assessments, even in these more procedural and factual domains, examine
whether and how specific elements of knowledge can be used in new contexts or to
solve new problems.

Beyond the use of computers as teacher aids, half the chapters in this volume discuss ways in which digital technologies allow us to embed formative assessment directly within curricular materials. In this approach, assessment becomes integral to
curriculum instead of an add-on or afterthought. Questions, increasingly supportive
hints, and peer-to-peer interaction can be built into the learning experience. At the
extreme, students may no longer notice that they are being assessed, a change that will
be particularly welcome to those who experience test anxiety. Students will simply
work their way through a unit or module, interacting with the teacher, with other students, and with the computer in ways that feel seamless, much like the learning that is
central to the success of commercial, often multiplayer, computer games.

One important effect of this ability to embed assessment materials directly within
the curriculum is the formative feedback that student interaction with the materials
provides to curriculum writers. Writers can see where students skimmed, where they
made no mistakes, where they floundered, or where their answers indicate that they
have misconstrued a concept that an earlier piece of curriculum and assessment seemed
to ensure they had mastered. Formative assessment can help to ensure that the process
of curriculum refinement is based on real data about how students respond to the materials and what the evidence indicates they are learning.

Another important effect of these embedded assessments is the conversations
that they can promote among learners and teachers outside of the curriculum. Technology-supported formative assessment has a lot to learn from the newest generation
of commercial video games. Video-game scholars like James Gee point out that much
of the learning that is central to the success of multiplayer games occurs in chats,
blogs, voice channels, hallways, and homes—areas outside the actual game. Indeed,

many of the assessment innovations described in these chapters could use indications of such extracurricular discourse as both developmental targets and compelling
evidence of success.

The Difficulty of Getting Formative Feedback and Next Instructional Moves Right

One consistent finding detailed in this volume is that even with good assessment instruments, teachers have difficulty figuring out how to respond effectively to what
they learn about students' understanding. Even the kind of feedback to give students is
often unclear for teachers. We know that grades on completed work can inhibit student learning. In chapter 12, Daniel T. Hickey describes his observation that feedback
that is too abstract and removed from the students' prior experience can quell their
participation and, therefore, their learning. This is one of the reasons that some technology programs build feedback directly into the assessment materials.

Beyond feedback to students, though, comes the question of what instructional
moves to make next when assessment results show that initial instruction has been less
than completely effective. Not all the chapters in this book reached this point; some
stopped with the assessment itself and the information it can provide. Other chapters
noted that this dilemma about what to do next leads to a perceived need for further
professional development, be it in the craft of writing, strategies for improving reading
comprehension, or new ways of presenting mathematical concepts. According to this
view, one benefit of formative assessment is that it stimulates teachers' interest in
learning more about the subject they are teaching. David Foster responded to the
"what-next" dilemma by creating "reengagement lessons." Reengagement lessons use
a variety of student responses to MARS tasks as the raw material for further class discussion of key concepts, approaches, solution strategies, and errors.

Key, then, to the question of what to do next after formative assessment is the
quality of teacher-student and student-student discourse. Students will disengage from
such discourse in many ways and for many reasons. Unfortunately, students who need
the most help are most likely to disengage, out of boredom, frustration, or ego-protec-
tion. In response, teachers may choose to rein in more experienced students who are
pushing the discussions so far that the struggling students cannot join in—hardly a
perfect solution. This is an ideal dilemma to address with digital technology. The Strategic Reader discussed in chapter 7 takes a different approach by building in digital
discussion forums. Such forums for student interaction offer a promising approach for
fostering student engagement in assessment-driven discourse because they promise to
make it easier for struggling students to "lurk" and find places to join in the conversation.

Leadership, Accountability, and Durability of Formative Assessment

The committed leadership of principals, district administrators, and department heads
is vital if the hard work of formative assessment in schools is to take off and continue
in ways that accomplish widely shared goals. Committed leadership means clarifying
that student learning involves more than success on standardized tests. It means communicating the fact that formative assessment is a high priority for the school. It
means providing the necessary time, professional development, and supports needed

for teachers to collaborate. In many cases, it means investing wisely in the right kinds of technology to allow all students access to the tools of instruction and assessment.

Accountability oriented achievement tests have tremendous power to distort the content of instruction. Formative assessment practices can help stand as a bulwark against such distortion, but only if there is genuine collaboration among classroom teachers, instructional leaders, and building administrators. The evolution of the professional learning communities approach described in chapter 2 seems like a promising framework for fostering such collaboration. One important requirement for the success of professional learning communities is the careful nurturing of a collaborative school culture, where teachers can reveal their areas of weakness with the confidence that their colleagues will respond helpfully. Unfortunately, the psychological safety provided by such a culture may be undermined by the current emphasis on each individual teacher's accountability. Teachers concerned about job security may be less willing to reveal gaps in their knowledge, and teachers competing against one another for limited bonus money may feel that collaboration is against their own interests.

For these and other reasons, we have serious concerns about negative consequences of value-added schemes that estimate each teacher's contribution to each student's annual achievement. These schemes seem particularly worrisome when tied to pay-for-performance policies that link compensation to achievement gains. Nonetheless, both are central elements of statewide accountability reforms currently being phased in across the United States. While many of these concerns take us beyond the scope of this book, it seems to us that worthwhile formative assessment practices may provide a promising means of palliating some of the damage. At minimum, leaders and administrators should help teachers thoughtfully consider the relationship between student growth on classroom assessments and external, high-stakes scores. Depending on the form these accountability schemes take, principled leaders may be able to advocate for performance on classroom assessments to feed into and inform value-added indexes. If this is so, then it is possible some variant of the multilevel model described in chapter 12 could ease teacher concerns and foster genuine instructional improvement.

The Difficulty of Finding "Proof"

Given the claims made in some literature about the effectiveness of formative assessment in boosting student learning, it is at first puzzling that empirical evidence of impact on achievement was not more prominent in many of the chapters in this book. The reasons are multiple and complex. Some projects, such as the efforts of Alison Bailey and colleagues with ELL kindergarten teachers (chapter 8), focused on changing teacher behavior rather than on measuring impact on students. Other projects are still at very early stages of development, directing their attention more toward perfecting their assessment instruments than to measuring the effect of their interventions with students. In other projects, teacher implementation of the assessment practices was spotty and difficult to document. As Hickey points out in chapter 12, the highly contextual nature of formative assessment and the accepted fact that feedback is useful points initially toward design-based research focused on finding strategies for improving outcomes and efficiency, rather than experimental research with control groups focused on proving impact. Controlled studies bent on proving efficacy become appropriate once a practice is refined and ready to be scaled up, but experimental studies are unlikely to generate the insights needed to identify and refine the needed practices from the outset. Perhaps more importantly, when studies relying on experimental design and external measures come prematurely, they are unlikely to show impact. Such "negative" studies may then discourage continued investment in new forms of practice. It may well be that large-scale, instrumented formative assessment is itself still at a stage where outcome studies should primarily be formative rather than summative.

Nevertheless, in a few of the chapters, the authors *were* able to document student achievement gains relative to comparison groups. These studies include those carried out in the Seeds of Science program, Foster's mathematics program, and Hickey's studies of GenScope. But even in these cases, confounding factors may cloud the picture. Foster chose districts for intensive work based on strong leadership; in other cases, entrepreneurial leaders may have enrolled early in formative assessment programs. Since strong leadership is a predictor not just of successful use of formative assessment but also of higher school achievement overall, such choices threaten the validity of comparison studies.

Most of the programs discussed in this book did show varying degrees of improvement in student performance according to their own measures. The real difficulty arose in confirming these gains with gains made on outside measures, such as standardized tests. This is where the alignment issues come in to haunt program developers. If genetics makes up one-ninth of the questions on a state science assessment, by how much should we expect scores to improve as a result of formative assessment in genetics? If a California writing test that is later abandoned as fatally flawed shows no particular achievement gains among students whose classroom writing had been the target of formative assessment, does that mean the program was ineffective?

Because of these difficulties and the practical and political importance of demonstrating student gains in ways that will be convincing to communities and state agencies, the editors strongly recommend that any school undertaking an initiative in formative assessment carefully consider what the summative assessment of the program will be. What gains in student learning are you looking to achieve, and how will you know if you have been successful in achieving them? While growth on the formative assessment instruments themselves is encouraging, an outside source of validation makes the case for a new intervention even more convincing. This additional confirmation can be anything from changes in student enrollment and success in subsequent classes to improvements on particular sections of state tests to gains on a selection of questions from the National Assessment of Educational Progress (NAEP) or Trends in International Mathematics and Science Study (TIMSS) to increases in the quality of written work graded by trained and blinded examiners. If practical, schools or districts should include a "wait-listed" group of control students to differentiate which portion of student growth comes with the passage of time and use of the regular curriculum and which portion comes from the practices of formative assessment. In wait-list designs, teachers or schools are recruited and organized into pairs or groups. Then half of each pair or a subset of each group can be randomly assigned to implement the innovation in the first year and the rest in subsequent years.

Student and Teacher Engagement

In spite of all these difficulties and barriers, most teachers in these chapters seemed pleased with and even excited about their new formative assessment practices. Again and again, teachers voiced their enthusiasm for looking at student work in a new way and for the intellectual excitement of diagnosing student thinking. For many teachers, formative assessment makes teaching an intellectual enterprise. Such an enterprise can engage beginning teachers, and it can provide renewal for seasoned teachers who have settled into predictable routines. Formative assessment practices invite teachers to learn alongside their colleagues, to share in a process of common inquiry, and to develop their expertise. It gives teachers a new set of tools to increase their effectiveness. All of these factors—collegiality, discovery, and the development of new skills—are likely to be motivating for the strongest teachers. Even more powerful are those moments when teachers realize that their students can meet higher standards than they had ever expected.

As for students, most of them are likely to find the kinds of assessments described in this book more motivating and more challenging than the standard mixture of mostly multiple-choice and one or two open response or essay questions. In some cases, assessment is so smoothly stirred into the curriculum that students may not feel any disconnect between instruction and assessment. Other assessments will feel more like homework, games, or group projects than the kind of tests that makes a student's stomach hurt and hands go clammy. After all, whatever written or technological tools teachers use to facilitate it, the best formative assessment should feel to students like nothing more than good instruction that challenges them, probes their thinking, and demands their best.

FORMATIVE ASSESSMENT AND ACADEMIC DOMAINS

Many books and papers written on formative assessment either address the topic generically without reference to specific subjects or focus on a single subject, most often mathematics. Because the chapters in this book explore the workings of formative assessment embodied in mathematics, science, and English language arts classrooms, they afford us the opportunity to examine whether and how formative assessment differs among these three subjects. Some of these issues were raised in the introduction. We return to them in detail here.

Mathematics

School mathematics tends to be a highly structured, hierarchically organized subject. Teachers of mathematics must constantly negotiate the balance between procedures and mathematical concepts. More than in reading or writing, student and teacher misconceptions threaten to derail progress through the curriculum. Misunderstanding a topic today is likely to lead to trouble tomorrow, next month, or next year. Given the widely acknowledged lack of teacher preparation at the lower grades, there is a particular danger in elementary or middle school mathematics that teacher feedback will be not just unhelpful but will actually promote misconceptions.

For students of mathematics, transfer is a perennial problem. Students may be able to apply a procedure such as figuring percentages correctly when studying the figuring percentages section of the decimals and percentages chapter, yet they may find the same kind of question difficult to fathom when asked at the end of another chapter or in the midst of a realistic scenario. While most students learn how to calculate the three primary measures of central tendency (mean, median, and mode) early on, many of them remain unable to articulate the consequences of using one or the other until many years later. Some never can. The various chapters in the first section of the book illustrate how formative assessments can help ensure that students master the crucial conceptual and contextual knowledge needed to use mathematical procedures appropriately.

Additional challenges arise from the way mathematics study is currently arranged. Even with multiple levels of mathematics taught in many middle schools and most high schools, there is still a great need for differentiation within the classroom. We are currently in a period of accelerating the American mathematics curriculum in order to compete with students in other countries. As a result, the danger of many students hurrying on with major unacknowledged holes in their understanding may be greater than ever. (Perhaps this rushed approach helps to account for the fact that even students who have passed precalculus or calculus routinely perform on the ACT at a level that predicts a high likelihood of failure in college algebra.) We are pleased that the new Common Core State Standards in Mathematics have addressed at least some of these problems. We further expect that these standards will provide enough stability and commonality to allow for building shared knowledge of effective formative assessment materials and strategies. In particular, this introduction of "crosscutting mathematical practices" that are stretched across the specific standards seems like precisely the sort of innovation in standard setting that lends itself well to formative assessment.

English Language Arts

An issue particular to English language arts may be the difficulty of clearly defining goals for instruction. Lisa Lineweaver describes in chapter 6 the challenges of breaking the construct of reading comprehension into subskills of finding evidence and making inferences so that these can be assessed, brought into students' awareness, and specifically taught. Similarly, in writing, teachers struggle to move beyond the two poles of either grading papers for adherence to conventions of grammar and punctuation or evaluating student writing by an intuitive, holistic feeling that does not allow for specific feedback. Learning to recognize the features of strong writing and the craft moves—transitions, descriptions that call on multiple senses, thoughtful use of repetition and rhythm, control of pacing, and the like—that create strong written work is the first step in the formative assessment of writing. The development of oral language among English language learners, too, requires careful delineation of what features of language a teacher must look for to measure progress.

Beyond these characteristics of formative assessment in language arts is the fact that so much of what happens in reading and writing goes on underground, out of sight. In chapter 7, it was only when middle school teachers heard students reading aloud within the Strategic Reader program that they realized that comprehension problems might be rooted in lack of basic reading fluency. Likewise, in writing, students may need help identifying specific features in sample pieces of writing before they can reproduce these features in their own work. The various chapters in this volume and work reported elsewhere show how formative assessment can help students as well as teachers recognize the component skills needed for proficient reading and writing.

Finally, reading, writing, and speaking cross all other academic areas. The new Common Core State Standards in English stress the importance of reading and writing in the content areas of mathematics, social science, and science. Most of the reading students will do after high school, whether in college or the workplace, will be nonfiction. Most of the writing they do will be analytical, informational, or procedural, and writing will increasingly occur in informal, digital, or multimodal contexts. For these reasons, reading and writing offer untapped opportunities for cross-disciplinary or integrated formative assessment. The way that a single assessment probe for both writing and science was used in chapter 9 introduces a promising strategy that could be readily taken up in other science learning contexts and other subject areas as well.

Science

More than other subjects, science offers opportunities for modeling and exploration within virtual environments. Objects within virtual environments can be programmed to obey the laws of physics and biology, and students can be empowered to explore how these laws work by interacting with objects in the environment. Virtual environments offer an opportunity to decrease the noise-to-signal ratio, eliminating some of the sources of error or complication (like friction) that operate in the real world. It is perhaps for these reasons (or perhaps because of National Science Foundation funding or because other developers share Paul Horwitz's sense that science is a game) that science has become one of the richest fields for technological innovation in embedded formative assessment.

The study and assessment of science has its own controversies. Chief among these is the proper balance between science content and the processes of scientific inquiry. Standardized tests have particular difficulty assessing science inquiry; past attempts to address this lack through standardized performance assessments have run into problems with cost and reliability. Formative assessment that comes through observing how students approach problems—observation made feasible by the ability of computers to capture and collate student moves—holds particular promise as a way of approaching the question of students' understanding of inquiry. The chapters in this book focused on science learning provide outstanding examples of ways that formative assessment can be used to improve learning within a conceptual and inquiry-oriented curriculum.

An unresolved problem in science, perhaps even more salient than in mathematics, is transfer. The question must always be asked whether students' interaction with and seeming mastery of a computerized model represent anything more than the younger generation's finely honed computer gaming ability. Efforts must be made to ensure that in the student's mind the concepts involved in the "game" have relevance in the world of reality and can be applied in written, spoken, and concrete physical contexts. This issue was a central focus of the refinements to the formative assessment for GenScope described in chapters 11 and 12 and remains one of the most fertile areas for continued formative assessment research in science.

AREAS OF CONTROVERSY IN FORMATIVE ASSESSMENT

Among the controversies in formative assessment, perhaps the foremost is what kinds of assessment qualify to be called *formative*. Among scholars in the field, periodic assessments closely modeled on summative standardized tests do not qualify and should properly be called interim assessments or mini-summative assessments. This distinction comes because such assessments, while useful for predicting student performance on later exams, are much less useful in guiding teachers on anything more than coverage of specific topics. Recognizing that the same test can be used for different purposes, Dylan Wiliam and other assessment scholars have helped move the field beyond assigning the formative label to any particular assessment. Instead, they assign that label to the assessment's purposes. In chapter 12, Hickey suggests that a broader conceptualization of learning associated with new situative theories of learning leads to assigning the labels of formative and summative to particular assessment *functions*. This approach highlights the fact that an assessment that might serve a formative function for policy makers (such as for making major curricular policy decisions) will necessarily serve a more summative function for teachers. Likewise, an exam that teachers might use formatively to make curricular decisions in their classroom will often serve a more summative function for the students who complete the exam.

The longer the time between student performance on an assessment and feedback given to the student in response, the less clearly the assessment serves a formative purpose or function for that student. Arguably, if the only person meant to act in a new or different way as a result of the assessment is the student, the assessment is not formative in the sense presented in this book. Formative assessment should change the teacher's way of thinking about what students know and can do and about where the teacher's approach so far has been successful and unsuccessful. It should lead to changes in what the teacher plans to do tomorrow, if not sooner. Ideally, it should enlist teacher and students on the same side in the next campaign for deeper understanding and more engaged participation.

Individual versus Situated Group Assessment

Daniel T. Hickey raises the question of whether formative assessment limits itself by adhering to a model of learning based exclusively on the growth of individual students' skills and conceptual understanding. He argues that much of our participation in modern life and even in knowledge generation occurs within a social and technological context, with knowledge distributed and shared among multiple individuals. In place of formative assessment that focuses on individuals, he argues for informal *participatory assessment* that encourages shared participation by student and teacher members of a learning community in a particular domain. Progress is seen here in increasingly successful participation in the domain, as reflected in discourse between student and teacher or between student and student, as mediated by the various assessment tools.

Needless to say, this notion of situated and shared assessment, where feedback focuses on participation rather than on answers or even correct concepts, is controversial. Most in the assessment community assume that shared discourse and participation in group projects are not ends in themselves but are meant as ways to boost individual understanding. It is this individual understanding, they would argue, that should be assessed; and if progress is insufficient, interventions other than group learning and shared discourse should be tried. Fortunately, these are assessment questions that actually can be answered with established empirical methods where both such approaches are employed in similar settings, and the ultimate improvement in individual understanding and group achievement is carefully compared.

Role and Nature of High-Stakes Assessment

As shown in many of the chapters and in the observations earlier, tensions and issues with high-stakes accountability testing permeate most aspects of formative assessment. Most proponents and practitioners decry the reductionist tendencies of standardized tests, with their focus on measuring only a single construct per question and their insistence that multiple-choice questions offer the best psychometric properties and efficiencies. Clearly, standardized tests serve a different purpose from the formative assessments described in this volume. But the question remains for many as to whether the process of formative assessment should be expected to contribute *anything at all* to student success on standardized measures.

Though some would disagree, we would argue that surely the answer must be yes. If we believe that standardized tests measure anything important about learning in a subject area and if we believe formative assessment contributes to student learning in that same domain, then we should expect to see the sort of patterns that Foster observed across the MARS summative assessments (which were oriented more to the MARS formative assessments) and the statewide mathematics achievement test (which were oriented more toward the content standards). This pattern is what Hickey characterizes as an echo: a positive impact, attenuated but real, on the standardized measure that mirrors the larger effect on the more sensitive assessment. When such an effect is found, it provides robust evidence that the formative assessment program is providing real gains in learning and not simply honing students' ability to respond to a certain kind of prompt in a certain way.

The tensions that arise over formative versus accountability purposes for assessment can sometimes become conflated with tensions over assessment *formats*, independent of purpose. Assessment purposes and assessment formats are distinct issues, and they interact in complex but important ways. In general, more open-ended assessment formats (especially portfolio, performance, and essay assessments) are more consistent with constructivist and inquiry-oriented instruction. These, in turn, reflect a view of knowledge as higher-order conceptual representations that each human mind uniquely constructs in order to make sense of the world. From this viewpoint, the specific associations used to recognize answers to multiple-choice items are seen as relatively meaningless. Furthermore, if any such associations were learned as a result of deliberate efforts to prepare students for those items, then the evidence they provide is meaningless as well.

A very different view of knowing supports the use of multiple-choice formats. More expository and direct-instruction approaches assume that knowledge consists of a mass of very specific associations. These associations, be they stimulus-response behavioral associations or if-then cognitive relationships, can be learned directly from the world, built up, and assembled into hierarchies. If this conception of learning is correct, then multiple-choice tests that efficiently assess a relatively large number of these associations are a sensible and trustworthy format. Conversely, open-ended formats are messy, inefficient, and inauthentic.

The purposes of assessment and the formats for assessment both raise serious questions. How educators answer these questions has important implications for theory, policy, and practice. Indeed, there are other volumes devoted to both issues. Continued progress in testing for accountability and assessment for learning demands careful consideration of both assessment purpose and assessment format.

FUTURE DIRECTIONS AND CHALLENGES

This book should have made clear to any practitioner that formative assessment carries with it plenty of implementation challenges, including the need for steady leadership, significant professional development, and persistence. But how do we expect formative assessment to develop in the next decade or two? How will this practice be affected by or perhaps contribute to changes in the educational landscape?

One seemingly safe prediction for change in education is that digital technologies will continue, however slowly, to penetrate the classroom. Even more slowly, social networks and other Web 2.0 technologies will eventually follow. Indeed, if teacher retirements continue as expected, if our ability to graduate new teachers in mathematics and science does not improve, or if working conditions and salary levels continue to drive new teachers out of the field, we may have no choice but to rely on computers to do ever more of the work of math and science teachers. Therefore, the role of assessments embedded in instructional materials should only increase. What is uncertain is whether these assessments will be the kinds of rich, complex examinations of student moves within a model-based environment envisioned here or whether they will be computerized drill and practice geared toward the digestion and regurgitation of discrete facts about the natural world.

So, one challenge is to guard the complexity and depth of formative assessment. Another is to continue to explore the degree to which two-dimensional models of how the world works translate into thoughtful contemplation of real phenomena in the three-dimensional nonvirtual world. Scholars will need to continue to scrutinize the question of transfer so that our assessments provide feedback for how to prepare students to succeed in the real world and not just the world of testing.

Another prediction about education is that even as we develop and embrace common state standards for the first time, the delivery of education is likely to continue to diversify. The number of home-schooled students in the United States now rivals the number attending charter schools. As the availability of digital technology and online delivery of open source or open access curriculum accelerates, more and more parents will opt for the ultimate in customized education for their children. Formative assessment tools may become increasingly important in helping students move through curricula at their own pace and following their own path.

A further challenge to scholars of formative assessment is the question of what kind of feedback to learners is most effective. Hickey refers to this problem in his chapter, revealing that some forms of feedback appear to be worse than no feedback at all. To do all the work of formative assessment only to harm student progress seems like a particularly grim sort of educational failure. Figuring out what kinds of assessment responses activate students, motivate them, encourage them to persist, and actually help them to take the next steps conceptually should be a priority for researchers.

Finally, there is the question Paul Horwitz refers to in his chapter—how can the science of psychometrics handle formative assessment, group assessment, or analysis of the branching student moves a computer tracks on a complex task? There is a whole playing field of possibilities for new mathematical investigation of how these kinds of student interaction with assessment materials can be measured and interpreted.

CONCLUSION

This book has attempted to provide a picture of formative assessment as it works on the ground in settings from kindergarten to high school, with tools from pencils to computers to handheld digital devices, and in the subject areas of mathematics, English language arts, and science. The chapter authors have discussed the design, implementation, and interpretation of formative assessments, along with the professional development needed to deploy these assessments usefully. They have presented a realistic view of the challenges and barriers associated with formative assessment, and they have provided an early view of the evidence that formative assessment practices change how teachers teach and students learn.

From a parent sitting with a child on his lap helping the child learn to read, to the designer of a sophisticated computer program that models the actions of atoms and molecules, every teacher realizes that learning happens more efficiently when the teacher can meet the learner at the leading edge of his knowledge. Knowing where that leading edge is and making the right choices about how to encourage and guide the student to take the next step lie at the heart of formative assessment and the heart of teaching. To diagnose and respond to student understanding remains a fascinating challenge, one that should make formative assessment an exciting field of study and practice for years to come.

Notes

Introduction

1. Paul Black and Dylan Wiliam, "Inside the Black Box: Raising Standards through Classroom Assessment," *Phi Delta Kappan*, 2004, no. 9: 9–21.
2. Lynn S. Fuchs and Douglas Fuchs, "Effects of Systematic Formative Evaluations: a Meta-Analysis," *Exceptional Children* 53, no. 3 (1986): 199–208; and Robert L. Bangert-Drowns, C. L. Kulik, J. A. Kulik, and M. Morgan, "The Instructional Effect of Feedback in Test-Like Events," *Review of Educational Research* 61, no. 2 (1991): 213–238.
3. Stuart S. Yeh, "Class Size Reduction or Rapid Formative Assessment: a Comparison of Cost-Effectiveness," *Education Research Review* 4, no. 1 (2009): 7–15.

Chapter 1

1. Paul Black and Dylan Wiliam, "Inside the Black Box: Raising Standards through Classroom Assessment," *Phi Delta Kappan*, October 1998, 1–13.
2. Robert E. Slavin, Gwen Carol Holmes, Nancy A. Madden, Anne Chamberlain, and Alan Cheung, *Effects of a Data-Driven District Reform Model* (Baltimore, MD: Johns Hopkins University, Center for Data-Driven Reform in Education, February 2010).
3. Marnie Thompson, "Tight but Loose: A Conceptual Framework for Scaling Up School Reforms" (paper presented at the annual meeting of the American Educational Research Association [AERA], Chicago, IL, April 9, 2007–April 13, 2007, p. 6).
4. Quoted in Lorrie A. Shepard, "Formative Assessment: Caveat Emptor," in *The Future of Assessment: Shaping Teaching and Learning*, ed. C. A. Dwyer (Mahway, NJ: Erlbaum, 2007), 279–303.
5. David Foster and Pendred Noyce, "The Mathematics Assessment Collaborative: Performance Testing to Improve Instruction," *Phi Delta Kappan*, January 2004, 367–374; and David Foster, Pendred Noyce, and Sara Spiegel, "When Assessment Guides Instruction: Silicon Valley's Mathematics Assessment Collaborative," in *Assessing Mathematical Proficiency* (city, state: Mathematical Sciences Research Institute, 2007), pp. 137–154.

Chapter 2

1. Richard DuFour and Robert Eaker, *Professional Learning Communities at Work: Best Practices for Enhancing Student Achievement* (Bloomington, IN: National Educational Service, 1998).
2. MLC materials are available at http://www.doe.mass.edu/omste/instructional.html. For more information on the MLC project and how to implement it in your own school or district, contact Sandra.Mayrand@umassmed.edu

Chapter 3

1. Mark R. Shinn and Suzanne Bamonto, "Advanced Applications of Curriculum-Based Measurement: 'Big Ideas' and Avoiding Confusion," in *Advanced Applications of Curriculum-Based Measurement*, ed. Mark R. Shinn (New York: The Guilford Press, 1998), 1–31.
2. Lynn S. Fuchs and Douglas Fuchs, "Effects of Systematic Formative Evaluation: A Meta-Analysis," *Exceptional Children* 53, no. 3 (1986): 199–208.
3. Julie Sarama and Douglas H. Clements, *Early Childhood Mathematics Education Research: Learning Trajectories for Young Children* (New York: Routledge, 2009).
4. Lev S. Vygotsky, *Thought and Language*, ed. Alex Kozulin (Cambridge, MA: MIT Press, 1986).

5. Herbert P. Ginsburg, *Entering the Child's Mind: The Clinical Interview in Psychological Research and Practice* (New York: Cambridge University Press, 1997).

6. Michelene T. H. Chi, Nicholas de Leeuw, Mei-Hung Chiu, and Christian LaVancher, "Eliciting Self-Explanations Improves Understanding," *Cognitive Science* 18 (1994): 439–477.

7. Russell Gersten, Nancy C. Jordan, and Jonathan R. Flojo, "Early Identification and Interventions for Students with Mathematics Difficulties," *Journal of Learning Disabilities* 38, no. 4 (2005): 293–304.

8. Herbert P. Ginsburg, Alice Klein, and Prentice Starkey, "The Development Of Children's Mathematical Thinking: Connecting Research With Practice," in *Handbook of Child Psychology: 5th ed., vol. 4. Child Psychology and Practice*, eds. Irving Sigel and Anne Renninger (New York: John Wiley & Sons, 1998), 401–476.

9. Elizabeth Fennema, Thomas P. Carpenter, Victoria R. Jacobs, Megan L. Franke, and Linda W. Levi, "A Longitudinal Study of Gender Differences in Young Children's Mathematical Thinking," *Educational Researcher* 27, no. 5 (1998): 6–11.

10. John M. Love and Yange Xue, "How Early Care and Education Programs 0-5 Prepare Children for Kindergarten: Is It Enough?" (paper presented at the Head Start's 10th National Research Conference, Washington, DC, 2010).

Chapter 4

1. National Council of Teachers of Mathematics, *Professional Standards for Teaching Mathematics* (Reston, VA: National Council of Teachers of Mathematics, 1991).

2. U.S. Department of Education, Office of Educational Technology, *Transforming American Education: Learning Powered by Technology: National Education Technology Plan 2010* (Alexandria, VA: Education Publications Center, 2010).

3. R. Correnti, B. Hansen, and B. Rowan, "Early implementation and student achievement outcomes in Texas schools using Agile Mind Algebra 1 services" (unpublished manuscript, University of Michigan, 2008).

4. Everett M. Rogers and Everett Rogers, *Diffusion of Innovations* (New York: Free Press, 2003).

5. Laura S. Hamilton, Brian M. Stecher, Jennifer Lin Russell, Julie A. Marsh, and Jeremy Miles, "Accountability and Teaching Practices: School-Level Actions and Teacher Responses," in *Strong States, Weak Schools: The Benefits and Dilemmas of Centralized Accountability* (Research in Sociology of Education, vol. 16), eds. Bruce Fuller, Melissa K. Henne, and Emily Hannum (Bingley, UK: JAI Press, an imprint of Emerald Group Publishing Limited, 2008), 31–66.

6. National Governors Association Center for Best Practices and the Council of Chief State School Officers, "Common Core State Standards for Mathematics," http://www.corestandards.org/the-standards/mathematics.

Chapter 5

1. New Standards Primary Literacy Committee, *Reading and Writing Grade by Grade: Primary Literacy Standards for Kindergarten Through Third Grade* (Washington, DC: New Standards, 1999).

2. Anonymous teacher participant, ECRW Summer Institute, 2003.

3. Marnie Thompson and Dylan Wiliam, *Tight but Loose: Conceptual Framework for Scaling Up School Reforms* (Chicago, IL: AERA, April 2007).

4. Katie Wood Ray, *Wondrous Words: Writers and Writing in the Elementary Classroom* (Urbana, IL: National Council of Teachers of English, 1999). Ralph Fletcher and Joann Portalupi, *Craft Lessons: Teaching Writing K–8* (York, ME: Stenhouse Publishers, 1998); Joanne Portalupi and Ralph Fletcher, *Nonfiction Craft Lessons: Teaching Information Writing K–8* (Portland, ME: Stenhouse Publishers, 2001).

Chapter 6

1. John T. Yun "Learning From the Test: Improving the Teaching of English Language Arts Using Systematic Diagnosis of MCAS Item-Level Information" (doctoral dissertation, Harvard Graduate School of Education, 2003), 95–102.

2. Barbara Neufeld, *Year II of CCL in the Effective Practice Schools: Expanding the Work* (Cambridge, MA: Education Matters, Inc., 2003).

3. Paul Black and Dylan Wiliam, "Inside the Black Box: Raising Standards Through Classroom Assessment," *Phi Delta Kappan* 80 (2008): 139–148, http://www.pdkintl.org/kappan/kbla9810.htm.

4. Achieve, Inc., *Measuring Up: A Standards and Assessment Benchmarking Report for Massachusetts* (Boston: Achieve, Inc., 2001).

5. Barbara Neufeld and Sara Schwartz, *Formative Assessment Pilot Implementation: Final Report* (Cambridge, MA: Education Matters, Inc., 2004), 7.

6. Marianne Perie, Scott Marion, and Brian Gong, "Moving Toward a Comprehensive Assessments System: A Framework for Considering Interim Assessments," *Educational Measurement: Issues and Practice* 28 (2009): 5–13.

7. Margaret E. Goertz, Leslie Nabors Oláh, and Matthew Riggan, "Can Interim Assessments Be Used for Instructional Change?" *CPRE Policy Briefs* RB-51 (2009): 1–11.

8. Robert Marzano and J. S. Kendall, *The New Taxonomy of Educational Objectives*, 2nd ed. (New York: Corwin Press, 2006).

9. Again, because the MCAS is considered a fairly rigorous exam, using the skills it requires of readers as the standard did not seem to compromise BPE and BPS's commitment to rigorous, authentic reading instruction.

10. Boston Plan for Excellence, "FAST-R Teacher Resource Guide" (working paper, Boston Plan for Excellence, Boston, 2008).

11. Neufeld and Schwartz, *Formative Assessment Pilot Implementation*, 13, 15.

12. Ibid., 15.

13. Ibid.

14. Ibid., 21–22.

15. Ibid., 19.

16. Edward Tufte, *The Visual Display of Quantitative Information*, 2nd ed. Los Angeles: Graphics Press, 2001).

17. American College Testing Service, *Reading Between the Lines: What the ACT Reveals About College Readiness in Reading* (Iowa City: ACT, 2006), 14–15.

18. A "considerate" text is one in which the author has built in support to help readers make sense of the text, such as by defining unfamiliar vocabulary parenthetically or using "signpost" words such as "first," "next," "last," or "in contrast," and "similarly." Being considerate doesn't necessarily mean the text is easy, but that it is crafted in ways that may provide help to a struggling reader. A "challenging" text, on the other hand, is more complex and does not tend to provide much in-text support to help readers deal with the complexity. Note that the ratings are in relation to the suggested grade levels for each passage: A text that would be rated "uncomplicated" or "considerate" for eighth-grade readers would likely be considered "challenging" for fifth graders. For more, see: American College Testing Service, *Reading Between the Lines: What the ACT reveals about college readiness in reading* (Iowa City: ACT, 2006), 14–15.

19. Susan Trimble, Anne Gay, and Jan Matthew. "Using Test Score Data to Focus Instruction," *Middle School Journal* 36, no. 4 (2005): 26–32.

20. Boston Plan for Excellence, *FAST-R Teacher Resource Guide*.

21. Boston Plan for Excellence, *Straight Talk About CCL: A Guide for School Leaders* (Boston: Boston Plan for Excellence, 2003).

22. Barbara Neufeld, *Year II of CCL in the Effective Practice Schools: Expanding the Work* (Cambridge, MA: Education Matters, Inc., 2003).

23. Neufeld and Schwartz, *Formative Assessment Pilot Implementation: Final Report*.

24. Ibid., 21.

25. Ibid., 6.

26. Janet C. Quint, Susan Sepanik, and Janell K. Smith, *Using Student Data to Improve Teaching and Learning: Findings From an Evaluation of the Formative Assessments of Student Thinking in Reading (FAST-R) Program in Boston Elementary Schools* (New York: MDRC, 2008).

27. Ibid., 72–76.
28. Ibid., 61.
29. Jerome Groopman, *How Doctors Think* (New York: Houghton Mifflin, 2007).
30. Neufeld and Schwartz, *Formative Assessment Pilot Implementation: Final Report*, 6–7.
31. Ibid., 19.
32. Quint, Sepanik, and Smith, *Using Student Data to Improve Teaching and Learning*, 58.
33. Goertz, Oláh, and Riggan, "Can Interim Assessments Be Used for Instructional Change?"

Chapter 7

1. David H. Rose and Anne Meyer, *Teaching Every Student in the Digital Age: Universal Design for Learning* (Alexandria, VA: ASCD, 2002).
2. Ibid.
3. Ibid.
4. Patricia S. Moyer, Deborah Niezgoda, and John Stanley, "Young Children's Use of Virtual Manipulatives and Other Forms of Mathematical Representations," in *Technology-Supported Mathematics Learning Environments*, eds. William J. Masalski and Portia C. Elliott (Reston, VA: National Council of Teachers of Mathematics, 2005), 17–34; Nicole Strangman and Tracey E. Hall, *Text Transformations* (Wakefield, MA: National Center on Accessing the General Curriculum, 2003).
5. Bridget Dalton and C. Patrick Proctor, "Reading as Thinking: Integrating Strategy Instruction in a Universally Designed Digital Literacy Environment," in *Reading Comprehension Strategies: Theories, Interventions, and Technologies*, ed. Danielle S. McNamara (Mahwah, NJ: Lawrence Erlbaum, 2007), 421–440; Skip Stahl and Marc Aronica, "Digital Text in the Classroom," *Journal of Special Education Technology 17*, no 2 (2002): 57–59; Robert P. Dolan, Tracey E. Hall, Manju Banerjee, Euljung Chun, and Nicole Strangman., "Applying Principles Of Universal Design To Test Delivery: The Effect of Computer-Based Read-Aloud on Test Performance of High School Students with Learning Disabilities," *Journal of Technology, Learning, and Assessment 3* no. 7 (2005), http://escholarship.bc.edu/jtla/vol3/7/.
6. Julie Alonzo, Gerald Tindal, and Leanne R. Ketterlin-Geller, "Curriculum-based Assessment," in *Handbook of Special Education*, ed. L. Florian (Thousand Oaks, CA: Sage Publications, 2007), 307–318.
7. Ann C. Schulte, Diane N. Villwock, Michelle S. Whichard, and Cheryl F. Stallings, "High Stakes Testing and Expected Progress Standards for Students with Learning Disabilities: A Five Year Study of One District," *School Psychology Review 30*, no. 4 (2001): 487–506.
8. Christine A. Espin and Anne Foegen, "Validity of Three General Outcome Measures for Predicting Secondary Students' Performance on Content-Area Tasks," *Exceptional Children 62*, no. 6 (1996): 497–514.
9. Lynn S. Fuchs, Stanley L. Deno, and Phyllis A. Merkin., "The Effects of Frequent Curriculum-Based Measurement and Evaluation on Pedagogy, Student Achievement, and Student Awareness of Learning," *American Educational Research Journal 21* (1984): 449–460; Douglas Fuchs, Lynn S. Fuchs, and Pamela Fernstrom, "A Conservative Approach to Special Education Reform: Mainstreaming through Transenvironmental Programming and Curriculum-Based Measurement," *American Education Research Journal 30*, no. 1 (1993): 149–178; Lynn S. Fuchs, Douglas Fuchs, and C. L. Hamlett, "Monitoring Reading Growth Using Student Recalls: Effects of Two Teacher Feedback Systems," *Journal of Educational Research 83*, no. 2 (1989): 103–110.
10. Annemarie S. Palincsar and Ann L. Brown, "Reciprocal Teaching of Comprehension Fostering and Comprehension-Monitoring Activities," *Cognition and Instruction 1* no. 2 (1986): 117–175.
11. An oral reading fluency procedure measures a student's accuracy and smoothness of a text read aloud; a maze is an exercise in reading comprehension where words are removed from a passage and the student fills in blank spaces. The maze is sometimes more formally referred to as a *cloze* test.

12. Although we mask the names for obvious privacy concerns, the case stories are three *real* examples that we chose from our sample of schools, teachers, and students implementing Strategic Reader.

13. The Gates-MacGinitie Reading Achievement Test is used to assess student achievement in reading. The test includes vocabulary and comprehension subtests and is used frequently with excellent reliability. See Robert B. Cooter, "Test Review: Gates-MacGinitie Reading Tests, Third Edition, Levels 5/6, 7/9, and 10/12," *Journal of Reading* 32, no. 7 (1989): 656–658.

14. Tracey E. Hall, Nicole Cohen, Maureen Kavenaugh, Ge Vue, and Patti Ganley, "Project Monitor: Combining Universal Design for Learning and Curriculum-Based Measurement in a Strategic Tool for Learning" (Manuscript in preparation, 2011).

Chapter 8

1. Ron Haskins and Cecilia Rouse, "Closing Achievement Gaps," *The Future of Children*, Policy Brief, Spring 2005; and National Research Council, "Language Diversity, School Learning, and Closing Achievement Gaps: A Workshop Summary," M. Welsh-Ross, Rapporteur, Committee on the Role of Language in School Learning: Implications for Closing the Achievement Gap, Center for Education, Division of Behavioral and Social Sciences and Education (Washington, DC: National Academies Press, 2010).

2. Kathleen E. Metz, "Reassessment of Developmental Constraints on Children's Science Instruction," *Review of Educational Research* 65 (1995): 93–127.

3. Richard A. Duschl, Heidi A. Schweingruber, and Andrew W. Shouse, eds., *Taking Science to School: Learning and Teaching Science in Grades K–8* (Washington, DC: National Academies Press, 2007);and Metz, "Reassessment of Developmental Constraints on Children's Science Instruction."

4. Alison L. Bailey et al., "Further Specifying the Language Demands of School," in *The Language Demands of School: Putting Academic English to the Test*, ed. Alison L. Bailey (New Haven, CT: Yale University Press, 2007), 103–156; Susana Dutro, "An Introduction to a Focused Approach to English Language Instruction" (paper presented at the California Reading Association Conference, San Diego, CA, October 2003); and Mary J. Schleppegrell, *The Language of Schooling: A Functional Linguistics Perspective* (Mahwah, NJ: Lawrence Erlbaum Associates, 2004).

5. Duschl, Schweingruber, and Shouse, *Taking Science to School: Learning and Teaching Science in Grades K–8.*

6. J. Myron Atkin, Paul Black, and Janet Coffey, eds., *Classroom Assessment and the National Science Education Standards* (Washington, DC: National Academy Press, 2001); Margaret Heritage, "Formative Assessment: What Teachers Need to Know and Do," *Phi Delta Kappan* 89, no. 2 (2007): 140–146; and Richard J. Stiggins, "Assessment Crisis: The Absence of Assessment FOR Learning," *Phi Delta Kappan* 83, no. 10 (2002): 758–765.

7. Paul J. Black and Dylan Wiliam, "The Formative Purpose: Assessment Must First Promote Learning," in *Towards Coherence Between Classroom Assessment and Accountability: 103rd Yearbook of the National Society for the Study of Education*, ed. Mark Wilson (Chicago: University of Chicago Press, 2004), 20–50; and Alison L. Bailey and Margaret Heritage, *Formative Assessment for Literacy, Grades K–6: Building Reading and Academic Language Skills Across the Curriculum* (Thousand Oaks, CA: Corwin/Sage Press, 2008).

8. Alison L. Bailey et al., "A Teacher-Researcher Collaboration for the Academic Language and Science Learning of Young English Language Learners: Facilitating the Transition from Pre-Kindergarten to Kindergarten," *California Latino Superintendents Association*, http://calsa.schoolfusion.us/modules/cms/pages.phtml?pageid=160518&sessionid=69c35e7cb84d481486f93fbba8aec8d7&sessionid=69c35e7cb84d481486f93fbba8aec8d7.

9. Richard Fry, *The Role of Schools in the English Language Learner Achievement Gap* (Washington, DC: Pew Hispanic Center, 2008).

10. Carolyn Edwards, Lella Gandini, and George Forman, eds., *The Hundred Languages of Children: The Reggio Emilia Approach to Early Childhood Education* (Westport, CT: Ablex Publishing Corporation, 1993).

Chapter 9

1. Carnegie Corporation, *The Opportunity Equation: Transforming Mathematics and Science Education for Citizenship and the Global Economy* (New York: Carnegie Corporation, 2009).
2. P. David Pearson, Elizabeth Moje, and Cynthia Greenleaf, "Literacy and Science: Each in the Service of the Other," *Science* 328 no. 5977 (2010): 459–463.
3. National Research Council, *Draft Conceptual Framework for New Science Education Standards* (Washington, DC: National Academy of Sciences, 2010).
4. National Governors Association Center for Best Practices (NGA Center) and Council of Chief State School Officers (CCSSO), *Common Core English Language Arts Standards*, www.corestandards.org/assets/CCSSI_ELA%20Standards.pdf.
5. Gina Cervetti, P. David Pearson, Marco Antonio Bravo, and Jacqueline Barber, "Reading and Writing in the Service of Inquiry-Based Science," in *Linking Science and Literacy in the K–8 Classroom*, eds. Rowena Douglas, Michael P. Klentschy, and K. Worth (Arlington, VA: NSTA Press, 2006), 221–244.
6. Note that the lessons surrounding drafting of this piece were not focused on grammar or mechanics, but rather on gathering evidence in order to make a logical explanation—a critical element of scientific writing. To take this piece further and if the intent were to publish the piece (such as in a class book or for inclusion in a writing portfolio), teachers might choose to have students revise for mechanics. This is especially effective if teachers already use an editing checklist or peer review for polishing a piece of writing, so that the focus of the instruction remains on the content and structure of scientific writing.
7. Jennifer L. Tilson, Jill Castek, and Megan Goss, "Exploring the Influence of Science Writing Instruction on Fourth Graders' Writing Development," in *59th Yearbook of the National Reading Conference*, eds. R. T. Jimenez, V. J. Risko, M. K. Hundley, and D. W. Rowe (Oakcreek, WI: National Reading Conference, Inc., 2009), 117–134.
8. Pete Goldschmidt, *Evaluation of Seeds of Science/Roots of Reading: Effective Tools for Developing Literacy through Science in the Early Grades* (Los Angeles: CRESST Center, University of California Los Angeles, 2009).
9. Marco Antonio Bravo, Gina N. Cervetti, Seth M. Corrigan, and Jacqueline Barber, "Seeds of Science/Roots of Reading: Research and Development for Accommodation of English Language Learners, Final Report to The Noyce Foundation," Berkeley, CA: Lawrence Hall of Science, 2010.

Chapter 10

1. Other significant contributors to the development of the MW software include Charles Xie, Robert Tinker, Boris Berenfeld, Barbara Tinker, Amy Pallant, and Frieda Reichsman.
2. NetLogo is developed by Uri Wilenski's group at Northwestern University (http://ccl.northwestern.edu/netlogo/), and Phet is developed by a group founded by Carl Wieman at University of Colorado (http://phet.colorado.edu/).
3. Lee Shulman, "Knowledge and Teaching: Foundations of the New Reform," *Harvard Educational Review* 57, no. 1 (1987): 1–22; and Punya Mishra and Matthew J. Koehler, "Technological Pedagogical Content Knowledge: A Framework for Teacher Knowledge," *Teachers College Record* 108, no. 6 (2006): 1017–1054(38).
4. D. Royce Sadler, "Formative Assessment: Revisiting the Territory," *Assessment in Education: Principles, Policy & Practice* 5, no. 1 (1998): 77–84.
5. John D. Bransford, Ann L. Brown, and Rodney R. Cocking, *How People Learn: Brain, Mind, Experience, and School* (Washington, DC: National Academy Press, 1999).
6. James D. Slotta and Marcia C. Linn, *WISE Science: Inquiry and the Internet in the Science Classroom* (New York: Teachers College Press, 2009).
7. Marcia C. Linn, Bat-Sheva Eylon, and Elizabeth A. Davis,, "The Knowledge Integration Perspective on Learning," in *Internet Environments for Science Education*, eds. Marcia C. Linn, Elizabeth A. Davis, and Philip Bell (Mahwah, NJ: Lawrence Erlbaum Associates, 2004), 29–46.

Chapter 11

1. For the technically inclined, ThinkerTools ran on the Commodore 64 computer. For efficiency purposes—i.e., to ensure that it could do the calculations rapidly enough to make the animations smooth—it was programmed entirely in assembler, using the simple instructions encoded in the hardware of the computer, rather than a higher-level programming language that would then have had to be compiled into those instructions.

2. Note that this arrangement would have been impossible to implement in a public school today, due to the necessity of preparing all students for standardized tests.

3. This reviewer's concern was that sixth graders had not reached a sufficient level of cognitive development to enable them to learn the targeted concepts. It is amusing, at this historical remove, to contemplate the hold that Piagetian concepts had on education researchers thirty years ago. With this in mind, we reproduce some relevant portions of the review here. "ThinkerTools is a formal operational system . . . It cannot be used *with meaning* by students probably below grade 12. Students can be *trained* in its use but research suggests understanding will not be developed. The system is making claims research says it cannot fulfill . . ." (emphasis in the original).

4. Barbara White, "Designing Computer Games to Help Physics Students Understand Newton's Laws of Motion," *Cognition and Instruction* 1, no. 1 (1984): 69–108.

5. Paul Horwitz, E. Neumann, and J. Schwartz, "Teaching Science at Multiple Levels: The Genscope program," *Communications of the A.C.M.* 39, no. 8 (1996): 179–196.

6. In the real world, not all changes in DNA have macroscopic effects, but GenScope's simple model of genetics did not include arcana such as introns and synonymous mutations.

7. Daniel T. Hickey, Ann C. Kindfield, Paul Horwitz, and M. Christie, "Advancing Educational Theory by Enhancing Practice in a Technology-Supported Genetics Learning Environment," *Journal of Education* 181, no. 2 (1999): 25–55.

8. Elizabeth A. Davis and Marcia C. Linn, "Scaffolding Students' Knowledge Integration through Prompts for Reflection," *International Journal of Science Education* 22 (Special Issue), no. 8 (2000): 819–838.

9. Barbara Buckley, Janice Gobert, Paul Horwitz, and Laura M. O'Dwyer, "Looking inside the Black Box: Assessing Model-Based Learning and Inquiry in Biologica," *International Journal of Learning Technologies* 5, no. 2 (2010): 166–190.

10. Camelia Rosca, Laura O'Dwyer, Trudi Lord, and Paul Horwitz, "Ready, Set, Go, Evolution!" *@ Concord* 14, no. 2 (2010): 4–6.

11. I am indebted to Edmund Hazzard for this anecdote.

12. Ann C. Kindfield, "Understanding a Basic Biological Process: Expert and Novice Models of Meiosis," *Science Education* 78, no. 3 (1994): 255–283.

13. Jean Lave and Etienne Wenger, *Situated Learning: Legitimate peripheral participation* (New York: Cambridge University Press, 1991); and Barbara Rogoff and Jean Lave, eds., *Everyday Cognition: Its development in social context* (Cambridge, MA: Harvard University Press, 1984).

14. Kate T. Anderson, Steven J. Zuiker, Gita Taasoobshirazi, and Daniel T. Hickey, "Classroom Discourse as a Tool to Enhance Formative Assessment and Practise in Science," *International Journal of Science Education* 29, no. 14 (2007): 1721–1744.

15. I am grateful to Barbara Buckley for emphasizing this point.

16. Jaekyung Lee, "Tracking Achievement Gaps and Assessing the Impact of NCLB on the Gaps: An In-depth Look into National and State Reading and Math Outcome Trends" (Cambridge, MA: Harvard Education Publishing Group, 2006).

17. Lisa M. Abrams, Joseph J. Pedulla, and George F. Madaus, "Views from the Classroom: Teachers' Opinions of Statewide Testing Programs," *Theory Into Practice* 42, no. 1 (2003): 18–29; Bruce Fuller, Joseph Wright, Kathryn Gesicki, and Erin Kang, "Gauging Growth: How to Judge No Child Left Behind?" *Educational Researcher* 36, no. 5 (2007): 268–278; and Frederick M. Hess, "Accountability without Angst? Public Opinion and No Child Left Behind," *Harvard Educational Review* 76 no. 4 (2008): 587–610.

18. Federal Communications Commission, "FCC Enables High-Speed, Affordable Broadband for Schools and Libraries," Federal Communications Commission, Washington, DC, 2010.

19. It is worth noting in this context that the U.S. Department of Education's Race to the Top Assessment Program has recently awarded approximately $350 million to two consortia of states to support the development of a new generation of assessments, some of which will be performance based.

Chapter 12

1. Paul Black and Dylan Wiliam, "Assessment and Classroom Learning," *Assessment in Education: Principles, Policy & Practice* 5, no. 1 (1998): 7–74.

2. James Pellegrino and Susan Goldman, "Beyond the Rhetoric: Realities and Complexities of Integrating Assessment into Classroom Teaching and Learning," in *The Future of Assessment: Shaping Teaching and Learning*, ed. Carol Anne Dwyer (Philadelphia: Lawrence Erlbaum Associates, 2007), 7–52.

3. Dylan Wiliam, "Keeping Learning on Track: Classroom Assessment and the Regulation of Learning," in *Second Handbook of Research on Mathematics Teaching and Learning*, ed. Frank K. Lester (Greenwich, CT: Information Age Publishing, 2007), 1051–1089; and Richard J. Shavelson, Donald B. Young, Carlos C. Ayala, Paul R. Brandon, Erin Marie Furtak, Maria Araceli Ruiz-Primo, Miki K. Tomita, and Yue Yin, "On the Impact of Curriculum-embedded Formative Assessment on Learning: A Collaboration Between Curriculum and Assessment Developers," *Applied Measurement in Education* 21, no. 4 (2008): 295–314.

4. W. James Popham, *Classroom Assessment: What Teachers Need to Know* (Boston: Pearson, 2011); and Lorrie A. Shepard, "Formative Assessment: Caveat Emptor," in *The Future of Assessment: Shaping Teaching and Learning*, ed. Carol A. Dwyer (Mahwah, NJ: Erlbaum, 2007), 279–303.

5. James G. Greeno, Allan M. Collins, and Lauren B. Resnick, "Cognition and Learning," in *Handbook of Educational Psychology*, ed. David C. Berliner and Robert C. Calfee (New York: Macmillan Library Reference USA, Prentice Hall International, 1996), 15–46.

6. James W. Pellegrino, Naomi Chudowsky, and Robert Glaser, *Knowing What Students Know: The Science and Design of Educational Assessment* (Washington, DC: National Academy Press, 2001), 54.

7. Drew H. Gitomer and Richard A. Duschl, "Establishing Multilevel Coherence in Assessment," in *Evidence and Decision Making. The 106th Yearbook of the National Society for the Study of Education, Part I*, ed. Pamela A. Moss (Chicago: University of Chicago Press, 2007), 288–320; and Mark Wilson, ed., *Towards Coherence Between Classroom Assessment and Accountability: The 103rd Yearbook of the National Society for the Study of Education* (Chicago: Chicago University Press, 2004).

8. Pellegrino, Chudowsky, and Glaser, *Knowing What Students Know*, 225.

9. Horst W. J. Rittel and Melvin M. Webber, "Dilemmas in a General Theory of Planning," *Policy Sciences* 4, no. 2 (1973): 155–169.

10. Stephen B. Dunbar, Daniel M. Koretz, and H. D. Hoover, "Quality Control in the Development and Use of Performance Assessments," *Applied Measurement in Education* 4, no. 4 (1991): 289–303; Richard J. Shavelson, Gail P. Baxter, and Jerry Pine, "Performance Assessments: Political Rhetoric and Measurement Reality," *Educational Researcher* 21, no. 4 (1992): 22–27; and William A. Mehrens, "Consequences of Assessment: What is the Evidence," in *Large-scale Assessment Programs for All Students: Validity, Technical Adequacy, and Implementation*, eds. Gerald Tindal and Thomas M. Haladyna (Mahwah, NJ: Lawrence Erlbaum Associates, 2002), 149–177.

11. Samuel Messick, "The Interplay of Evidence and Consequences in the Validation of Performance Assessments," *Educational Researcher* 23, no. 2 (1994): 13–23.

12. Willam A. Mehrens, W. James Popham, and Joseph M. Ryan, "How to Prepare Students for Performance Assessments," *Educational Measurement: Issues and Practice* 17, no. 1 (1998): 18–22.

13. Ibid., 20.

14. James G. Greeno, "The Situativity of Knowing, Learning, and Research," *American Psychologist* 53, no. 1 (1998): 5–26; and James P. Gee, *Situated Language and Learning: A Critique of Traditional Schooling* (New York: Palgrave Macmillan, 2004).

15. Jean Lave and Etienne Wenger, *Situated Learning: Legitimate Peripheral Participation* (Cambridge, MA: Cambridge University Press, 1991).

16. James G. Greeno and Melissa S. Gresalfi, "Opportunities to Learn in Practice and Identity," in *Assessment, Equity, and Opportunity to Learn*, eds. Pamela A. Moss, Diana C. Pullin, James Paul Gee, Edward H. Haertel, and Lauren Jones Young (Cambridge, MA: Cambridge University Press, 2008), 186.

17. Ann C. Kindfield, "Understanding a Basic Biological Process: Expert and Novice Models of Meiosis," *Science Education* 78, no. 3 (1994): 255–283.

18. Daniel T. Hickey, Edward W. Wolfe, and Ann C. H. Kindfield, "Assessing Learning in a Technology-supported Genetics Environment: Evidential and Systemic Validity Issues," *Educational Assessment* 6, no. 3 (2000): 155–196.

19. Richard A. Duschl and Drew H. Gitomer, "Strategies and Challenges to Changing the Focus of Assessment and Instruction in Science Classrooms," *Educational Assessment* 4, no. 1 (1997): 37–73.

20. Daniel T. Hickey, Ann C. H. Kindfield, Paul Horwitz, and Mary Ann T. Christie, "Integrating Curriculum, Instruction, Assessment, and Evaluation in a Technology-supported Genetics Learning Environment," *American Educational Research Journal* 40, no. 2 (2003): 495–538.

21. Paul Cobb, Jere Confrey, Andrea diSessa, Richard Lehrer, and Leona Schauble, "Design Experiments in Educational Research," *Educational Researcher* 32, no. 1 (2003): 9–13.

22. This has implications for science education more broadly because ninth-grade biology is a "gatekeeper" course for more advanced college-prep science courses. Many students find genetics so confusing that it deprives them of the grades and/or the desire needed to pursue advanced science courses in subsequent years.

23. Daniel T. Hickey, Steven J. Zuiker, Gita Taasoobshirazi, Nancy Jo Schafer, and Marina A. Michael, "Balancing Varied Assessment Functions to Attain Systemic Validity: Three is the Magic Number," *Studies in Educational Evaluation* 32, no. 3 (2006): 180–201.

24. Daniel T. Hickey, Adam A. Ingram-Goble, and Ellen M. Jameson, "Designing Assessments and Assessing Designs in Virtual Educational Environments," *Journal of Science Education and Technology* 18, no. 2 (2009): 187–208; and Daniel T. Hickey, Gita Taasoobshirazi, and Dionne Cross, "Assessment as Learning: Enhancing Discourse, Understanding, and Achievement in Innovative Science Curricula," *Journal of Research in Science Teaching* (accepted for review, March 2011).

25. Daniel T. Hickey, Michelle A. Honeyford, Katie A. Clinton, and Jenna McWilliams, "Participatory Assessment of 21st Century Proficiencies," in *Innovative Assessment in the 21st Century: Supporting Educational Needs*, eds. Valerie J. Schute and Betsy Jane Becker (New York: Springer, 2010), 107–139; and Daniel T. Hickey, Jenna C. McWilliams, and Stephen Bishop, "Participatory Design for Engagement, Understanding, and Achievement in University e-Learning Contexts" (paper presented at the annual meeting of the American Educational Research Association, New Orleans, April 2011).

26. George Siemens, "Connectivism: A Learning Theory for the Digital Age," *International Journal of Instructional Technology and Distance Learning* 2, no. 1 (2005): 3–10.

27. Melissa S. Gresalfi, "Taking up Opportunities to Learn: Constructing Dispositions in Mathematics Classrooms," *Journal of the Learning Sciences* 18, no. 3 (2009): 327–369.

28. At www.workingexamples.org. These are being developed as part of a project funded by the MacArthur Foundation's Digital Media and Learning initiative.

About the Editors

DANIEL T. HICKEY is an associate professor in the Learning Sciences program at Indiana University in Bloomington, and a research professor with the Indiana University Center for Research on Learning and Technology. He completed his PhD in psychology at Vanderbilt University, where he studied with James Pellegrino and the other members of the Cognition and Technology Group at Vanderbilt. He also completed postdoctoral training at the Center for Performance Assessment at the Educational Testing Service. He studies participatory approaches to assessment, feedback, evaluation, and motivation. He primarily works with technology-supported learning environments including video games, digital networks, and e-learning. He has directed projects in these areas funded by the National Science Foundation, NASA, and the MacArthur Foundation, and has published both practical and theoretical papers in leading journals.

PENDRED E. NOYCE is a physician, author, and trustee of the Robert Noyce Foundation, which supports innovation and improvement in public education in mathematics, science, and literacy. She was educated at Harvard, Stanford, and the University of Minnesota Hospitals, and she practiced internal medicine in the Boston area before pausing from medicine to work full-time on education issues. For eight years, she helped lead the NSF-funded Massachusetts State Systemic Initiative, PALMS, which inspired the development of curriculum frameworks, assessments, professional development, family involvement, and strategic planning for districts in mathematics and science statewide. As a founding funder and chair of the Rennie Center for Education Research and Policy, Noyce has helped formulate and write policy papers on value-added assessment, opportunity to learn in science, and alternate math pathways to college readiness. She also serves on the boards of the Concord Consortium, where she is past chair; TERC; the Consortium for Mathematics and Its Applications; the Libra Foundation; and the Boston Plan for Excellence. She is the author of the *Lexicon* series of middle-grade fantasies for children and is a founder of Tumblehome Learning, Inc, which publishes science-based mysteries, biographies, and accompanying kits and activities for young people ages eight through sixteen.

About the Contributors

ALISON L. BAILEY, EdD, is a professor in the Department of Education, University of California, Los Angeles, and a faculty associate researcher at the National Center for Research on Evaluation, Standards and Student Testing (CRESST). She is principal investigator of the Center for Community Partnerships/Para Los Niños science and language learning project. A graduate of Harvard University, her research focuses primarily on language and literacy development and English language assessment. She serves on the advisory boards of the California Department of Education, the twenty-six-state WIDA consortium, and commercial publishers developing language and literacy assessments for English language learners. Bailey is the author of numerous books, chapters, and articles, including as editor and contributing author to *The Language Demands of School: Putting Academic English to the Test* (Yale University Press, 2007), and coauthor with Margaret Heritage of *Formative Assessment for Literacy K–6: Building Reading and Academic Language Skills across the Curriculum* (Corwin/ Sage Press, 2008).

JACQUELINE BARBER is the coprincipal investigator for *Seeds of Science/Roots of Reading*, and serves as associate director of the Lawrence Hall of Science (LHS), responsible for LHS's Curriculum Center. She has worked in K–12 science and mathematics education for over thirty years, in curriculum and professional development, and is the author of many science curriculum units and student books. Prior to her work in education, she conducted research in neuroendocrinology on a Fulbright scholarship at the University of Strasbourg, France.

ALISON K. BILLMAN is a literacy research specialist for the *Seeds of Science/Roots of Reading* development team at the Lawrence Hall of Science with a special focus on development of curriculum for the primary grades and supporting literacy assessment efforts. Her research interests are rooted in fourteen years of teaching experience and focus on language and literacy development across the curriculum, particularly in the primary grades. She also has expertise in instruction and assessment of primary-grade children's informational text comprehension.

LINDA J. CHAPUT is founder and chief executive officer of Agile Mind, Inc. The company was created to support instructional innovation at scale, by equipping educators and students with Inbox exemplary programs, tools, and services—most delivered using Internet technologies—that enable educators to teach more effectively, that foster high academic achievement and persistence in mathematics and science, and that use technology to achieve these goals more effectively. Since 2004, 20,000 educators and 2 million students—80 percent in underserved areas—have used Agile Mind programs, which are developed in intensive and continuing collaboration with leading education research organizations.

Chaput has worked for more than twenty years leading initiatives to develop and disseminate educational programs, tools, and services in mathematics and science for adolescents and adults, as well as for the educators who serve them. Before founding Agile Mind, Chaput was president of Scientific American Inc.'s education, general, professional, and reference publishing enterprises for ten years. She was also founder and CEO of Cogito Learning Media, Inc., a pioneering provider of multimedia and Internet-ready learning tools authored by leading authorities. In 2010, she was named by *Fortune* as one of the top-ten female small-business entrepreneurs in the United States.

CYNTHIA CHIONG received her doctorate degree in developmental psychology from the University of Virginia, where she was also in the Institute of Education Sciences (IES) fellowship program that focused on an interdisciplinary approach to educational research. Her research interests focus on how the design of educational media can affect young children's learning, the way they interact with them, and how parents and teachers use them to teach. Chiong is currently the director of research for Sirius Thinking, the creators of the Emmy Award–winning children's literacy show, *Between the Lions*. She also works with the Joan Ganz Cooney Center at Sesame Workshop to explore young children's use of digital media and with Teachers College, Columbia University, and Wireless Generation on research that incorporates new approaches in creating math assessments for young students.

WENDY CLEAVES is the mathematics coordinator at the Regional Science Resource Center at the University of Massachusetts Medical School. A former middle school math teacher, Cleaves has spent the past nine years providing professional development to mathematics teachers in grades preK–12. She is a codeveloper of the *Mathematics Learning Community* materials and *MLC Facilitator Training*, both of which support the development of math-specific, school-based professional learning communities facilitated by lead teachers or coaches. Cleaves is also a mathematics consultant for Teachers21 and serves as a peer reviewer for the NCTM journal *Mathematics Teaching in the Middle School*. She holds a bachelor's degree in mathematics from Assumption College, a master's degree in education from Fitchburg State University, and a master's degree in mathematics for educators from Worcester Polytechnic Institute. She is most interested in developing teachers' mathematical pedagogical content knowledge, as well as in finding ways to provide more access to math for all learners.

NICOLE COHEN is a doctoral student at Boston University's School of Education, in the special education program. Her dissertation work focuses on instructional design for students with high-incidence learning disabilities. While in her doctoral program, Cohen has been involved at the Center for Applied Special Technology (CAST) as an intern and research assistant, and was a teaching fellow in Boston University's School of Education. Before starting her doctorate, Cohen was a special education teacher for students in middle school at University of Chicago's Hyde Park Day School. In addition, she had the opportunity to design and create a learning center at the Foote School in New Haven, Connecticut. Cohen's undergraduate degree is from Bradley University, in Peoria, Illinois.

KATHI COOK leads the Charles A. Dana Center's online services team, which designs instructional materials, assessments, and professional development to improve student access to— and success in—challenging course work so that every student leaves high school ready for college or career. A special focus of her team's work is the Dana Center's collaboration with Agile Mind, Inc., to develop comprehensive online instruction, assessment, and professional development materials that support a cohesive, vertically articulated mathematics program from middle school through Advanced Placement Calculus and Statistics. She has nearly thirty years of experience in mathematics education, including nineteen years of mathematics teaching experience at the university, high school, and middle school levels. She has taught courses ranging from algebra and geometry to precalculus, AP calculus, and AP statistics.

SETH CORRIGAN is a research and assessment specialist for the *Seeds of Science/Roots of Reading* development team at the Lawrence Hall of Science. He leads development of the project's curriculum assessments as well as its research measures. He has taught elementary, middle school, and high school science and math, and has worked as a teacher and researcher on numerous projects sponsored by the National Science Foundation and the U.S. Department of Energy. His graduate training is in program design and evaluation at the University of California at Los Angeles.

DANIEL DAMELIN is currently a curriculum and technology developer at the Concord Consortium (CC). As principal investigator for the Rhode Island Information Technology Experiences for Students and Teachers project, he collected and analyzed data from over one hundred teachers and thousands of students across Rhode Island who used computer models to better understand core science concepts. For the past ten years, he has been involved with many projects at CC, most related to development of software and curriculum utilizing the Molecular Workbench. He has an undergraduate degree in chemistry, computer science, and environmental studies, as well as a master's in education from Tufts University. He has also taught high school chemistry for fourteen years and worked as a professional software engineer.

MARYLOU ESCOBAR, MEd, is a kindergarten teacher at Para los Niños Charter Elementary School in downtown Los Angeles. She was a focal classroom teacher during the final phase of the Center for Community Partnerships/Para Los Niños Project when the kindergarten supplemental curriculum and formative assessment practices were implemented. Escobar has a master's in education with a reading specialty and a California State Clear Multiple Subject K–12 credential. She has taught kindergarten for six years, with twenty-three years in K–12 teaching overall. She has received extensive professional development in science while teaching at Para Los Niños.

DAVID FOSTER is the executive director of the Silicon Valley Mathematics Initiative (SVMI), comprised of forty-three member districts in the greater San Francisco Bay Area. Besides the intensive work in California, SVMI consults across the United States, including in New York, Illinois, Massachusetts, Ohio, Tennessee, and Georgia. SVMI is affiliated with programs at the University of California, Berkeley, Stanford University, and San Jose State University. Foster established SVMI in 1996 working as mathematics director for the Robert N. Noyce Foundation. Foster is the primary author of *Interactive Mathematics: Activities and Investigations* (Glencoe/McGraw-Hill, 1994). He was a regional director for the Middle Grade Mathematics Renaissance of the California State Systemic Initiative. Foster taught mathematics and computer science at middle school, high school, and community college for eighteen years. He also works part-time for San Jose State University. He is codirector of the Santa Clara Valley Math Project. He is also cochair of the advisory committee of the Mathematics Assessment Resource Service/Balanced Assessment. He is a consultant to the Urban Math Leadership Network that works with the twenty-five largest school districts in America.

PATTI GANLEY MEd, is a senior product development manager at the Center for Applied Special Technology, CAST. She utilizes many years in education as a teacher, administrator, and as a curriculum product developer at EBSCO Publishing to inform her work at CAST. She is especially interested in the design process, user interface, and visual literacy. Ganley is project manager for both federally and foundation-funded projects in which she works to develop interactive online writing environments based on the principles of UDL to support all users. Additionally, Ganley works with teams as a part of collaborative projects in schools and across partnering institutions. She manages the National Center on Universal Design for Learning, focusing on the development of online communities of practice and professional learning materials. Ganley received an undergraduate degree from the University of New Hampshire and a master of education in curriculum design from Antioch University.

HERBERT P. GINSBURG, PhD, is the Jacob H. Schiff Professor of Psychology and Education at Teachers College, Columbia University. He has written, with Sylvia Opper, a widely used account of *Piaget's Theory of Intellectual Development*, as well as introductions to early mathematical thinking (*Children's Arithmetic*), and to clinical interviewing (*Entering the Child's Mind*). He has conducted basic research on the development of mathematical thinking, with particular attention to young children, disadvantaged populations, and cultural similarities and differences. He has drawn on cognitive developmental research to develop mathematics curricula (*Big Math for Little Kids*) and storybooks for young children, tests of mathematical thinking, and video workshops to enhance teachers' understanding of students' learning of mathematics. Currently, he is developing a model course on early mathematics education for use in colleges and universities. The course makes use of Web-based computer technology (Video Interactions for Teaching and Learning [VITAL]) designed to help prospective teachers improve their craft by making meaningful connections between research and theory and the analysis of individual children's learning and thinking. Also, he is engaged in creating computer-based systems (mCLASS MATH) for helping teachers to conduct basic clinical interviews to assess children's mathematical knowledge. He is developing computer software, MathemAntics, to foster young children's (from three years to grade three) mathematics learning. He has served as a consultant for various children's television programs, including *Sesame Street* and *Blue's Clues*, and has been a member of several National Academy of Science committees, including the recent panel on Mathematics Learning in Early Childhood: Paths Toward Excellence and Equity.

TRACEY E. HALL, PhD, is a senior research scientist in the area of assessment and instruction at the Center for Applied Special Technology, CAST. Hall's work over the past eighteen years has focused on curriculum-based measurement, professional learning in education, and instructional design of curriculum for all students applying the principles of Universal Design for Learning. Before joining CAST, Hall was an assistant professor at Pennsylvania State University in the Department of Educational and School Psychology and Special Education. Her public school experience includes teaching as a special educator, administrator, and consultant. Hall received her PhD from the University of Oregon in special education with research emphases in formative assessment and instructional design.

PAUL HORWITZ, PhD, is a theoretical physicist with broad interests in the application of technology to science and math education. He directs the Modeling Center at the Concord Consortium and is also the president of Educational Network Services, Inc. (ENS), a company he founded in 2003 to commercialize technology resulting from educational research. In a career spanning twenty-five years, he has used computer-based interactive models to create challenging learning activities that pose problems and then monitor and react to students' actions. He was the principal investigator on the ThinkerTools Project, which pioneered the use of such activities for teaching Newtonian mechanics. RelLab, a simulated "Relativity Laboratory" that he designed, won two EDUCOM Higher Education Software Awards in 1992, one for Best Natural Science Software (Physics), the other for Best Design. He directed the design and implementation of GenScope as well as its successor program BioLogica—multilevel models of genetic processes ranging in scale from DNA to populations. At the Concord Consortium, he directs two projects. One has created activities for teaching "evolution readiness" to fourth graders; the other uses simulations of electronic circuits and test equipment to create formative assessments for college students. Through ENS, he is working with Teachers College at Columbia University to develop MathemAntics, a sequence of interactive games for teaching mathematics concepts to children from preschool to third grade.

YICHING D. HUANG, MEd and MA, is a doctoral candidate in the Department of Education, University of California, Los Angeles. She is the senior graduate student researcher on the Center for Community Partnerships/Para Los Niños Project. She has master's degrees in education from Harvard University and the University of California, Los Angeles. Before returning to graduate school, Huang was an early childhood educator for several years and has extensive professional development and research experience in the area of early childhood education and child development.

KIMBERLE KOILE, PhD, is a senior research scientist at Concord Consortium, where she directs the LOOPS project. She also leads an educational technology research group at the MIT Center for Educational Computing Initiatives, where her research focuses on the use of pen-based interaction and wireless communication to support formative assessment in K–12 settings. She has designed and implemented software for over twenty years in a variety of domains, including education, chemistry, and molecular biology, and has taught undergraduate and graduate computer science and high school chemistry. She has an undergraduate degree in chemistry from UT Austin and a PhD in computer science from MIT.

YOUNG-SUN LEE is an associate professor in the program of measurement, statistics, and evaluation within the Department of Human Development at Teachers College, Columbia University. Her training is in the field of educational and psychological measurement, with specific emphasis on test construction/scale development and item response theory. Her research has focused on applied statistics and psychometric theories to solve practical problems in educational settings: (1) the application of psychometric models in the development/evaluation of mathematics assessments, and (2) the application of cognitive diagnosis modeling in international comparative studies.

LISA LINEWEAVER, currently director of accelerated improvement working to turn around one of Boston's lowest-performing elementary schools, led the team at the Boston Plan for Excellence that developed the FAST-R assessments and supported their use in Boston Public Schools. She helped teams of teachers become savvy users of data about their students' reading skills as an instructional data coach; then, as program director for FAST-R, she oversaw the creation and refinement of the FAST-R teacher support materials and the spread of FAST-R use into nearly sixty schools in Boston. A former fifth-grade teacher in Williamsburg, Virginia, she currently serves as an elected member of the Chelsea, Massachusetts, School Committee.

SANDRA MAYRAND, founder and executive director of the Regional Science Resource Center at the University of Massachusetts Medical School, has a BA in microbiology and an MBA in business development. She has twenty years experience as a biomedical researcher in cell and molecular biology with special emphasis on gene expression. She is actively involved with the advancement of science education in Massachusetts. She is currently the director of the Central MA STEM Pipeline Network and chair of the Massachusetts State Middle School Science and Engineering Fair. She is a member of the Massachusetts State Science and

Engineering Fair, Inc., board of directors, and serves on its executive committee. She received the Bruce Alberts Award in 2002 from the American Society for Cell Biology for her distinguished contribution to science education. In 2003, the Worcester YWCA recognized her with the annual Katherine F. Erskine Award for medicine and science. In 2008, she was awarded the Commonwealth Citation for Outstanding Performance and the Manuel Carballo Governor's Award for Excellence in Public Service.

SANDRA PAPPAS received her doctorate degree in developmental psychology from Teachers College, Columbia University. Her research interests focus on developing ways to enhance young children's metacognition during problem solving. In particular, she focuses on identifying whether young children are capable of accurately expressing thinking, recognizing and correcting mistakes, and adapting problem solving strategies to meet the demands of the task. Pappas is currently a research associate at Wireless Generation, Inc. where she works in collaboration with Teachers College, Columbia University, to develop cognitive-based comprehensive mathematical assessments for young children.

AUDREY E. POPPERS served as the director of the Noyce Foundation literacy program, Every Child a Reader and Writer, from 2001 through 2009. During her forty-four years in California public education, she worked in a variety of roles, including middle-school language arts and reading teacher, elementary teacher, director of instruction for the Millbrae School District, and associate superintendent for instruction, San Mateo–Foster City School District. She holds a BA in elementary education, an MS in administrative supervision from California State University at Hayward, a reading specialist credential, and an EdD in educational management.

CATHY SEELEY, EdD, is a thirty-five-year mathematics educator and change facilitator at the local, state, and national levels. Seeley has taught mathematics at the middle and high school levels, worked as a K–12 district mathematics supervisor, and served as K–12 director of mathematics for the Texas Education Agency, where she worked on the state's development of the highly recognized Texas Essential Knowledge and Skills for mathematics. She spent from 1999 through 2001 teaching mathematics as a Peace Corps volunteer in Burkina Faso. After her return from the Peace Corps, Seeley served as senior adviser for a distance education online algebra project with the University of Texas. Seeley has a range of experiences in assessment, including service on the National Study Group on Assessment for the Mathematical Sciences Education Board of the National Academy of Sciences, resulting in the 1993 publication of *Measuring What Counts*. She is a prolific author of textbooks and professional articles and book chapters, most recently authoring the 2009 book *Faster Isn't Smarter—Messages About Math, Teaching, and Learning in the 21st Century*, a resource for teachers, leaders, policy makers, and families.

JENNIFER L. TILSON is a literacy curriculum specialist for the Seeds of Science/Roots of Reading project at the Lawrence Hall of Science. She is a former first- and second-grade teacher, and holds an MA in language, literacy, and culture from the University of California, Berkeley. Tilson was the lead author on several Seeds of Science/Roots of Reading curriculum units for grades three through five, and has written several student books

GE VUE, EdM, is an instructional designer/research associate at the Center for Applied Special Technology, CAST. He is interested in developing social learning technologies and is instrumental in the development of Universal Design for Learning (UDL) digital literacy environments to support reading, writing, and assessment. Currently, Vue works on two national centers and is focused on integrating accessible collaborative tools and social media practices into the development and implementation of the National Instructional Materials Accessibility Standard (NIMAS). He also serves on the DIAGRAM board (Digital Image and Graphic Resources for Accessible Materials), a research and development center to transform the production of digital images. Vue received his undergraduate degree from Carleton College and a master of education in technology, innovation, and education from the Harvard Graduate School of Education.

Index